Laura Wyatt-Smith is an International Coaching Federation certified coach with twenty years' experience in leadership at some of the UK's foremost children and family organisations, including as a current trustee for the UK's national charity for working parents, Working Families. She is also a certified digital wellness educator, a Churchill Fellow and qualified teacher. Laura, a mum of two, lives in London and loves outdoor family adventures in her campervan, Captain Barnacles. *Screensaver: A Judgement-Free Guide to Your Child's First Smartphone* is her first book. For further support or information about Laura visit www.laurawyattsmith.com.

Praise for *Screensaver*

'An important and careful guide to the contentious world of smartphones and screens. Laura writes without judgement, taking you through all the major decisions you'll have to make. As the parent of a nine-year-old, I found a number of very useful ideas that will hopefully help us navigate the (tricky) path ahead'

Jack Thorne, playwright, screenwriter and creator of the *Adolescence* series

'*Screensaver* offers extremely helpful and practical suggestions that will not only be invaluable for parents of children and young people, but also for adults with learning disabilities'

Professor the Baroness Hollins, founder and chair of Beyond Words

'The book every parent has been waiting for – wise, kind, meticulously researched and full of the type of practical advice we all need and can put into use immediately, regardless of how old our kids are and whether or not they have a smartphone yet'

Rebecca Seal, journalist and author of *Solo*, *Be Bad, Better* and the *Leon* cookbooks

'Laura's book combines valuable tech knowledge with a heartfelt understanding of what children and parents need ... Laura gently guides us through the feelings of guilt and helplessness, offering no judgement – just plenty of practical ideas and tips'

Lauren Seager-Smith, CEO of the For Baby's Sake Trust

'*Screensaver* is an excellent and non-judgemental guide for parents navigating the challenges of smartphones. It offers a balanced and nuanced perspective, providing thoughtful support for the immensely difficult task of raising children in the digital age'

Nova Eden, founder of One Collective Power

'WOW! This is precisely the book that parents need ... Most of us know about the challenges of smartphones, but the beauty of this book is that it truly provides practical, realistic strategies to navigate this tricky subject with your children. It's backed by research, real-life conversations and Laura's lived experience of working with youth and being a parent'

Rachel Vecht, director of Educating Matters

'This is an easy and enjoyable read covering everything from when to get your child a first phone and navigating tricky social media situations to talking about pornography with your kids. Laura has provided a roadmap for setting up a custom family phone agreement which will help families who are looking to personalize their rules around screen time'

Claudia Erickson, co-founder of Unplug Collaborative

'*Screensaver* asks and answers the critical questions and provides a clear lesson plan that will ease parental anxiety and help parents make screen choices in a complex world of AI, online education, ear buds, virtual reality and all the technology that has erupted in the last decade... a clear guide to raising healthy children who will thrive in a world replete with screens'

Dr Larry D. Rosen, professor emeritus of psychology at California State University

'Drawing on the latest research, this book adds valuable insights and weight to the growing and increasingly compelling body of evidence that children and young people's use of internet-enabled digital devices poses enormous risks to all aspects of their physical and mental health, and can also impact significantly on their cognitive, social and emotional development'

Dr Carol Homden CBE, CEO of Coram

'Laura's book is not a simple read. But it is practical and grounded in an understanding of the theory and the algorithms that underlie smartphone use. It provides a range of practical solutions without any hint of telling off parents or advocating only one way of managing smartphone use'

Jane van Zyl FRSA, CEO of Working Families

'Stop with the guilt! Almost every parent alive thinks they are doing the phone thing wrong. Whether your child already has a phone or you shudder to think of the day, here's a road map to sanity, safety, health and hope, by a mom who is also a dogged sleuth'

Lenore Skenazy, author of *Free-Range Kids*

'Finally, a balanced, grounded and child-centred contribution to the raging phone debate. Free from moral panic, this book is rooted in evidence and nuance, and recognises the real-world implications of phone use – both positive and negative – across a diverse range of children. A book politicians and policymakers would do well to read, alongside parents'

Molly Forbes, founder of the Body Happy Organisation

'A fabulous, accessible and refreshingly judgement-free primer for all those navigating parenting in the age of distraction, tech-harm and content overwhelm ... Highly recommended reading'

Jess Butcher MBE, CEO and founder of ScrollAware

Screensaver

A judgement-free guide to your child's first smartphone

LAURA WYATT-SMITH

SOUVENIR
PRESS

First published in Great Britain in 2026 by
Souvenir Press,
an imprint of Profile Books Ltd
29 Cloth Fair
London
EC1A 7JQ
www.souvenirpress.co.uk

Copyright © Laura Wyatt-Smith, 2026

Typeset by seagulls.net
Text design by CC Book Production

1 3 5 7 9 10 8 6 4 2

Printed and bound in Great Britain by
CPI Group (UK) Ltd, Croydon, CR0 4YY

The moral right of the author has been asserted.

All rights reserved. Without limiting the rights under copyright reserved above, no part of this publication may be reproduced, stored or introduced into a retrieval system, or transmitted, in any form or by any means (electronic, mechanical, photocopying, recording or otherwise), without the prior written permission of both the copyright owner and the publisher of this book.

A CIP catalogue record for this book is available from the British Library.

Our product safety representative in the EU is
BGC Sustainability & Compliance, 7 avenue du Général Leclerc,
Paris, 75014, France https://baldwinglobalconsulting.com

ISBN 978 1 80522 6475
eISBN 978 1 80522 6499

For my daughters, Esmie and Tilly.

Contents

Introduction   1

THE BASICS

Chapter 1: When Should a Child Get a Smartphone?   11
Chapter 2: Choosing Their First Phone   41
Chapter 3: Setting Yourself up for Success   58
Chapter 4: The Right Time for Your Child   84
Chapter 5: Buying Yourself More Time   94
Chapter 6: Why It's Not Too Late if Your Child Already Has a Phone   108

THE FIVE LESSONS

Lesson 1: Master Your Attention   124
Lesson 2: Become a Critical Thinker   146
Lesson 3: Know Your Digital Ethics   208
Lesson 4: Find Your Balance   242
Lesson 5: Keep Learning   264

Conclusion   278

Resource library   282
Acknowledgements   287
Notes   289
Index   299

'Making the decision to have a child – it's momentous. It is to decide forever to have your heart go walking around outside your body.'

Elizabeth Stone

Introduction

Sooner or later your child will get a smartphone. This is neither good, nor bad. It is simply an unavoidable reality in our ever-more digitised, online lives. Need to plan your journey on public transport? There's an app for that. Want to listen to music while you study? Book gig tickets? Manage your finances? Arrange a meet-up with friends or let Dad know you'll be late home? There's an app for all of these, as there is for every aspect of modern life. This means that while parents may struggle with the push and pull of 'real life' vs screens, we also need to accept that eventually a smartphone will almost certainly be how our child facilitates their so-called real life. Not only this, but smartphones will also become where our children conduct large parts of their 'real life' – not just organising but relaxing, socialising and learning. While there are many valid reasons to delay giving your child an adult smartphone, delaying is not enough. We owe it to our children to help them learn how to use one safely, healthily, happily – because use one, they will.

Getting your first smartphone has become a modern-day milestone for our children. How many of us are wheedled into

INTRODUCTION

promises of phones by our primary school kids, sometimes as early as five or six?[1] And it's been hard to ignore the media firestorm around the potential dangers of smartphones that has led to worried conversations around what is the 'right' age. In just a few months, the #smartphonefreechildhood (SPFC) movement motivated tens of thousands of parents to pledge to delay giving their child a smartphone until at least fourteen. The SPFC community is currently 350,000 parents strong and still growing. Are you one of those parents?

The publication of Jonathan Haidt's book *The Anxious Generation* in 2024 lit up academic debate and fuelled parental concern – if you didn't read the book yourself, you certainly saw the write-ups that surrounded it. Here was a global expert telling parents, 'it's not your fault – you have been set up to fail by unscrupulous tech designers' and making it safe for parents to share their concerns with one another openly, united against a shared enemy. Some notable academics have criticised his data analysis and emotive tone, but even so, his message really hit a nerve for anxious parents. It was recorded that over half of parents wish they had waited for longer to give their child a smartphone; two thirds have concerns about their child's phone use and the impact on their mental health and almost half say that mobile phone use has changed their child's personality.[2]

Haidt's book made four key recommendations: wait until age fourteen to give a smartphone, wait until at least sixteen for social media, keep schools phone-free, and cultivate more freedom and responsibility for kids in 'real' life. For all the controversy, his work has opened eyes and minds to the shady and manipulative technology designers that seek to profit from our attention, with scant consideration – and often blatant disregard – for children's safety or wellbeing.

When *The Anxious Generation* was released I had recently received a prestigious award from the Churchill Fellowship to investigate the impact of smartphones on children's mental health. The Churchill Fellowship promotes international learning to inspire positive change in the UK as the living legacy of Sir Winston Churchill, and they were funding me to take a one-month visit to California where I could better understand how Silicon Valley tech bros were raising their own children. I was in town at the right time to attend Haidt's San Francisco book launch, and had the pleasure of meeting him.

My America trip was the culmination of several years of informal research, all sparked by a podcast I had started in the shadow of the Covid-19 pandemic. After the best part of twenty years working in some of the UK's foremost youth organisations, including as a senior leader at the Prince's Trust (now the King's Trust) and the Sex Education Forum, I had become increasingly intrigued by the changing nature of modern childhood. I started *Childhood Heroes*, a podcast project, to interview experts on the big issues affecting young people today and try to find out if childhood today is better or worse than a generation ago. What struck me most was how so many of the experts were talking about the parallel loss of freedom that children were experiencing 'in the real world' and the simultaneous migration of childhood to the indoors, where children were spending increasingly long hours on screens. Statistically speaking, they said children had never been physically safer – yet they were now being increasingly exposed to all sorts of new online experiences that, as both professionals and parents, they simply did not yet have the playbook to deal with.

Meanwhile, my eldest was approaching the age when most kids were getting a phone, and I was beginning to worry. I knew of the potential harms they posed, yet when I looked for advice, the support I found online was disparate and contradictory. I am a parent, not an academic or a 'techy', and nowhere could I find the down-to-earth advice I needed. I knew many other parents of tweens who felt the same way. Soon enough I had applied for my research grant and retrained as a digital wellness educator – and this book is the result.

Haidt's work has been criticised for being too one-sided and for messaging that incites moral panic, and it is absolutely right that academics continue to interrogate and debate the detail and nuances behind the data. Yet, when reports show that half of children have accessed violent pornography on a screen by the age of thirteen,[3] that one in five 9–12-year-olds have had sexual interaction online with someone they believed to be over the age of eighteen[4] and studies have linked excessive smartphone use in children to problems with mental health and poor sleep,[5] only the most cynical of parents wouldn't have a small knot in their stomach thinking about the challenges ahead as their family enters the 'smartphone years'.

Still, the media narrative can certainly be unhelpfully alarmist and depressing, and good decisions are never made from a place of fear. So while it is great that we now recognise children's smartphone use as a societal challenge, not a personal parental failing, attention-grabbing, dread-inducing headlines have left swathes of parents feeling even more afraid and unsure of what to do next.

INTRODUCTION

Delaying to age fourteen is a good idea in principle – and it will be the right call for many families – but the reality is there are many reasons why parents and carers so often decide to give their child a phone earlier. Besides, even for those who do wait, what then? Your child will still see others' phones meanwhile, and they will still need help to use theirs responsibly when eventually they do get one. Worse yet, many have been left feeling like failures because they have already given their child a phone, which is so unhelpful when we heap more than enough guilt, judgement and pressure on ourselves already. Never mind our children being the anxious generation – we the parents have become increasingly anxious too.

It's understandable. While our children are physically safer and healthier than at any other moment in history, the pace of change today is so much faster, and life is much more complex for parents today than it was for our parents and grandparents. Besides, adult smartphones were designed by adults for adults and parental controls are limited, complicated and easily circumvented. There is also plenty of evidence to suggest that children's rights have been not just overlooked but wilfully ignored by technologists. Smartphones and social platforms should have young people's rights built in from the outset – something that is both technically possible and the least they deserve – but until that time, it is on us parents to figure this out. This is why I sincerely hope that *Screensaver* will be a reassuring guide to help you navigate your family's smartphone journey.

The good news is that all the campaigning and media coverage means that parents are feeling better able to question what phone they want to buy and when, rather than simply following the crowd. Virgin has reported that sales of 'dumb' phones doubled

INTRODUCTION

over 2024 (also known as brick, simple or flip phones)[6] and new, much more family-friendly smartphones are being released regularly as tech companies recognise the profit-making potential of parents. These are internet-enabled phones that offer more features than simple or 'dumb' phones and enhanced in-built protections for peace of mind; when my daughter and I reviewed three of these models for *The Times* newspaper, we concluded they could be great follow-on options for any teenagers who are ready for more digital freedom. Despite this, many parents will continue to pass down old adult smartphones to save the expense of buying a new handset, which is why *Screensaver* is about supporting you to understand all your options and help your family to thrive whatever path you pick through this digital jungle.

The conversation may start with 'What age are you getting your child a phone?', but it must not end there. The truth is, *how* a child uses a smartphone is as important as *when* they get one; spreading this message is my mission with this book.

I first became interested in smartphones because I was searching for answers for myself and my own children. I wanted a careful but kind, more nuanced, more balanced approach that felt achievable for me as a parent, as well as my kids. Meeting experts in California and across the UK, I realised that, more specifically, I didn't just want to protect my children, I wanted to empower them to become the master of their smartphone, rather than its servant. To get the best out of it, as well as avoid the worst.

This is what I want for you too, which is why I have trawled through the research, interviewed the experts, and amassed the best tips and resources. I've spoken in depth to a wide range of experts and academics, psychologists and mental health researchers to uncover what really matters when it comes to smartphones and mental health.

In the first section I will guide you through the key decisions you need to take – including when to give a phone, what features to choose, and how to set your family up for success (or refine your current approach). In the second section, I outline Five Lessons to underpin your decision-making and help your child to have a long and healthy relationship with their smartphone. I'd no sooner promise a single solution to this subject than I would buy a 'one size fits all' T-shirt, and anyone that does so is oversimplifying the issue. This book is about giving you the facts so you can make informed decisions and trust your own instinct as a parent to do what is best for your child, even if that means going against the crowd.

My aim is to provide universal, timeless principles that speak to the ethics and education of smartphone ownership that every family will have to grapple with, no matter the current technological trends. I have tried to keep references to specific tech to a minimum and where I do refer to named software or phones it is because at the time of writing they are so ubiquitous that it is hard to imagine them not being relevant in a few years.

Don't feel you have to read this book from start to finish if you don't have the time or your brain doesn't work like that. All parents today are perennially time poor. You will find 'Top takeaways' at the end of every chapter summing up the key points, and you can flip straight to relevant sections by navigating via the contents page or index at the back. The Resource library is also helpful if you are in an acute situation, and you want to dig into the details with help from a specialist.

INTRODUCTION

Finally, it's important to say that this book is for all parents and carers, no matter your child's age or smartphone stage. Whether your child already has their own phone or that day is still years off, it is never too early or too late to think about teaching safe and healthy usage. It is my sincere hope that you will finish this book feeling reassured and confident about how you'll handle this phase in your child's life. You do not have to do this alone, and your children absolutely can thrive, rather than simply survive, during their smartphone years.

SECTION 1
THE BASICS

Chapter 1

When Should a Child Get a Smartphone?

When I visited California in 2024 to research the impact of smartphones on young people's mental health, I held an informal workshop with some older students at an expensive private school in the heart of Silicon Valley, popular with the families of technology executives. I wanted to find out what these parent-experts know that we don't and, in light of this, how they are choosing to raise their children.

The first and most important thing to note was that the school – and other similarly exclusive schools in the Silicon Valley area – permits the children very little access to technology, and certainly no smartphones. In fact, as if in a parody of themselves, this mature and articulate group of students was crocheting as part of a textiles lesson at the time we spoke. Have you ever seen a group of eighteen-year-old young men chatting over crochet? Me neither. In an age where the British Netflix series *Adolescence* could be made it was a charming and intriguing sight, but it shouldn't be. (*Adolescence* is the cautionary and depressing story of how a thirteen-year-old boy could fall prey to toxic online influences and end up murdering a female classmate. Watch it. Then read the section in this book on social media to know what to do about it.)

As the students' fingers worked the wool, the students smiled warmly but wryly, alive to the irony of their parents being responsible for developing the technology that the rest of the world's children now use yet raising their own with very minimal technology in their homes. They told me that they mostly all started with text-and-call-only flip phones, before receiving their first smartphone around age fourteen, when the pandemic began. This is much later than the average American or Brit, who typically get their first smartphone around eleven years old (and in America, usually a smartwatch much earlier).[1] The students recalled how they begged to be given phones earlier, like friends from other schools had, and how their requests fell on deaf ears, and how they now believe their parents did the right thing. They went on to enthuse about their low-tech school, grateful for freedom from the pressure of needing to be constantly online, and I detected a hint of pity in their voices as they described how they felt this had enabled them to learn superior social skills to their friends from other schools, who they felt were obsessed with their phones, using them as a confidence crutch in social situations. Making conversation was clearly not a problem for these children, however. They even laughed about how comfortable they felt calling each other out when digital etiquette was breached; 'Hey! Put that phone away, we're hanging out here!'

It had not all been plain sailing though. Reflecting on the pandemic, when technology became the only way they could maintain social contact, they described how their parents were forced to soften their approach to technology, which was when, aged fourteen, most of them got their first smartphone. They said they needed this gateway to the world at that time and were excited to get online, but shadows fell across a few faces as they recalled darker days, including the prevalence of violent footage (such as beheadings) being circulated. As they spoke, I could not help but feel that if even these families aren't safe from these issues, it is telling for the rest of us – if not reassuring – that parenting through this stuff isn't easy for anyone, no matter how expert you may be.

Fast-forward four years and these mature and well-balanced young adults reported that while they feel they still use their phones 'too much' outside of school, they were generally happy with their digital balance. Despite feverishly protesting at the time, they are now grateful for their parents' relatively cautious approach. When I asked how they would raise any future children of their own, I was surprised that they planned to be even stricter than their own parents had been on them. Their advice to me with my tweens? 'Stay strong. Even if they beg, don't give in.'

Yet these savvy students weren't merely advocating for abstinence, which is never a sustainable solution, especially when it comes to wilful and rebellious young teens. They also knew from first-hand experience that parental relationships and education were key. One added, 'It's so important that you explain to your kids why you are taking these decisions so that they understand. My parents didn't do that, they just said: "If it's good enough for Steve Jobs, it's good enough for us", and that created real resentment for me.' Another told a cautionary story of a peer who was completely denied a smartphone until they turned eighteen who then went to college, got his own phone but didn't know how to cope with it all so became 'completely addicted',* staying up all night, suffering with his mental health, and eventually seeking professional help.

In Britain, most comprehensive (non-fee-paying) schools have been slower and softer in their response to publicity around the impact of smartphones. Parent campaigners for the SPFC community have been lobbying hard to change this – often with great success – yet while many schools claim to be smartphone-free, communication and enforcement of these policies is patchy. Without clear guidance from schools, parents continue to give their children hand-me-down adult smartphones, typically before the end of primary school.

Who can blame them? Phones provide welcome reassurance to parents raised in the 'Stranger Danger' era of the 80s and 90s, who want to know their child is safe and contactable on their commute to secondary school. Culturally, children often now expect to be in constant contact with friends in messaging groups, just like their parents are, although we forget this is still a very recent phenomenon. They also serve as a cheap and convenient form of entertainment or childcare, especially for parents who are working full-time jobs, parenting solo, or coping without support of nearby family – a list which covers most of us nowadays.

---

* Digital addiction is a contentious concept as the medical basis for addiction when it relates to technology is not clear cut. The term 'addiction' is commonly used in public discourse around smartphones, but 'smartphone obsession' may be a less controversial description of the compulsive behaviours that can result from manipulative technological design features.

But the question remains: why are those who could most afford the latest tech – including those who actually helped to create this same technology – opting for text-and-call-only phones, or none at all? There is much that Silicon Valley executives have known for years about smartphones and children that the average parent does not. It's time to level the playing field.

Smartphones vs other screens

If you are thinking, 'My child has been using screens their whole life and never had a problem; why all the fuss about smartphones?', it is a fair question. Most young children have been online in some form almost since birth, featuring in photos on social media or family video calls, watching TV, playing games on an iPad, tablet or console, reading Kindles, listening to music on Alexa or simply searching the internet on a laptop. What makes smartphones so special?

Two reasons. Firstly, they are transportable, which means they are omnipresent. The fact that you can take a smartphone anywhere and at all times means that the temptation to be entertained is a constant presence in our lives, like never before. You may enjoy gaming or TV, but if the console is fixed in the living room then it's not competing with concentration at school or conversation at the dinner table; you also need to negotiate use of the space or the screen with your family. This not only limits the time available for its use but makes it a less private act. You simply cannot watch what you like, wherever you like, whenever you like the way you can with a smartphone. The same could be said for laptops, iPads and Alexa-type devices; of course, it is possible to access inappropriate content or become obsessed with certain activities, but they are not typically carried around on our bodies at all times of day and night in the way that smartphones are.

Smartphones are everywhere and have become socially acceptable in almost all contexts. When once it would have been unthinkable to hear a phone in a restaurant or see a phone on a desk during a meeting, this has become the norm. It used to be a common courtesy to put your phone away during a conversation or charge your phone downstairs at night, but those days are gone. There are almost no boundaries to their role in our lives now, unless we actively create and enforce them. What this means is that even if a child may not be thinking about using their phone, if all their friends are using theirs, they will be more inclined to get their phone out and use it too. Phones quickly become inescapable.

The second reason is omnipotence. Not only have our phones become our constant companions, but they are so powerful and multifunctional that they have become extensions to our brains and bodies. We outsource innumerable functions to our phones. Google is our memory when we forget that name for that thing. Texting is our (false) courage when we struggle to say the words we want to express to someone's face so we type them instead. Deliveroo or Uber Eats become our legs when we can't be bothered to go to the shops. Citymapper soothes our impatience when we can't bear to wait for the bus for an unknown period. TikTok videos distract our dysregulated brains at the end of a stressful day. ChatGPT replaces our creativity in the kitchen when we use it to generate a recipe from random ingredients in the fridge.

Obviously other devices can provide some of these functions, but none can do them all the way our smartphones do at any given moment, day or night: our personal digital butler. It is wonderful to have the advantages of technology at our fingertips, but we must be careful of unintended consequences. If our children mindlessly default to using their phones for any and all challenges they face, there is a risk that they may become overly dependent on their device and fail to develop the essential skills and attributes that they need to cope in life. Consider how reliant we have all become on satnav to undertake relatively simple journeys. Now imagine you are a teenager who has never navigated a journey without it; you are a long way from home and your battery dies or you lose signal. You may well be terrified. It's not just our children. We have become so attached to our phones that most adults would struggle to be without theirs for a 24-hour period. Have you tried it? I have; it's really hard. I strongly recommend giving it a go as an experiment; you learn lots about the integral role smartphones play in your life, how 'naked' you feel without it, and how much forward planning is required to live life without one.

How old should they be? The bottom line

Researchers are divided on the data surrounding smartphones and children's wellbeing, and every month that passes seems to bring a new study and new headlines that generate fresh debate. I welcome and support more research in this field and yet, when it all boils down, these are my key takeaways:

THE BASICS

- Phones are not all good or all bad.
- Every child is unique and so is their phone use and its impact on them.
- The support and supervision that a parent gives a child with their phone makes a tremendous difference.

For all these reasons, I believe how a child uses their phone is as important as when they get one. With all that said, analysis of comprehensive mental health data collected across forty-one countries for Global Mind Project found that – on average and in general – the older the age of first ownership, the better a child's mental wellbeing is later in life, especially for girls.

This mega study suggested that the earlier a child gets a phone, the bigger its potential impact on how they feel about themselves, and life in general. While there are multiple complex factors that play into this data, strikingly, it found that children who get smartphones later appear to like themselves dramatically more than those who get a phone earlier on.[2] (Liking yourself is a great indicator of self-esteem, which is key for happiness.) For girls, mood, outlook, adaptability and resilience all improved sharply with age of smartphone acquisition.

So does this mean it's all the phone's fault? Of course not. Does it mean that if you give your child a phone earlier they will struggle with their mental health? Not at all. Does it guarantee that if you delay giving your child a phone they will be happier? Unfortunately, no – if only it was that simple! There will be many reasons for these results that we don't have time to dig into in this book, and anyway, your child is a unique human being, not an average data point.

What experts do tend to agree on is that, at one end, smartphones are unsuitable for primary school children and, at the other, by age 15 or 16, most teenagers are ready for their own (with support and controls). The start of secondary school, between ages 11–14, is the real flashpoint for debate, and this is where the Global Mind Project data offers some helpful perspective.

You need to make your own decisions about what will work best for your unique child and circumstances in full knowledge of all the pros and cons but, in my view, the level of supervision, parental controls and emotional support required for tweens and younger teens to safely use an adult smartphone means that there are better, safer, solutions available. Times have changed, and the discussion needs to move away from 'what age should a child get a smartphone?' to 'what is the right type of phone for what age and stage?'. For example, we gave our 11-year-old a text and call phone before she started secondary school for peace of mind, and so she can organise social meet-ups with friends now that she is out and about more. (It also has a basic camera, as she was keen to have the same one as her friends). When she reaches the point she needs more features – perhaps aged 13 or 14 – we will upgrade her to one of the purpose-built child-friendly smartphones with the specific apps we need, and none that we don't. Finally, when we feel she is ready to take adult-level responsibility for her digital life, she will get her adult smartphone and gain the greater freedoms and privacy that come with it.

We are lucky. A few years ago this wasn't an option for parents, who were forced to confront all-or-nothing decisions, but the tide is changing, and the market has come on hugely. The range of simple feature phones, hybrid and family-friendly smartphones is infinitely better than it was. Of course, no phone will exonerate parents of their responsibilities to support their child's digital life – your child will still require your active support as they explore the world via their new phone – but these more tailored products do make life a bit easier for us, and safer for our kids, during those in-between years.

With all this in mind, let us now unpack some of the specific reasons why the Silicon Valley tech bros who build smartphone technology are delaying giving them to their own children until typically at least 14, and why you might want to do the same.

The impact on attention or 'inner peace'

We now know that the mere presence of our smartphone impacts our brain's ability to fully focus on demanding tasks[3] because part of our unconscious mind is preoccupied about the possibility of what could be happening elsewhere while we are absent.

Our children may be spending time wondering if they have a reply on a group chat, any likes on social media, or what is happening on that live online game. This means they may struggle to feel fully present or peaceful. It is no accident that our phones make us feel this way. Phones have been designed to tempt us back to them using a 'variable reward' mechanism, a clever technological design feature that means when we check our phone we never quite know what we are going to get. Just like playing a slot machine this is exciting as there is a possibility (but not a promise) of a prize (the prize in this case being a hit of dopamine, a feel-good hormone) and it means that our brains are not fully on task, even when we think we are, because a small part of our mind is wondering, 'What might I win if I check my phone now?'

Even worse is that every time we interrupt our focus to check our phone, we typically take twenty-three minutes to return to our previous task – and that does not even account for the effect of 'attention residue', whereby part of your brain is still left thinking about what's just happened.[4] It's like when you have too many apps open at the same time on your phone, each one is pulling on the phone's operating system at the same time, slowing everything down and draining your battery.

This isn't just about sorting out your notification settings (although you should, and we cover how in Lesson 1: Master Your Attention). It is also a much deeper change that is occurring to our brains. Research proves that, just like Pavlov's dog, humans have, over time, been conditioned by our phones to anticipate an interruption, even when there isn't one.[5] Ever experienced a 'phantom vibration', where you thought you heard a buzz so you check your phone, only to discover there was nothing there? Then because you're there anyway, you can't help but go in and check every app, just to satiate that dopamine craving? It happens to the best of us and when everyone around us is checking their phones we are nudged into doing the same, which unwittingly reinforces the behaviour loop. Even if you planned to read your book on the commute, on boarding the train you see everyone staring at their phone so you 'have a quick check' too; before you know it the journey is over and the book remains unread in your bag.

If this resonates, then know that you are not the only one; studies have found more than half of parents feel they spend too much time on their smartphone,[6] but our phone use is not a personal failing or something to feel guilty about. Our lives are inextricably interwoven with technology. Humanity's relationship with technology is symbiotic – we created it and it reshapes us, in an ever-evolving cycle; it happened with the invention of the wheel, the written word, the radio, the internet, then smartphones, and most recently, artificial intelligence. Even so, we must set boundaries for our children that protect and channel their attention towards the things that matter most when they are too young to do this for themselves. At the same time, we must prepare them for a digital future by teaching them – and ourselves – how to remain in conscious control of our smartphones and use these remarkable tools in ways that further our aims and ambitions.

The trade-off of time spent online vs IRL (in real life)

One underlying fear we parents have about smartphones is that it marks the beginning of the end of childhood.

Heads bowed, their little faces glowing with blue light, we imagine them slipping away into this new and private world of flashy lights, emojis and pinging notifications. We worry our children will, little by little, forget all about the world outside their phone and the wholesome real-world activities we associate with childhood – playing outside, mucking about with mates and healthy hobbies all falling away in favour of The Phone. Is this future inevitable? And if it is, are smartphones to blame? Adolescence is, after all, defined by the slow ending of childhood. Setting aside the fraught and emotive concept of digital 'addiction' for now, let us begin by exploring the data around typical smartphone use, and the concept of screen time displacing IRL activity.

Would you be surprised if I told you the typical teen spends almost five hours a day just on social media,[7] and that this increases to between seven and nine hours a day if you add all other phone and screen time together?[8] (For tweens aged 8–12 the total time is around five hours). We all know screen usage soared during the pandemic, but what is weird is that it has remained that high and continues to rise to the point that nearly half of teens say they are online 'almost constantly'.[9] We also know from US data that screen usage varies across the population, with children living in cities, Black and Hispanic/Latino children, and those from lower-income households all spending longer online on average than their suburban or rural, White and wealthier counterparts.

But if you look closer, the picture is much more nuanced than it seems on face value because screen usage also varies with both your child's personality and your parenting approach. Researchers at US firm Gallup have shown that agreeable, extrovert, more emotionally stable children who are open to new experiences spend less time on social media.[10] Conscientious children – those with good control and self-regulation skills – typically spend 1.2 hours less on social media per day. If your child is not the conscientious type, don't panic – they also found that where parents restrict screen time, adolescents spend nearly two hours less a day on social media compared with those who don't. In other words, this is as much about your child's personality as anything else, and in any case, you really can influence how this all plays out as a parent by limiting their usage.

So what are the kids doing online for all this time? Studies show that watching online videos is what children do the most and YouTube is the one thing they'd most struggle to live without.[11] Girls spend nearly an hour more on social media than boys (although both are still crazy high at 5.3 and 4.4 hours respectively) and this increases as they age, from around four hours per day for thirteen-year-old girls to nearly six hours for seventeen-year-olds! They also found that the use of social media among tweens (aged 8–12) is growing, despite tweens feeling conflicted about social media.

If you are thinking, 'but where on earth are they finding the time for this?!', me too. Data directly answering this question is tricky to find, but during my research I asked children in the UK and US about this and their reply was, essentially, that they were on their phones almost whenever they possibly could be – before school, on the way to school, on the way home, on weekday evenings, and longer at the weekends, at school break times and in lessons if they can get away with it. Smartphones may also be used for homework or be on in the background while they are doing other things, like playing music when studying or to aid sleep, of course.

Many of us reminiscence about our own childhoods and worry that our kids are missing out on other important life experiences, which is a fair concern. Haidt argues that there are more nourishing – and developmentally critical – IRL experiences that have shaped the evolution of humanity over eons that we need to prioritise above screens.[12] He defines these as being: embodied (using hands and facial expressions to communicate), synchronous (interacting at the same time as others makes us feel closer to the other person), involving one-to-one communication or in a small group (as opposed to large groups where we feel we need to 'perform') and in communities that have a 'high bar for entry and exit'. This last point is important because in real life, people are usually strongly motivated to invest in relationships and work through issues, whereas online people can be quick to block others or quit a conversation, which makes our relationships more fragile, shallow and disposable – and makes us more insecure.

The important thing is that your child is getting enough of these meaningful real-life experiences and has the usual building blocks of a healthy life – things like a good diet, exercise, hobbies, responsibility, education, friendship, sleep. We then need to ensure that what they are doing online is harmless and age-appropriate.

Beyond these two considerations, I think we need to remove our rose-tinted spectacles and avoid demonising screen time. There is always something else our children could be doing and there is nothing inherently wrong with digital leisure time. Growing up, I climbed trees, skated, hung out at shopping centres, and played *Street Fighter* on the Sega Mega Drive with my brothers; the screen time was every bit as important and special as the rest of it. Now, as an adult, I enjoy browsing holiday destinations online and chatting with my friends on WhatsApp. My husband plays word games and reads football websites on his phone. It's digital leisure and it's all healthy in moderation, as long as it complements, rather than detracts from, our broader life and relationships. It's the same for your child.

Plus, if we can be open-minded about what a phone might be adding to our child's life this can also help us better understand and connect with our children – and drop some of the parenting guilt too.

The impact on sleep

The one area that I do feel strongly about is sleep. While certain apps may be used to aid sleep (think meditation, reading and music), poor smartphone use results in less, and worse quality, sleep for our children.[13] This is a huge problem because the link between sleep and our mental and physical health is indisputable; according to mental health charity Mind, without the right sleep, our children are more likely to:[14]

- Feel anxious or depressed, and existing mental health problems will worsen.
- Feel lonely and isolated, especially if they don't have the energy to see friends.
- Struggle to concentrate in school or make plans and decisions.
- Become irritable and not have energy to do things.
- Have problems with day-to-day life, their family and friends.
- Create or worsen physical health problems.

Experts say children aged 6–12 years should sleep 9–12 hours a night, and teenagers 8–10 hours,[15] yet one study found that on a typical weekday six out of ten children are using their phone between midnight and 5 a.m. – mostly on YouTube, social media and gaming.[16] Young people called out TikTok in particular as 'way more addicting' than other apps, saying that it led them to have difficulties in falling asleep. We should not be surprised; it's what Big Tech has wanted all along, and if this sounds cynical then it's because I am. But you don't have to take it from me; in 2017, the chief executive of Netflix admitted that sleep was their main competitor: 'You get a show or a movie you're really dying to watch, and you end up staying up late at night, so we are really competing with sleep.'[17]

My experience backs up this data. The children I spoke to in both California and the UK told me that when they had their phones in their bedrooms, their parents had no idea how late they we are staying up at night. They described being exhausted the next day after staying up to the early hours, incessantly group messaging as the FOMO makes it impossible to disengage. (Incidentally, I have heard of this happening with those as young as nine or ten, and via apps on tablets, not just phones.)

If I was a teen today, I can imagine being the same. Luckily I just had a text-and-call-only phone and the option of four channels on my TV. I was a sensible kid, but if I could have watched anything I wanted, on demand, without my parents knowing and all my friends were all up at the same time messaging each other all night, and that was all they spoke about the next day, then I know that degree of willpower would have been beyond me. I am convinced it is beyond most tweens and teens, which is why we need to provide the boundary for them. No smartphones in bedrooms overnight, no excuses, and all screens off at least an hour before bed to assist the wind-down process, ideally longer.

This isn't just about protecting their sleep or restricting access to opportunity for illicit usage (we cover pornography later in the book). Removing their phone from their bedroom also prevents it being the first thing they think of, reach for, or interact with when they open their eyes, so that they can properly wake up and greet other members of the household first. Doing this sets the tone for the rest of the day and sends our brains the subliminal message that we do not need our phones with us every waking (and sleeping) moment.

To help instil this habit, you can put a basket next to a charging point that acts as the 'home' for family devices whenever they are out of use. Use it for mealtimes, playdates, family gatherings or any other time that you decide phones should be stowed away. It could be in the kitchen or – if there is any chance your teen would sneak out to check it after you go to bed – then in a box in your bedroom. Just make sure all devices are fully switched off so that they don't disturb your own sleep by tempting you to 'have a quick check' yourself!

For more information about smartphones and sleep, including advice on how to get phones out of your bedrooms, read Lesson 4: Find Your Balance.

The influence of social media

When you break it down, often parents' biggest worry around smartphones is not the phone itself but social media. The US Surgeon General has blamed social media for a 'crisis' in young people's mental health,[18] describing our children as having 'become unknowing participants in a decades-long experiment'. Social media use among young people is nearly universal, with up to 95 per cent of teenagers and four out of ten 8–12-year-olds on social media, despite the minimum age for most platforms being thirteen.

Just like parenthood is a messy mixture of beauty and hardship that, once discovered, we would never be without, so social media offers young people a bewildering tangle of tantalising highs and potentially devastating lows. We need to take a closer look to understand what attracts our kids to this curious world, but first, let's get clear on what we mean by 'social media'.

By social media, I mean any websites and computer programs that allow people to communicate and share information, opinions, pictures or videos on the internet. This definition includes not just the likes of TikTok, Instagram, Snapchat, X (previously Twitter) and Facebook, but also popular apps and sites that you may not necessarily have considered as social media, like YouTube, Messenger, WhatsApp, Pinterest, Reddit and live-stream video games. New apps are being developed and launched all the time so it is inevitable that this list will feel laughably out of date by the time this book is printed, but the point is that social media is anywhere your kids can communicate with others online, from local friends to global strangers. Basically, anything with a chat function where information, opinions, pictures or videos can be shared, means it is both 'social' and 'media'.

Whatever your views on social media, it will be a part of your children's future so we need to understand the role it plays, and why its appeal is so strong. Perhaps the most obvious function of social media is entertainment, but it's more than that. At its best, social media can offer acceptance, support and connection. The US Surgeon's report revealed that roughly two thirds of adolescents say social media helps them feel more accepted, and that they have people who can support them through tough times. They also felt it gave them a place to show their creative side. For marginalised young people who lack access to real-world support, such as some in the LGBTQ+ community, or those with health conditions or disabilities, or those living in an area where they are the ethnic minority, social media can lead to finding a meaningful online community, provide positive and affirming content that helps create a sense of belonging and acceptance, and even increase access to mental health support.

And yet, it can also be incredibly harmful for many children, much of the time. In a world designed to prey on human insecurities (which teens have in spades) and extract value from users whatever the personal cost, we find popular social media platforms proactively serving deeply inappropriate, and often very distressing content to children via their feeds, even when children do not search for it or want it. Content related to suicide and self-harm, including live depictions of self-harm acts, toxic and dangerous 'beauty' advice, misogyny, violence and abusive sexual practices are commonplace, and in certain tragic cases has been linked to childhood deaths.[19] The recent flood of AI-generated 'brainrot' content is the latest trend to look out for, with a single video that can stack up millions of views across the globe. Created using the latest technology, these deepfaked moving images of celebrities and cartoon characters doing obscene and disturbing things are designed to optimise algorithms by compelling you to hover just long enough to exclaim, 'what the f***?' in horror, before sharing with a friend; sadly, it is the natural evolution of an unchecked social media marketplace to serve your child not what they want, but what makes them stop and stare. The question to ask is therefore not, 'should I trust my child with social media?', but 'should I trust social media with my child?'

The correct answer, in case you aren't sure, is no – you should not trust social media with your child – not for a minute. Young people themselves are telling us this, if only we would listen. American nonpartisan think tank Pew Research found nearly half of teens say that social media has a mostly negative impact on people their age (which, intriguingly, is dramatically higher than the third of young people who said the same in 2022) and a similar amount say it hurts the amount of sleep they get, and worsens their productivity.[20] Girls in particular (but boys too) consistently report that social media makes them feel worse about their bodies, and this should not surprise us because insecurity sells.[21] Sarah Wynn-Williams, a former Facebook executive, and author of *Careless People: A Story of Where I Used to Work* claims that when teen girls deleted selfies, the company would use that behaviour as a prompt to serve beauty ads because the act of deletion flagged them as feeling vulnerable and more easily influenced.

We also know heavier social media users double their risk of anxiety and depression,[22] that two-thirds of children are routinely exposed to online hate[23] and teenage girls are fending off unwanted sexual advances on Instagram every week.[24]

Social media companies know all this better than anyone. Jonathan Haidt's research team aggregated evidence from fourteen separate lawsuits against TikTok, concluding that it was 'harming children at an industrial scale' and that 'company insiders were aware of multiple widespread and serious harms and were often acting under the orders of company leadership to maximise engagement regardless of the harm to children'.[25] He highlighted that its actions had fuelled compulsive and problematic use, contributed to youth depression, anxiety, body dysmorphia and

THE BASICS

self-harm, and provided a platform for suicide, porn, violence and drugs, sextortion, child sexual abuse material and sexual exploitation. If there is any good news, it is that much of this is solvable, right now – we only need the industry to decide to act.

Frustrating as all this is, remember that getting your child a smartphone does not mean you need to allow them access to any or all social media. Also, that it is excessive, not mild or moderate, use that is most closely linked to anxiety and depression, and there is still much that you can do to protect your child. Research proves that parenting patterns strongly predict youth mental health and that children whose parents invest heavily in discipline, monitoring and loving support have (on average) better mental health than children whose parents have a weak relationship with their child, leave them unsupervised, and do not try to restrict screen time.[26] This means that when your kids do start with social media you can insulate them from the worst of the negative impacts with the warmth and quality of your relationship and support to them, both off- and online – just ensure that if you do allow them on social media, you take the time to educate, support, supervise and regulate their use.

There is much more on the solutions in Lesson 3: Know Your Digital Ethics, but first, how did we get to a point where Silicon Valley billionaires have such a chokehold on childhood? Permit me this short lesson on the history and mechanics of social media design; it'll be easier to support your child if you fully understand what you're up against.

Before social *media* was social *networking*. When Facebook first launched, its purpose was to help maintain and build pre-existing personal connections. Essentially, it was a glorified digital address book and photo album that helped you maintain contact with friends you otherwise might lose touch with. But around 2009, when smartphones began to take off and Instagram launched, the focus shifted towards sharing content, which the platforms would push beyond your immediate personal network using algorithms. By resharing content we amplified others' voices, and 'influencers' were born. 'Friends' swiftly became 'connections' or 'followers', and our posts became more polished as we cultivated public-friendly online personas. Unconsciously, unintentionally, we had morphed into mini content producers.

How does this shift relate to children's mental health? In sociological terms, maintaining and developing pre-existing 'strong ties' (i.e. relationships we are at least somewhat invested in or have a meaningful connection to) can strengthen and deepen relationships. Whereas publishing and consuming 'content' to higher volumes of 'weak ties' means that the time our children spend online is not necessarily an investment in people who already know, like or love them, but a performance where they are both actor and audience, either awaiting judgement or delivering it. In this environment, mistakes or misdemeanours can be harshly judged and exploited by insecure onlookers who feel little loyalty to our child. Worse yet, the fearful anticipation of judgement shapes how our children and their friends show up in the first place, as they post more of what they think will be liked by others, than what they themselves truly like. Inevitability, individuality, courage and kindness become riskier than conformity and cowardice. This is why we all carefully curate an attractive, culturally approved, safe online persona for ourselves; we hope it will shield us from the pain of rejection. Ironically this is exactly why social media can feel so uniquely depressing[27] – what we all share is not an honest representation of what our lives are really like and so when we compare ourselves to our peers, we feel lacking.[28]

When our children's first exposure to social media occurs during adolescence, its impact is even more potent. This is because adolescence is a critical time for forming our identity and sense of self. Indeed, the prefrontal cortex – the area of the brain that is responsible for decision making, reasoning, personality expression, maintaining social appropriateness and other complex cognitive behaviours – is still developing into our twenties.[29]

On the other hand, those who grew up before social media took hold had the chance to develop more realistic internal frames of reference based upon what they saw in real life, meaning that their sense of self today is less likely to be so profoundly affected by what they see online than someone with a social-media-warped view of reality. I count myself fortunate to be one of this generation – perhaps you do too.

Even if you teach your child to be careful with who they follow and what they share (and you should certainly do that) there remains a monumental power imbalance between your child and the power of the algorithms. Knowing this helps us to judge our children less harshly for what they end up watching and doing online. We all have moments we feel powerless to our phones. Drawn magnetically into echo chambers of content based on our personal data and online behaviours (our age, our gender, what made us click like and comment, or how many seconds we watched that video before scrolling away), we are fed more and more of what we hover over or click on. Sometimes it makes us feel good, sure, but make no mistake: the algorithms do not discriminate between positive or negative engagement. This is the attention economy, where engagement of any type makes money, irrespective of whether it helps or harms us. The platform's only objective is to keep you online for as long as possible, no matter the harm.

This means that if your child 'likes' a cute cat video, they can expect to see more of them. Equally, if they pause for a few seconds to watch violent or sexist footage, they will also be fed more of that and recommended relevant accounts to follow. If they make a typo in their spelling, stare for a few seconds, or click through – just once – to adult or inappropriate content – they will be pushed more of it. In fact, various experiments have shown that no matter how impeccably your child behaves online, they will still be pushed inappropriate content, based purely on their age and gender. This is why the suggestive power of algorithms can be so dangerous; they mercilessly exploit our vulnerabilities. This is how our otherwise sensible sons and daughters end up following superficial influencers who open their eyes to 'imperfections' and insecurities they never even knew they had, before offering them increasingly extreme 'solutions'. Social media is a primarily visual experience so obsession over their appearance and prematurely sexualised behaviour are natural responses to the lessons social media teaches our children. Children are clever and quickly learn what will make their 'friends' hit 'like'. Why be you, when you can be popular?

The struggle of girls growing up in today's society were captured aptly in Dove's Self-Esteem Project, a viral video advertising campaign with a message about the toxicity of today's beauty industry. In the videos Dove promoted online, horrified mothers sat together with their daughters, watching deepfaked footage of themselves giving out the same inaccurate and harmful beauty advice that the children were absorbing daily from popular social media influencers. Advice included filing down your uneven teeth to encouraging them not to 'put up with their thin lips' when they could invest in 'at home lip filler kits'. Yet the most striking thing about this campaign was how matter of fact the daughters were about it: one simply said, 'This stuff is on every girl's feed'.

Dove's follow-up tear-jerking 'Cost of Beauty' video, in which Mary progresses from carefree little girl, to being hospitalised with an eating disorder as a result of toxic beauty culture, showing where absorbing this content daily can lead. Even where the outcome is not so extreme, the insidious messaging that tells our little girls how to dress, pout and pose for maximum approval is where the damage is done. Look like this to be liked; look like this and you are ignored, irrelevant, worthless. For those interested in learning more about this topic, the film *I Am Ruth*, starring Kate Winslet, provides a deeper character study of both parent and child's parallel experience of social media.

Social media is also guilty of popularising online hate and misogyny. Young people may not actively seek out damaging ideologies, but social media can manufacture demand and create a market where one did not previously exist. Tragically, researchers from the University of Kent[30] found that lonely boys and men were being fast-tracked on to a highway of harmful extremism as algorithms initially served content focused on loneliness and a desire for belonging, but would progressively push harmful hyper-masculine, hyper-toxic ideology. Needless to say, the consequences of this are terrible for all genders.

This goes to show that although girls spend longer on social media and have poorer mental health outcomes during their teenage years,[31] boys also see their insecurities exploited. Another example of this is the looksmaxxing trend in which boys are shown perceived 'imperfections' that they then feel obliged to 'correct' through soft and harder aesthetic fixes, all in the name of increasing their 'SMV', or 'sexual market value'.[32] Pornography culture (which we explore more in Lesson 3: Know Your Digital Ethics) is even worse for ensuring boys grow up with a hugely warped sense of what is normal or desirable, both with regards to their bodies and sexual behaviour, and social media frequently acts as a young person's first main gateway to this world. With all these risks, it is no wonder that campaigners and politicians in the UK, Norway, Australia and nations across the EU have been seeking to increase the minimum age to access social media to sixteen.

Social media has so much potential for good, and locking children out entirely sits very uncomfortably with me, but the truth is, social media today is not child-friendly, and we parents don't have time to waste waiting for Big Tech to develop a conscience. Longer term, I believe rights-based legislation is the answer, but while the rusty cogs of governments around the world continue to grind, I am afraid that change will come too slow for most parents reading this book. Meanwhile, the reality is that it's up to us to make decisions about how and when we allow our children to access social media, and to talk to them about it so they can make sense of what they see.

I want the final word on this social media chapter to go to young people, whose true preferences were revealed in a fascinating study of 1,000 American college students by the University of Chicago.³³ Despite initially saying that they would pay to remain on social media (i.e. if their friends were still on it but they were not), upon deeper questioning it emerged that almost two thirds of TikTok users and almost half of Instagram users said that *they would pay to get rid of the platforms if others also weren't using them.* In other words, social media is worth less than nothing to many young people, and while they may personally hate many of these platforms, they still feel compelled to use them.³⁴ This shows that our children need our support and protection when it comes to social media, but as they get older they will also need our empathy, as rejecting social media out of hand may not feel like a plausible option. Parenting is tough, but so too is adolescence.

The 'not-my-child' thinking trap

A brief word of caution. As you read this book it is likely that you will have moments where you think, 'sure, but *my* kid would never do that.' Notice this thought and look at it closely. While it may well be true, it may also be that you are falling into the 'not-my-child' thinking trap.

It is tempting to believe that your child would be wiser, kinder or perhaps more innocent than their peers. It is comforting to believe that they would never make the 'mistakes' that we will cover in this book. I do it myself. But the truth is that the digital world is complicated and messy, just like adolescence itself, and our kids – and we – *will* make mistakes on the way.

If your baby was one of those who 'couldn't roll yet' but then rolled off the changing mat or whose toddler 'couldn't crawl yet' then crawled up a full flight of stairs when your back was turned, you'll know how easy it is to underestimate your child's abilities when they are growing and changing as fast as they do. This applies to the digital realm just as much as to real life. Take overall screen usage. When Rebecca Jackson, co-author of *The Learning Habit*, asked parents how much screen time their child was having, they estimated between 90–120 minutes per day but the reality was between 6–8 hours per day.[35] And despite being presented with the evidence, parents were unable to believe that this could be so high. It is the same when reading negative statistics – we simply don't want to believe these could apply to us, so we don't. This is understandable but unhelpful, because if we can't accept that our own child may face these challenges, then we won't be able to help or be there for them when they need us most.

We also tend to want to view our offspring as innocent and childlike even as they mature. We worry about them being lured into reckless or inappropriate behaviour by others, but how often do we view them as sexual or risk-taking beings in their own right? Everyone develops at different rates, and although some children will not engage in risky or sexual activity, plenty do. The question we therefore need to ask ourselves is why would this *not* be my child? Do I have an objective reason to believe my child would not be typical among their peers?

The aim is to find the parenting middle ground, where neither do we angst about something that may never happen, nor do we automatically push away uncomfortable ideas with a defensive 'not-my-child' knee-jerk. We can achieve this by remaining curious and open-minded, calmly asking ourselves, could this also be true for us?

THE BASICS

> **TOP TAKE-AWAYS**
>
> We know that smartphones are uniquely compelling because they are everywhere and unavoidable; they are also designed to be 'addictive' and Silicon Valley parents know this well enough to deliberately delay their own children's smartphone use. Smartphones affect our inner peace because they are distracting and impact our attention – this can be very problematic for a child's developing brain. The typical teen spends five hours a day on social media alone. Excessive smartphone use can reduce the quality and quantity of their 'real life' experiences, expose them to harmful content and impact sleep and self-esteem, especially for girls.
>
> The data is complicated, but the most comprehensive global study to date suggests that, on average, the older a child gets a phone, the better they like themselves overall. The good news is that parents can make a huge difference to a child's smartphone years. Aim to remain curious, open-minded and non-judgemental; try to avoid 'not-my-child' thinking. Limit what your child can do online and for how long – in particular, ensure bedrooms are smartphone free. Most of all, invest in your parent–child relationship and be their safe place during difficult times.

Chapter 2

Choosing Their First Phone

Imagine your seventeen-year-old learning to drive for the first time in a Formula One car. *Maybe* they will be all right with a lot of help and support (and quite a lot of skill), but for most kids, most of the time, a Nissan Micra will make a more sensible choice for a first car. That's a lot like how I see smartphones. You *could* just let your child loose with the full top-of-the-range model, but I strongly suspect that without a heck of a lot of coaching and commitment from you – and probably even with that – someone or something is likely to get hurt.

It might feel like giving them an iPhone will stop the whining, but for most children that just seems to quickly morph into a new pining – for more access, more permissions, more time online. What parents don't always know is that giving a smartphone is just the beginning of more work for you; you will have to educate, support and safeguard them on this steep learning curve. You may well have added parental restrictions, but these aren't foolproof and can never replace strong boundary-setting and a relationship of trust and openness.

The better way to select a phone is to first consider what features you want your child to have, and then to find a phone that does those things – and no others. When they need more features, and they have proved themselves as reliable phone users, you can upgrade the phone. Technology and times move fast, so remember: this is not a *forever* phone, it is their *first* phone. That is why I generally suggest you start them off simply with a basic 'brick' or 'feature' phone while they master the essentials, then move to a more family-friendly phone when you are ready to increase responsibility and need extra functionality, before finally graduating to an adult smartphone.

It's so easy to run ahead and overlook the basics of teaching younger children about good phone use. Things we take for granted but which are new skills and responsibilities, like how to take care of their phone, not lose it, keep it charged, not get distracted while crossing the road. With a simple phone you can learn how well they uphold their commitments, like texting you when they arrive safely somewhere, switching off their phone (or handing it in) while in school, giving it back to you without arguments at dinner and bedtime with less jeopardy. Likewise, we can ensure their messages to friends or family are polite and friendly, before upping the ante by adding in group messaging.

The key idea here is about gradual release of responsibility – stage-gating their digital journey – rather than dropping them in at the deep end, and feeling surprised, disappointed or guilty when they sink.

When you have established that the basics are going well with a simple feature phone, your child might graduate to one of the newer family-friendly smartphones that have more recently hit the market. What I like about these is that they further break down the 'all or nothing' mentality that has forced parents into a corner for so long. You want text, calls, the ability to track your child, a music player, GPS-powered map, journey planner and weather app, but no social internet browsers or social media? You got it! Your older teen now wants internet browsing but you want inbuilt content filters? Got it. The idea is that these phones can be tailor-made from the bottom up by you, adding features you want as your child goes, excluding those you don't, and by linking your child's phone to yours you can remotely monitor and manage their use, if you like. These phones are internet-enabled so obviously they are never going to be entirely risk-free (and when not successfully paired with your phone, be aware that they may operate like any other unrestricted smartphone), but they do offer much more visibility and control over your child's experience than we have had before. About time too.

While newer to the UK, these phones have been around for some years in America, and yet adult smartphones remain by far the top choice, which I am sure is because the money-saving option of passing on your old iPhone or adult Android phone will always be tempting. All I would say is, if you are able to buy new then family-friendly smartphones are often cheaper than the adult phones and offer much easier set-up and monitoring. Consider them the final step before total digital freedom.

Bear in mind that tech development moves fast and new models are being released all the time. My aim with this section is not to provide product reviews (you can easily find these online) but to give you a broad overview of the pros and cons of your headline hardware options to help you make decisions about which could work best for where you are at.

THE BASICS

Basic or 'feature' phones

If all you want is for your child to be able to call or text, and you don't feel the need to track their location, then you just need a simple 'feature' phone. Also called brick, dumb or flip phones, generally these phones have an old-school 'T9 keyboard', i.e. nine keys on a phone number pad that you repeatedly press to text letters – just like you may have had when you were a teenager.

Simple phones have very limited features but some have a camera (typically rear-facing), radio, or MP3 music player. Most do not have internet browsing or apps but some simple T9 keyboard phones do in fact have WhatsApp, video calling and even AI-assisted search technology embedded in them so read the specification to make sure you're clear on exactly what you're getting and avoid any surprises!

In the UK, Nokia are popular and have a range of retro phones, complete with the original 90s *Snake* game, whereas flip phones are particularly popular in America. Alternatively, if a modern smartphone-style look is important to your child, then consider The Phone, designed and produced in France but available internationally – this is a simple text-and-call-only phone that looks very similar to an iPhone. (Note – this is different from 'The Light Phone'.)

Pros

- Affordable – from as little as £20 for a new handset and a £6 monthly subscription for unlimited texts and calls.

- A wide range of models, colours and designs your child can choose from, from retro to newer models that look just like iPhones.
- Easy to audio call friends and family as you can assign quick-dial numbers to key contacts.
- Less stress if lost or damaged.
- Much less likely to be stolen, making your child less of a target for theft.[1]
- Longer battery life than smartphones so more reliable if your child forgets to charge it.
- (Generally) no camera, social media, internet browsing, app store or video calling (these could be pros or cons, depending on your priorities).
- Less distracting for your child when in school, social situations or crossing the road.

This last point is an important one: road safety is no small issue. Children's newspaper *First News*' 'Look Up!' campaign seeks to warn young people about the dangers of looking at your phone while crossing the road.[2] They say that road accidents are one of the main reasons that young people die and point to government experts who say 'the largest number of child pedestrian injuries take place between 8 a.m. and 9 a.m. and between 3 p.m. and 7 p.m.' and that 'children aged 12 are the most likely to be involved in an accident, as they are walking independently to, and from, school for the first time.' The easiest way to preventing your child from becoming a 'smombie' (smartphone + zombie) is to talk to them about the risks, and not to give them a smartphone until you are confident they will take road safety seriously. Similarly,

THE BASICS

smartphone snatch theft is increasingly affecting children in urban areas, with rates more than doubling in just one year to 2024, so if this is an issue in your community, a basic phone will make your child less of a target.[3]

Cons

- No option to GPS-locate your child.
- Trickier to text and fewer accessibility features than smartphones. (T9 keypads can be more time-consuming to master than the QWERTY keyboards on smartphones so might be inaccessible for some children.)
- Limited parental controls, e.g. it would be possible for your child to add new contacts without permission.
- Some models may lack the 'cool factor'.
- No maps or travel planning apps to help your child navigate.
- If you live in an area with terrible mobile signal and need an internet-enabled phone for your child to text or call you, this will rule out certain basic phones. In this case, try a minimalist family-friendly model with limited features instead.

Family-friendly and 'hybrid' smartphones

If you need more than a super simple model, but your child is not ready for the full-on Ferrari version, this is your best bet. There is (finally) a decent selection of smartphones to choose from that retain the convenience and functionality of adult smartphones but benefit from inbuilt, customisable parental controls and protective features, making your life an awful lot easier. This combination offers a potentially winning middle ground – peace of mind for you, essential functionality and some 'cool factor' for your kid.

At the time of writing, Pinwheel is available internationally, including in the UK, HMD (the makers of Nokia) now produce a new Fusion model aimed at the teen market, which they developed in partnership with parents and teenagers, and the Barcelona-born Balance Phone has a model designed for teens, whereas Gabb (which is big in the US) and Troomi have not yet made it across the pond.

There is also a growing range of 'hybrid' phones aimed at adults who want to live a more digitally minimal life and remove the distracting temptation of internet browsing and social media, or just want to take a break from their smartphones over the weekend, all while retaining the practical convenience of smartphones (think Google Maps, Uber and a camera). While these can be great, be aware that they can be more expensive and may not have parental controls or monitoring options.

Naturally, features vary between models so consider the specification carefully to find the right one for you. These are some typical features, benefits and drawbacks to look out for.

Pros

- A 'smartphone with guard rails'.
- Set-up process designed with parents in mind to build 'from the bottom up'.

THE BASICS

- Customisable so they grow with your child; you choose which functions are allowed and release more as your child matures.
- GPS tracking.
- Limit usage remotely through silent, night or school mode scheduling.
- Typically, there is an app store with a wide selection of pre-approved 'safe' third-party-provided apps that all require parental-approval so you can enable/disable accordingly. These include internet-based maps and travel planning apps to help your child navigate.
- Option for no or limited social media.
- Internet browsing with various levels of age-appropriate protections.
- Typically cheaper than a new adult smartphone.
- A growing range of attractive models, colours and designs to choose from, with trendy add-ons like cases with a flash feature.
- Camera – depending on model, rear- or front-facing options available (which may deter/encourage selfie-taking).
- 'Safe' video calling modes available (e.g. no ads, no in-app purchases, only with pre-approved contacts).
- Option for parental monitoring of contacts, messages and calls.
- 'Clean' music streaming options.
- Some may offer 'smart' filtering of messages, e.g. automated scanning for inappropriate content.
- Games library.

Cons

- More expensive than simple phones.
- Less likely that you have the option of a free 'hand-me-down' because the technology is still new (but the second-hand sales market should grow).
- Less common currently, so some kids may still feel FOMO or want an adult smartphone.
- An internet-enabled phone is never entirely risk-free.
- Interfaces will vary – bright and colourful options and designs may still feel compelling/'addictive' for our children.
- Often requires a monthly subscription to ensure parent-child phone pairing and safety features work.

Smartwatches

Smartwatches are essentially a wearable family-friendly smartphone and are popular with security-conscious parents in America for younger children. Current models include the Garmin Bounce, Xplora Go, Verizon Gizmo and the Gabb Watch. Compare models judiciously to ensure that you're getting all you want and nothing you don't.

Pros

- If all you want is to be able to call and text your child and know where they are with GPS-tracking, these will probably be everything you need and more.

- Contacts must be approved by parents.
- Some have extra features like extra-long battery life, timers, calculators, SOS buttons, 'safe zone alerts' (so you can see if your child goes beyond agreed parameters), silent/school mode schedule, games, cameras (and video calling).
- Generally cheaper to buy than a smartphone.

Cons

- Monthly data subscription required.
- Parents contacting children during school hours can interrupt learning. In America, where there are greater fears around shooting incidents, parents can also create confusion in emergency situations by messaging their child. Depending on school policy they may be asked to remove them at the door, which is entirely reasonable, given they are, in essence, 'wearable phones'.

Regular adult smartphones

Adult smartphones are not really phones, but pocket-sized computers that act as your child's gateway to the world; for the reasons I outlined under Chapter 1, I would not recommend them for a child's first phone without good reason, especially now we have more family-friendly options available. Consider them the Ferrari option that we all know, love and occasionally hate – iPhones, Samsung Galaxy, Google Pixel, etc. You almost certainly own one yourself so you know what they can do, which is pretty much everything. You probably have an old model handset (or three) sitting in a cupboard and have considered (or already) passed this on to your child as a convenient and affordable option, but there are downsides to this. We all know that technology ages rapidly, and badly. It's likely that not only is the battery life shorter on your old phone, but it will have inbuilt limits preventing you from updating the operating system beyond a certain point. This means apps will be riskier for your child as they will not be using the latest versions, which means not benefiting from the latest security features. A better alternative may be to sell the old phone online and put the money towards buying a newer, family-friendly smartphone.

If your child has passed the smartphone readiness test (see page 90) and you are looking for an adult smartphone for your child then be ready to put some significant time and effort into configuring permissions, controls and monitoring under 'settings'. This is all covered later in the book, but the key point to note is that while adjusting their settings adds a layer of protection for your child, these are merely hurdles to jump over, not brick walls. I cannot begin to tell you how many relatively easy ways there are for a determined child to overcome your restrictions; use them, but please do not rely on them to keep your child safe.

This is why The Five Lessons are so important. If you are opting for an adult smartphone, agreeing clear expectations around usage, instilling some supportive boundaries and being open about any monitoring that you plan to do is essential. You will need to keep the conversation flowing around their digital lives from the moment they get the device; always assume they are one step ahead of where you think they are.

Some tech experts say that Androids may be a little less intuitive and engaging (i.e. 'addictive') than iPhones, but, speaking as a non-techy parent, I think that choosing the model you are personally most familiar and comfortable navigating will be more helpful when it comes to set-up and monitoring. There is so much to consider already that being an 'Apple family' or 'Google family' is one less thing to think about as you can more easily link devices under a family plan.

Pros

- Your child is likely to be delighted to have a 'proper' phone!
- Access to every feature you could ever need or want – texts, video calls, maps, internet browsing, online banking, online ticketing, music streaming, emails, school-related apps, etc.
- Front and rear facing cameras.
- Phone settings to limit app downloads, set usage limits and add parental safety controls are available – although most parents struggle to set them up properly and they can be circumvented anyway.
- GPS tracking.
- Easy to set up and go (without parental controls, that is).
- Possible that you have an older model lying around that you can pass down to save money (although a monthly contract still required).

Cons

- May counter initial pester power, but children likely to continue to lobby for more or different use of phone.
- The most expensive option, if bought new.
- Higher financial risk if lost or damaged.
- Your child is more likely to be a victim of theft than with feature phones.
- Hand-me-down phones have suboptimal security and performance.
- Parental control and monitoring settings difficult to understand and set up and may create a false sense of security.
- Harder ongoing work for parents; need to regularly 'MOT' their phone to ensure settings haven't been changed, or supervise usage and check in about phone habits, for example, ensuring the phone has not been taken to bedroom.
- Exciting colourful interface and 'addictive' design features will distract and encourage compulsive use. Risk of children becoming secretive as they are tempted to stretch the rules or circumvent your systems.
- Access to social media, AI chatbots and inappropriate or adult content, including via messaging apps.
- New app features added by tech companies without any warning to parents (e.g. Spotify added videos and WhatsApp added an AI-powered chatbot and 'secret chat' features to hide messages without advance notice to users) so apps you originally deemed safe may become unsafe without your knowledge.

THE BASICS

- Ineffective content filtering. App ratings and explicit content warnings are generated by the app producers themselves and not correctly applied or moderated, so an app rated 4+ or 'clean' can easily include adult material or dangerous features for children.

Making your choice

It is essential that you are clear on why your child is or is not getting a smartphone, both for your own sake as well as your child. Here are a few common reasons parents give smartphones as first phones and my advice on how to address them.

- **Pressure from your child to 'be like everyone else'.** If this is your main reason for getting a phone then it's time to press pause and take a breath. Ask yourself is this really what YOU think is best for them right now, or are you just being swept along by the tide? Fitting in is important to tweens and teens, and we need to take their feelings seriously, but if peer pressure is your only reason for going along with something that feels wrong to you, reflect on what message this is sending your child about your family values. Do they even know what they want to do with the phone? Are you aligned with your child on what beneficial or useful phone use looks like? Is it even true that *everyone* else is getting one or does it just feel like that to them? Dig for the facts before reaching for conclusions.

- **Fear of your child being left out of chats and social plans.** Show me a parent who isn't worried about their child becoming the social pariah! Buddying up with other parents to take a similar approach can be hugely empowering; even just one other child in the class that is doing the same as yours may be a game changer for your child's courage and – just as importantly – yours. But even if they are the only one, agreeing workarounds with your child, and involving other parents in this can help, so that they don't miss out on key information and digital social hangs. Turn to Chapter 5: Buying Yourself More Time for advice on how to tackle this topic.
- **Ability to track your child.** You can do this with smartwatches, family-friendly smartphones or a very simple tracking chip, such as an AirTag. I would also query whether this is completely necessary or helpful or if making an agreement with your child to text or call when arriving or leaving would be sufficient. Turn to Chapter 3: Setting Yourself up for Success for more advice on the pros and cons of tracking your child.
- **Keeping in touch with family living apart.** Would texts and audio calls on a simple feature phone do the trick instead, plus video calls and picture messaging via your (or your co-parent's) phone, as needed? If not, a family-friendly phone would provide better inbuilt protections than an adult smartphone.
- **Travel apps for public transport.** Bus companies usually have a number you can text to find out the next service on your route. Perhaps you can also reframe not being

permanently connected to the internet as a valuable opportunity for your child to learn some problem-solving skills and develop their confidence by having to rely on their own initiative or the kindness of strangers to get by, just like we had to growing up! They can always text or call you if they really are stranded and in trouble. If this feels too wild (and I would challenge, is it really that wild!?) look for a family-friendly or hybrid phone that offers the app you want, without everything else.
- **Essential apps for supporting health conditions or disabilities, like diabetes, asthma, hearing loss or low vision.** Now here are some great applications for technology! I recommend identifying the precise app(s) you need first and researching whether a family-friendly smartphone can give you the access you need, before assuming you must have a full adult model.

If you decide to delay, reassure your child that 'not now' does not mean 'not ever' and that they will get an adult smartphone when the time is right. Meanwhile, your child can earn your trust by taking care of the devices they do have, upholding any family agreements about screens, and generally showing you that they are socially and emotionally mature enough to handle this responsibility when it comes. Reassure them that you intend to release more responsibility and functionality over time and you are always open to their feedback and ideas, even if you can't always say yes straight away.

When you decide that it is time for the smartphone, have confidence in yourself. You have thought carefully about this – you even read the book! – so give yourself some credit that you know what is best for your child and reassure yourself that there is loads you can do to support your child to use it safely.

Step by step, we cover everything you need throughout this book, and a family smartphone agreement (see Lesson 4: Find Your Balance) will help pull this all together nicely.

If you are finding the decision difficult, be kind to yourself. All you can do is weigh up your different priorities and make the best call you can with what you know today. Whatever way you go, hold your decision lightly. While prevention is always easier than cure, you remain the adult, and you always retain the right to change your mind any time, on any of this.

TOP TAKE-AWAYS

When choosing your child's first phone, don't just do whatever everyone else is doing. Decide what features you want your child to have and then find a phone that does those things – and no more. Increase responsibility progressively as your child learns and matures. Starting off simply with a simple feature (brick) phone while they master the essentials is advisable for tweens. After this, the new purpose-built family-friendly smartphones offer greater parental control and visibility for teens who are ready for the next step. Finally, when you feel your older teenager is ready for greater independence and privacy, they will have developed the skills to graduate to a full adult smartphone.

Chapter 3

Setting Yourself up for Success

Choosing the right phone to begin with matters, but how you set it up will also make a tremendous difference to how your child experiences it.

From the absolute basics of setting sensible PIN numbers and passwords, to navigating the minefield of parental settings and grappling with the ethics of GPS tracking your child, this section covers those fiddly details that, while tedious for you or me, will help to set your child up for success. I appreciate that this is a pain, but taking some time to understand this stuff now will save you so much trouble later. (I know – I hate it too, but I promise it *is* worth it.)

Medical information and emergency contacts

Did you know that smartphones typically allow you to store medical information that can be used in case of an emergency? This includes things like allergies, medical conditions and your emergency contacts. It takes mere moments to set up and this function is a potentially life-saving tool if your child ever needed first aid. To set up your Medical ID on your iPhone you need to go to the Apple Health app; on other phone types search under settings for 'medical information' or search online for 'emergency information on my [insert brand] phone'. Ensure that you have applied settings to enable someone to access this information while the phone is locked.

While you are doing this, add a couple of emergency contacts so that emergency services will know who to call if your child needs assistance. Many phones allow you to apply an 'emergency bypass' feature that allows emergency contacts to ring straight through to your child's phone, even if their phone is on silent, which can be very handy. If you use this feature make sure that these contacts (most probably you and anyone else who has caring responsibilities for your child) know not to call at awkward times, like if your child is in class or at the cinema!

Should I use parental restrictions?

It seems that almost all parents feel overwhelmed by the idea of their child's internet safety, which probably explains why just one in four of us use the safety settings.[1] Even if we know the settings exist, it all just feels too much on top of everything else for busy, hard-working parents, including me. The good news is that if you feel like this too, you can eliminate most of this stress by choosing a family-friendly smartphone. You will still need to configure your preferences at the outset, but as this technology was designed with parents in mind, with inbuilt filters and controls, it should feel somewhat easier than reverse-engineering settings on an adult smartphone.

When it comes to full adult smartphones, there are two schools of thought. The first is that applying parental restrictions is a sensible precaution that will provide some welcome peace of mind. The counter view is that restrictions are largely a futile game of cat and mouse that promote a false sense of security because controls are never totally watertight (even on a so-called family-friendly model). Besides, your kids will still see bad stuff elsewhere. This so-called 'no controls, no complacency' school of thought says that it would be a better use of your time and energy to simply focus on discussing the risks and supporting your child to develop the good judgement to avoid harmful content and make sensible decisions in the first place.

It is true, no matter what the marketing teams say, that a determined and curious child will always find ways to get around restrictions. It is often as simple as memorising your PIN but it could also be pasting the banned website address into a free web proxy site that instantly removes the content block; deleting and reinstating apps; creating an additional false adult account; using a new VPN; forcing a factory reset; 'sideloading' apps (using alternative sites to download apps or transferring from other local devices); using private browsers, private chats features or the 'shared notes' function as a chat room ... the list of clever tricks is infinite.

If you want to learn more about this topic, simply google 'How do I hack [insert name of parental control product or approach]' and you will quickly see how enterprising, ingenious – and deceptive – children can be when there is something they want.

Or visit the website of ex-Google employee and mum of teens, Miranda Wilson, who has created an illuminating list of how kids get around parental controls on her website (teched-off.com) and offers tips on staying one step ahead. It has loads of fantastic videos that show you the ins and outs of installing controls on the most popular games, apps and handsets. All you really need to know though, is that it's a minefield out there. The bottom line is that if you do opt to use parental controls, you must remember that while they set useful boundaries, they can also be circumvented.

To level with you, researching this chapter left me feeling downbeat for a while; all this work we're supposed to do as parents and these controls are still ineffective! Is the effort even worth it? Yet, as imperfect as they may be, I do still feel it's sensible to apply some basic safety settings. While there is no silver bullet to keeping your child safe online, parental controls offer one more welcome layer of protection – just don't sweat over them or expect too much from them. Nothing can replace quality conversations with your child.

There are several ways you can approach parental controls and I outline the main ones below. As well as teched-off.com, both the UK Safer Internet Centre website and Internet Matters provide detailed guidance on setting up controls, and I recommend setting aside a few hours when the kids aren't around to get your head around the information without too many distractions. I won't lie – it's a headache and I struggle with this stuff too, so just do what you can and don't beat yourself up about it. You will also want to regularly test the settings yourself to see how they are working.

THE BASICS

Applying parental controls on your home network

What? Configure your internet provider settings (EE, BT Mobile, Sky Mobile, Vodafone, Plusnet, etc.) to block inappropriate content, set time quotas and even shut down the internet at bedtime. Most providers give options to create different rules for individual profiles, so adults need not be subjected to the same rules as kids. Services may carry additional fees.

How? The UK Safer Internet Centre website (or Internet Matters, globally) has a guide on how to set up controls for many of the major network providers, or you can visit your provider's website for instructions. Applying controls using individual profiles at network level means you can protect all the devices you want to on that network (including children's laptops and tablets) so it is great if you have multiple or younger children. A more hard-core option is to buy a specialist parental-control router that will filter absolutely everyone and everything in your home, including *your* access.

Limitations? Applying protections to your home network is great, but your child will be unprotected the second they walk out your front door and connect to any other network, which is why you will also want to apply parental controls on the phone itself too.

Applying parental controls on a phone

What? If you have multiple phones of the same brand (Apple, Google, Samsung, etc.) you can set up a 'family of phones' and apply age-based content filters, time limits, request activity reports or opt for 'live' notifications delivered to you when they attempt to make an in-app purchase or if they want to request additional time that day.

How? Popular options include Apple Family Sharing; Samsung Family Hub; Android Family Link and Google Family Link. You can also apply settings within your child's individual phone (simply search for 'settings' under the phone menu and apply a password), although this offers less control and visibility than with a family account. Another popular option to consider is a ParentShield All-Network SIM card; this goes into their phone and works by piggybacking off several of the top major network providers with lots of built-in protections, which means your child is protected across several networks. Some individual providers, like EE, are also now offering child-friendly SIMs with safer default settings, but the difference is that these will only work on their own network. AI-powered parental control apps that monitor and filter harmful activity and explicit content in real time, sending you live alerts when they find reasons for concern, are also becoming increasingly available but with mixed reviews, so please do your own research.

Limitations? As settings are based on your child's unique user ID, protections *should* apply wherever your child goes. However, when your child connects to a different provider or someone else's Wifi, they may still be unprotected, so complacency remains your nemesis! Equally, AI-powered live filtering is a new and evolving entity so please proceed with caution.

THE BASICS

WHAT'S WRONG WITH JUST GIVING THEM MY OLD IPHONE, IF I STRIP IT BACK FIRST?

Lots of parents plan to pass on an old adult smartphone as their child's first phone but don't want them to have full access to the internet. These parents ask me, 'What's wrong with just applying parental controls on my old iPhone and removing the apps I don't want them to have?' The truth is, I think a lot of parents feel that this will be an easy option then later discover that it creates more issues than it solves. This is why if your child is not ready for the internet, I don't recommend you give them an internet-enabled phone, especially not for their first device. Below I explain some of the reasons why a locked-down smartphone is not as simple a solution as you might hope it is, and some of the pitfalls you'll need to dodge if you do go down this route ...

- They're not as easy to set up and monitor as you'd expect, which means that most parents won't have the headspace or know-how to keep on top of it.
- Sometimes settings simply don't work the way they say they will. Protections often only work on the apps created by the phone maker and not those you download independently. Apps you permitted that you thought were safe then quietly add in new AI-powered or other inappropriate features without warning. Harmful content simply falls through filters.
- They create a false sense of security: just when you think you have it all sorted your child may well discover

one of the many workarounds that we mentioned earlier in this section.
- When your child turns thirteen, tech companies are legally allowed to remove your safety settings because this is the current age of 'internet adulthood', so you may lose any supervision rights, 'downtime' schedule or GPS tracking, and apps may be unblocked without notice. (You can turn these settings back on, but you would have to notice that it's happened first and then your child has to accept them!)
- The smartphone interface is still very colourful and enticing, which opens up a world of excitement and temptation. At even the most basic level, i.e. with no apps allowed, gifting them a front-facing camera, with photo and video editing technology, and even just the GIFs and emojiis available within standard messaging apps, begin to draw kids into the device more than a simple, monochromatic feature phone would.
- It's a slippery slope that will end up increasing the requests/demands on you, not reducing them. As you cannot delete the app store (even if you switch off their ability to download apps without permission) they can still see everything that you are not allowing them to have. This means that their nagging for a smartphone simply levels up to nagging for 'just one app', which levels up to 'just one more app', and so on.

There are other challenges we have already covered too – like distraction leading to road safety risks, the higher risk of theft, and more recently, the fact that increasingly schools are not permitting smartphones on-site anyway. For all these reasons, I believe that it is easier for the parent and better for younger children to make their very first phone a simple feature phone. That said, if you are not persuaded and choose to opt for a smartphone, please do work with your child to closely monitor their usage; apply – and regularly review - the parental control settings (something is always better than nothing); and stay alert and strong in avoiding that slippery slope ...

Amending settings on individual apps and games

What? It may feel like a nuisance but taking the time to configure the settings on the individual apps your child uses, including YouTube, Google, Netflix and any social media is important. Applying stricter content and data-sharing settings and using private (not public) profiles on internet browsers, social media and online games will reduce the quantity of adult, violent and harmful content that algorithms push towards them, lower the risk of contact with strangers and mitigate some of the most addictive design features. Put the work in now, reap the rewards later.

How? Where available, select the child or teen account option for each app; don't expect these to be safe, but they should at least provide enhanced features like setting accounts to private by default. Then go through the specific settings one by one. Ideally you will do this before you agree to let your child have the phone so you can explore it and make your decisions based on what you see, but doing it later is always better than never! If you let them have YouTube or internet browsers (Safari, Microsoft Edge, Google Chrome, etc.) start by switching these to safe mode. It's not about whether you trust them or not – innocent searches often yield far from innocent results. Next, tackle any messaging apps, games and social media accounts by adjusting privacy and permission settings to the max. If you can't find 'settings' it may be called parental controls, assistive access, family features, privacy or security.

Limitations? Configuring settings on individual apps may sound brain-bendingly tedious, but if you do it one by one, as you go, it will feel easier. As with all parental controls, a determined child could undo your hard work, but if you explain your reasons to them, it should help to create a safer and more positive experience for your child online. Perhaps the biggest benefit though, is that by walking through the steps to set it up you will personally understand more about the world you are about to unlock for them.

Do we really need rules and restrictions? Won't they learn to self-regulate?

What you allow them to see and do online, when and how, is entirely your choice, but all the research says that children absolutely do need us to create clear boundaries around smartphones. By all means, take your child's views into account when creating these, and review your arrangements regularly as your child

THE BASICS

matures, but ultimately, as the adults, it is our responsibility to set standards that support our children's wellbeing and development. It is too much to expect a child to navigate this new digital landscape alone, and the risks too high.

I prefer to set 'standards' instead of 'rules' and I explain why, give examples of standards you can consider, and explain how to create a family phone agreement, in Lesson 4: Find Your Balance. Whatever standards you set, never assume that your expectations are implicitly understood; spell them out clearly, using examples of what is and is not okay. Explain your reasoning behind each standard so that your child understands your positive intentions; remember, they do not have to like them, but they do need to adhere to them if they want the privilege of having their own phone. Agreements around use should evolve as your child matures, and if you can model the positive behaviours you are expecting from your child – like no phone at the dinner table or in the bedroom – this will make it much easier for your child to respect the rules (and you).

Which apps should I allow/ban?

Giving your child a smartphone does not mean you need to let them have whatever apps they want. One day they will be old and wise enough to make these decisions for themselves, but with their first phone it is important to agree app by app what they are allowed to have.

Here is my step-by-step guide to deciding which apps to permit, and which to refuse.

1. **Configure settings to require a password or PIN before downloading new apps.** You need to control what they can download for this to work. Approving apps on a case-by-case basis will also help avoid a shocking phone bill. Remember that your passwords and PINs are discoverable and your child isn't silly; assume they will discover them and set a reminder to update them often. If you have the option to approve download requests from your child in real time, this will be convenient for your child, but do not be pressured to agree to a new app before you have researched it.
2. **Before approving an app check it out on the Common Sense Media website.** It provides free impartial expert reviews on all the major apps and is a great first port of call.
3. **Do not trust app age ratings.** They have no reliable meaning because they are entirely fabricated by the app creators and there is no independent reviewing body. This allows toxic and outright dangerous apps to be categorised as safe for ages 4+ or 12+, including chat rooms where children can meet and 'flirt' with anonymous strangers, have their sexual attractiveness rated by others, apply 'skinny' filters or participate in 'sexy photoshoot dares'. In the US, the App Store Accountability Act is aimed at regulating the age rating of apps just like we do with TV, film and adverts, but change will take time.
4. **Remember that blocking an app doesn't stop a child viewing the website.** It is usually possible to view a link on a website without having created a profile. If you

don't want them to visit a site at all you need to be clear that this is not allowed and use other parental controls to limit their access.

5. **Don't overlook 'innocent' apps.** You would be forgiven for thinking nothing of giving your child access to practical or professional productivity apps like Notes, Dropbox, OneDrive or Google Docs to help them collaborate over school projects – their school may even require it. What you or they might not have considered is how they can also be used in less salubrious ways. Google Docs is a cloud-based app where users across multiple locations can co-create and edit documents in live time and is frequently used by children to collaborate on homework assignments. It's also a great makeshift chat room, safe from unsuspecting parents, where text and image uploads can be shared and deleted with no record of a conversation ever happening. iPhone's seemingly innocent Notes also works perfectly for text chats if you simply tag a friend, and Dropbox works for sharing private images and videos. Special 'icon-hiding apps' are used to conceal banned apps in plain sight from parents under the beard of a boring icon; a fake calculator icon is a classic.

6. **Understand any fees.** Does it have an initial free trial leading to a paid subscription, or are there in-app purchasing options to watch out for? Agree spending limits with your child, but remember that paid-for does not mean bad, and there's no such thing as a free lunch. Free apps fund themselves through advertising and selling

your child's data to external parties so your child may be slammed with adverts or unhealthy algorithms. Conversely, the paid apps tend to be based on offering a straight-up exchange of service for payment, which means you get what you pay for without the perverse influences or time-wasting ads. I have loyally been paying for a meditation app for eight years because I value the quality content and don't want the pop-ups disturbing my peace.

7. **Seek out positive apps.** Like my meditation app, some apps are designed to promote wellbeing, support our focus and help us learn new things. For example, content-blocking apps can help your teen carve out focus or study time. Habit-tracking apps can support healthy behaviour IRL. Others can support hobbies or help you learn new skills, like the app I have that supports my family learning the piano ... at £20 a month it isn't cheap, but it can be used by five different users and is much more affordable than paying a private tutor. That said, even 'positive' apps usually deploy 'addictive' design features to keep you hooked so you don't quit, which carries the risk of compulsive behaviour or stress for some. For instance, my daughter started learning Spanish on Duolingo, but the pressure of daily reminders to 'maintain her learning streak' felt way too intense so we had to quit. Similarly, habit-tracking apps can also lead certain personalities to become unhealthily obsessed with their weight, diet or exercise. Also, as I mentioned earlier, unwelcome new features can be added without warning – like the 'channels' feature and the AI-powered chatbot

on WhatsApp or the video feature of Spotify, which caught many parents off guard – so just keep everything under review. Ask yourself regularly: is this still what we signed up for? Is this still working for us the way we originally hoped it would?

8. **Beware of duplicate accounts.** Many children have a 'clean' social media profile for family and a 'real' account, with all the stuff they don't want you to see. Regularly reviewing your child's 'clean' account and believing that all is well, only to later discover a nasty surprise, is a relatively common experience among parents; for me, this is another reason to delay opening the Pandora's box of social media for as long as you can. If you don't want them to use social media, explain your reasons why, do not allow them to download the app, and take care to block the website too.

9. **Be the bad guy.** If you are not ready to investigate the request, set up the app safely, check in with your child regularly and pay for it, say no. If your instinct tells you it doesn't feel right, or it's too soon for your child, say no. Explain your reasons so they understand, but back yourself. Just because they do not like your decisions – or you! – it does not mean you're wrong. As I frequently need to remind myself, our job is to be their parent, not their best friend.

10. **The bottom line? Do your own research.** Search online to see what other parents and professionals are saying about it. Do you know any parents of older children who already have the app who can tell you about it? I have found older teenagers and young adults to be very keen

to share stories of what it's really like on these apps – but only once they are free from any risk of their parents removing it from them!

What notification settings do you recommend?

In short – switch off every single notification that is not absolutely time sensitive, and while you're at it, do the same on your own phone. To safeguard them in case of emergency, allocate priority VIP status to your own contact number and other key family members so that a phone call from you will ring through regardless. For a fuller explanation as to why and how, see Lesson 1: Master Your Attention.

Should I get PAYG or contract?

Whatever phone you choose – hand-me-down or new – you'll need to get them a SIM card. As you probably know, this small chip goes inside the phone and allows it to connect to the internet and make phone calls. With a pay-as-you-go SIM you top up their account with credit, which they spend down until they need another top-up. If you don't expect your child to use the phone much or want to avoid a shock with the bill you might prefer this option, but it tends to be more expensive overall.

A contract SIM offers a set monthly allowance of minutes, texts and data. Contracts range from thirty days to two years and are cheaper than PAYG in the long run. Exceeding your data limits costs extra, though, and if your child is spending hours streaming

THE BASICS

videos or gaming, they may end up using more than you would imagine, so ensure that you block additional spending without prior permission. ParentShield All-Network SIMs have in-built protections to prevent overspending, including providing daily limits to help manage their monthly usage, while also allowing unlimited calls to two 'safe' numbers. Alternatively, having your whole family on a single network provider may reduce admin if it means you can have everyone on the same monthly bill. Some networks offer discounts if you take out multiple plans with them, but shop around; Money Supermarket has a great guide on the best value deals.

Whichever option you go for, a phone can be a good opportunity to teach your child how to pace and budget their data spend. They will make mistakes as they learn, but if you have applied spending restriction settings, you can evade financial disasters.

Should I spy on my child?

Monitoring your child's usage could involve reading their messages, reviewing their social media accounts, checking their search history or buying software like Norton or Qustodio (search online for the latest independent reviews of the best products) that sends you real-time alerts that flag inappropriate language or images.

A survey of 1,000 American parents found that more than half of parents say they check messaging and social media accounts frequently using monitoring tools, and three quarters of those who monitor their children online felt that 'it had led their children to make better decisions, either because they know they're being watched or because they've been caught before'.[2] Nearly half of parents also felt that tracking their children's activities has had a positive impact on their relationship with their children, so monitoring your child has benefits and is certainly popular with parents. But ... isn't it spying?

There are two schools of thought on this. Some argue that parents' lack of knowledge around how much time their children are spending online and what exactly they are doing leaves them open to risks; monitoring this provides parents with valuable insights on what their kids are up to so they can take action to support and protect them. Others, like Emily Cherkin, author of *The Screentime Solution*, advocate against it. Cherkin emphasises that parents who 'spy' on their children risk eroding trust and discouraging honest communication, and that children could be tempted to become more secretive, creating false social media accounts, joining a VPN to avoid your home network settings or simply using coded lingo to hide meaning in plain sight. In any case, monitoring software is fallible and does not work consistently across every app or platform. For example, at the time of writing, no third-party software can monitor Snapchat on iPhones.[3] Plus, most search engines offer private search modes (like Google Incognito mode) or they could simply delete their search history, so even if you do decide to check in on their activity, you may not be getting the full picture. An alternative solution? Develop super clear shared family values and expectations about phone use – and don't give a smartphone to a child who is too immature to handle that responsibility.

Personally, I feel there is a balance to be struck that is neither spying, nor relinquishing any right to ever see what your child is up to online. To me, spying means digitally snooping on your child online without their knowledge, and I definitely do not recommend that. Devorah Heitner, PhD, author of *Growing Up in Public: Coming of Age in a Digital World* agrees.[4] By spying on your child: 'You could do *more* damage by monitoring covertly and intrusively and miss the chance to build a stronger relationship by discussing the ups and downs of digital life,' she says. Instead, ask yourself, what is your goal here? What are you worried about? Then focus less on trying to catch them doing the wrong thing and instead teach them how to do the right things. She suggests swapping spying for observation. Do they seem stressed by some aspect of life online? She also highlights how reading your child's friends' messages will probably cause your child to worry for their friend's privacy and create a dilemma for you about what to do with this information. Heitner argues that adolescence is a messy, complicated time when teenagers need space to experiment with creating an identity independently from us and that examining their interactions too closely risks robbing them of this opportunity. Instead, we need to trust that they will share personal information 'when they are ready, in their own way'.

So far, so sensible, especially for older teens, but what if you really are committed to giving your younger teen or tween a smartphone? You will certainly want to regularly review what they are up to online until you can be confident that you can trust that they are coping well. If you do decide to monitor their use – and this applies whatever age they are and even if you are only checking their phone very occasionally – then you must let them know what you are doing and why. Explaining the terms and conditions you are attaching to a new phone *before* you give it so that they know what you will see will help you avoid issues later – but, as always, better later than never. Be specific. Describe when and how you will check in on their online use. You can record this in your Family Agreement (see Lesson 4: Find Your Balance on how to create this). Remind them that your number one job as a parent is to keep them safe and, because this phone is a new privilege and you are both learning, you need to know that they are applying the lessons you have taught them about being safe and well online, until they are mature enough to gain complete technological independence. This way, you can never be accused of spying – because it was never a secret in the first place.

In the same manner that it is polite to knock on your child's door first before barging in, let your child know what you are checking and why *before* you check it. You can even review your child's usage – like screen time statistics or websites visited – together with them and use it as the launch pad for conversation about how things are going. The key is approaching this in good faith and with the transparency needed to build, rather than undermine, trust between you. It should go without saying, but as your child ages and proves their maturity as they enter early adulthood, they deserve and need much greater privacy. Equally, if they already have a phone, it is never too late to begin this practice – just give them advance notice so that they don't feel on the back foot with it. Of course, this means they may hide or delete things they don't want you to see, but you are playing the long game here by starting the conversation, rather than trying to catch them out.

Whatever approach you take with monitoring, I strongly recommend having a record of all their phone and social media passwords so that in case of a genuine emergency you can gain access to what could be vital information. Your child should know you have these and the conditions under which you would want to gain access. (You can also consider securing their accounts with a password manager.) Bluntly – this is important because if anything serious happened to your child you would want to know everything you could about what they have been doing online. Sadly, Big Tech have proved themselves to be unresponsive, unhelpful and even obstructive in sharing information with parents in cases of troubled, missing and deceased children.

Ellen Roome learned this in tragic circumstances when her son, Jools Sweeney, passed away in April 2022, aged just fourteen. Ellen had many unanswered questions about the role social media might have played in his death but found it impossible to access her son's accounts, with one MP describing her treatment by social media companies as 'cruel and inhumane'. Her tireless efforts to seek better legal rights for grieving parents with 'Jools' Law' has provoked debate in parliament, and we remain hopeful that both British and international law will eventually catch up.

Should I track my child?

The American survey revealed that 80 per cent of parents check their children's location and a third of these do it without letting their children know.[5] Admittedly, nearly two in three had caught their children doing something they shouldn't, but just because we *can* track our children (and catch them out), *should* we?

Tracking software has obvious benefits for rare higher-stakes situations – like locating your child in an emergency. Plus, if it means you are more likely to give your child more real-world freedoms that can also be great – but using it for day-to-day surveillance of what your child is up to can be problematic. While it may be comforting to know your child has arrived at their destination safely or is where they said they would be, tracking is never 100 per cent reliable. Batteries run out, your child may leave their phone behind, coverage can be patchy, tracking tools can be inaccurate or slow to update, and discrepancies between the technology and your child's account can lead to arguments. But for me, the even more important issue is when technology fails – do we still believe in our child's resilience to cope? Do *they* believe in their ability to cope?

Imagine that you have never left the house without either a parent by your side or a phone in your hand that constantly transmitted your live location to said parent. How afraid might you feel if that phone was stolen or ran out of battery, and you found yourself away from home, completely alone and disconnected? In this way, constant geolocation of your child effectively serves as an extended digital umbilical cord between parent and child, connecting them to you at all times, not something that any of today's Millennial or Gen X parents experienced growing up. Our parents trusted us to make sensible decisions, and for the most part, we did. Over time, those experiences helped us to see ourselves as strong, capable, independent beings who were not overly scared of walking out alone into the big wide world.

We must take care that tracking technology does not become an emotional safety blanket for our own fears as parents and so accidentally undermine our children's ability to develop this real-world resilience and inner confidence. We must not allow it

THE BASICS

to undermine our relationship with our child by inadvertently replacing trust and meaningful conversation. We must accept that our child will make mistakes and misjudgements. At some point – within healthy boundaries – our children need the space from us to have independent experiences and the chance to take responsibility for themselves, make good judgement calls, solve their own problems and – ultimately – grow.

When deciding whether to track your child, be honest with yourself about your personal motivations for doing so. Which are real and helpful age-appropriate precautions? Which are more about our own anxieties? Consider how you can support them to develop coping strategies and confidence for living life disconnected from their phone or GPS signal. Rather than tracking them, could you have an agreement where they text you to say when they have arrived or when they will be home, and use this as an opportunity to build trust and communication instead?

If you do decide to track your child, be open and honest with them about when and how you will use this function. There are several ways you can do this. If your child has a basic phone or no phone at all, an affordable and simple solution is to just pop a Bluetooth or GPS gadget like Apple AirTag or Tile Mate on their keyring or bag (note that some offer more precise locations than others). Family-friendly smartphones usually have this feature built in. Apps like Find My Friends, Life 360 or Google Family Link also work for adult smartphones. The challenge for nervous parents may be: once this tracking information is available on your phone, will you be able to resist checking it?

What about phones at school?

Curiously, schools in Britain (and around the world) have wildly different rules around phones, ranging from zero tolerance – with no phones allowed on-site, spot checks and strict sanctions for rule-breakers, or compulsorily locking away phones in lockers or pouches on arrival – to light touch 'not seen, not heard' policies with highly patchy enforcement. Schools who take the latter approach often present this as being 'phone-free' when the reality is that without strong leadership, phones remain in pockets and are used under tables, at breaktimes and in the toilets.

A review of smartphone policies in schools by several well-respected experts concluded that a lack of clarity on this topic leaves parents confused and teachers frustrated; meanwhile, 'children are clear that meeting and learning "in person" is far preferable, and that unless everyone is "off", they cannot be "off"'.[6] While children are positive about the digital world, they typically feel phones in schools exacerbate social pressures just at the time when they are learning and building their relationships. Schools can help reduce this pressure by banning smartphones from sites completely or ensuring they are locked away during the day (medical or special exceptions permitting).

Whatever the policy, I believe schools should never require children to have a smartphone to access learning or assume children own one by building their use into lessons or requiring them for homework (e.g. through doing online quizzes in class or inviting children to take a photo of the board) as this puts pressure on parents to give a phone earlier than they might want to. Of course, schools may expect families to have internet access for completing homework, booking clubs, managing dinner money etc., but if your school requires access to certain apps or websites for learning or practical purposes, these should be accessible via their parents' phone, tablet or laptop, or a school computer. Being able to complete homework or access school-related apps should not be the reason to give a child a smartphone before they are ready.

If you are unhappy with your school's policy you might find the #smartphonefreechildhood resources helpful. Many parents have had success in changing the norm in their school community by connecting with others who feel the same and acting together to raise concerns.

TOP TAKE-AWAYS

Choosing the right phone to begin with matters but so does how you set it up. Even though it's a hassle, it is worth putting the time and effort into understanding the phone settings so that you can make it as safe as possible, including adding medical information, emergency contacts and parental controls. There are several ways you can do this and if you feel overwhelmed, just do what you can, or consider getting a family-friendly smartphone instead, as these should be easier to set up.

Think carefully about which apps you let your child have and do your own research first. Ensure they are clear on any rules around what they are allowed to access or do online, and keep talking with them about how it's going. Switch off all their non-time-critical notifications to avoid distractions and always tell your child if you plan on tracking them or monitoring their use to preserve the trust between you. As for school – smartphones are best kept out of schools to reduce distractions and social pressures.

Chapter 4
The Right Time for Your Child

We have covered the reasons why you may wish to delay giving your child a smartphone, including the nature of the adolescent developing brain, the risk-to-reward ratio, and the level of effort required by you to enable their safe usage – but how do you know when the time is right to go for it?

First, if you have not yet read the section, 'How old should they be? The bottom line', where I explain the general consensus among experts around smartphone-readiness by age and stage, flip back to page 17 before reading on. This chapter is about your individual child and digs deeper into the individual attributes that inform a child's experience of smartphones, and the circumstances that might influence your own personal decisions. This is because the truth is there is no magic age that is 'right' for every child, and no expert knows your child better than you do. What is right for your child will not necessarily work for mine.

Like learning to ride a bike, while yours may have hopped on a balance bike and sped off competently, mine might have felt safer with stabilisers. It's the same with smartphones. The social media platform that feels like a welcome hug of support for one child may be a source of profound angst and insecurity for another. The news website that one child uses for helpful information for school projects may be a source of microaggression for another. An online game that fosters one child's sense of belonging may be the source of a terrible safeguarding incident for another.

The point is that we are all different and there are many factors that can influence our child's experience of phones and the internet. We have already covered the evidence around how a child's broader personality may inform their experience of the online world, including their relative conscientiousness and confidence, pre-existing mental health conditions, and any previous or ongoing experiences of bullying. This section offers a few more factors you may wish to consider, and a checklist to help your decision making so that you can feel good about whatever you choose to do.

Neurodiversity

Dr Meryl Alper, author of *Kids Across the Spectrums*, highlights that there is relatively little research around the everyday tech use of autistic children, although her work suggests that – perhaps contrary to popular belief – what autistic young people do with technology is not radically different from their non-autistic peers.[1] As for all children, the internet can be a double-edged sword for neurodivergent children. Online gaming can offer predictability and structure, which can be reassuring compared to the uncertainty of social interactions at school. The online world can also provide a richly informative and imaginative environment that offers joy, creativity and kinship. Equally, some children may struggle with this new and unfamiliar environment or find it harder to interpret social cues on group chats, such as when to speak, how to respond to humour, or other unspoken social norms. Some may feel stressed by the unnatural and unachievable expectations of social media. For others, perhaps including those with ADHD, the fast-paced nature of the internet might feel even more compelling, while also being overwhelming. A child that struggles to regulate their attention may find it hard to switch off their phone when asked or find the constant notifications and rapid conversations in group chats distracting and frustrating, especially if they feel that they can't keep up or respond quickly enough. Every child is unique.

If you believe your neurodivergent child would struggle with a smartphone, you may wish to delay giving them a phone. In the meantime, you could start by observing closely how their existing screen usage is working (playing or watching with them is even better) to see what you can learn from this. Which media results in dysregulation, which is going well, what practices already work for you to maintain a healthy balance? When the time comes, help them with strategies to take care of their phone – agree a place where it is stored and charged, and consider insurance if they are prone to losing things. For their first smartphone, consider a family-friendly model and be highly selective in what apps or features you allow at first. Set time limits and parental controls (especially if impulsivity is a challenge) and monitor how it is going. Children may need help with learning how to budget their time allowance so boundaries but also empathy are equally essential. Add more features only when you are happy they are coping well. A family phone agreement will ensure that expectations are clear from the outset and ongoing two-way communication will be key, including an awareness of how their phone use is shaped by their emotional needs. For instance, paying attention to whether they are turning to certain apps or games on their phone for relaxation after a hard day at school, and whether this is soothing or antagonising for them, then helping them identify better coping strategies, if needed.

Deeply Feeling Kids

Popular Instagram influencer and child behaviour expert Dr Becky uses the phrase, 'Deeply Feeling Kids' to describe children who are more sensitive than average. She says you can recognise these children easily as they 'tend to have more explosive moments, take longer to calm when upset, and tend to push us away in the moments they struggle the most'. They are more attuned to – and therefore more stressed by – social drama or conflict, both IRL and online. They may worry about what it means, why it is happening, how they are viewed or how to respond, and smartphones will only heighten their exposure to such situations. Deeply Feeling Kids may also be more profoundly disturbed than others by seeing harmful content online, such as violence, bullying or global events, as these will more deeply imprint on them and linger in their minds. Be aware that some have voiced concern about the Deeply Feeling Kids definition preventing or delaying some children from getting a neurodivergence diagnosis, so it shouldn't replace clinical support if you think your child needs it. The point is that we all respond differently to what we see, and what is harmful for my child may not be for yours and vice versa.

Discrimination

The internet can be a lifeline for young people questioning their identity or seeking belonging – it can provide role models, helpful information and a community where there may be none locally. Yet it is also a magnifying glass of humanity that exposes society's ugly side, thanks to unethical algorithms and the bravado of cowardly trolls and bullies who hide behind screens, shielded from witnessing the impact of their actions of real people.

Sadly, this magnifying effect means that those who are at risk of experiencing prejudice IRL, such as the LGBTQ+ community, are also at greater risk of experiencing abuse and harm online. Research by Glitch, a charity on a mission to end online abuse and champion digital citizenship, reveals that Black females receive by far the most – and the most toxic – online abuse.[2] Glitch encourages individuals at risk of discrimination to maintain strong boundaries and asks others to challenge discrimination where they see it. (For more on how to help your child stay safe and help others, see Lesson 3: Know Your Digital Ethics.)

It is also worth being aware of 'digital self-harm', a phenomenon where people use social media and the internet to harm themselves. This often starts unintentionally, like seeking out arguments with others who will fight back against your beliefs, or checking sites where you know you will find toxic opinions, but it can escalate to the point where individuals end up sending *themselves* hateful and abusive messages. There are many reasons why a young person might digitally self-harm; if you want to find out more, the LGBT Foundation has a great guide on its website.[3]

Children living apart from their parents

A phone can provide peace of mind and connection for both parent and child when you cannot be together. Perhaps you have separated from your partner, or your child is living away from another significant family member, or you are a single parent with little family support so you have to leave your child alone for longer periods than you'd like while you are at work. In these cases, it may be very helpful for your child to have a phone, but the functionality of that phone can still be limited to what they need and no more. If budget is an issue, it will be tempting to pass down your old second-hand iPhone or equivalent, but before you do, bear in mind that a text-and-call-only phone can cost as little as £20. It will also not require your time and effort to manage the safety concerns presented by full internet access, which could be especially challenging if you cannot be with your child as much as you would like or if you or your co-parent are on different pages with this topic. (Turn to 'What if my co-parent and I feel differently about smartphones?' on page 255 for more information on this.) If video calling you is important for the days that you do not see them, can this be done using the other parent's phone, or via a tablet that can be left at home? If that really won't cut it, go for the most family-friendly smartphone model you can find in order to minimise the risks to them (and the workload for yourself).

THE BASICS

Smartphone readiness checklist

Giving your child a smartphone should feel like an exciting next step that marks the beginning of a new chapter in their development, not something to fear. These ten questions are offered as thought prompts to help you consider how comfortable and confident you feel about giving your child a smartphone. Where you feel less confident, flip to the relevant section of this book to swot up on what you can do about it and revisit this checklist again when you feel that things have moved forward.

Please note that this checklist primarily relates to adult smartphones, and choosing a family-friendly smartphone should lower many of the risks involved.

1. **Are you clear on your reasons** for giving a smartphone now, and have you carefully considered alternatives that could provide the functionality you need?
2. **Are you okay with the digital behaviours you are modelling for your child?** Kids do as we do, not as we say. Have you health-checked your own habits and do you feel good about the example you are setting?
3. **Have you agreed what apps, websites, social media and artificial intelligence (AI) they are allowed to access, and how to use these safely?** Have you discussed: the potential pitfalls of group messaging and how to be an upstander, not a bystander when things go wrong; the power of algorithms to create echo chambers; the risks and opportunities of both social media and AI? Have you

clearly explained any rules and boundaries around use and your reasons for these to your child?

4. **Have you identified which parental controls you will use?** Do you feel confident setting these up and managing them on an ongoing basis? Knowing that no system is flawless and things will go wrong, are you still happy to proceed?
5. **Have you discussed online privacy?** Including what is or is not appropriate to share online, the importance of privacy settings and protecting your personal data, active consent in image-sharing, and how you plan to monitor your child's usage?
6. **Is your child mature enough to handle this responsibility?** Have they demonstrated maturity and responsibility in other areas of life, like homework and chores? Do they look after their possessions, treat others kindly, keep their promises and adhere to other screen-time rules? Do they conduct themselves respectfully in disagreements and know how to step away or stand up for themselves when needed?
7. **Have you discussed the 'tricky topics' with them?** Including what to do when they see pornography, violence, bullying or sexting? Could they spot and respond safely to sextortion or a scam? Would they turn to you or another trusted adult if they encountered problems online? As Protect Young Eyes founder Chris McKenna would say, would they feel confident and know how to walk away from a digital conversation with a 'nice' predator?
8. **Have you set clear standards in a family phone agreement?** Does it cover phone-free bedrooms, phone-free

times, including mealtimes and sleepovers, settings and notifications, and IRL responsibilities, like completing homework or chores before phone time starts? Are all family members on board with this?

9. **Are you genuinely interested and able to support your child with their digital life?** This decision isn't just about your child – it's also about what it means for you in supporting them with it. Are you able to uphold the checks and balances you've implemented? Will you make time to discuss what they have seen and done online and how it's going? Your child may be ready, but you too need to be ready to support them with this.

10. **Does this decision feel right in your gut?** To check in with your intuition, place your hands on your stomach. (Seriously, do it now.) Breathe deep and slow. Notice any sensations. What is your body communicating to you? Do you feel clear and calm in this decision, or is your tummy doing little nervous flips? Pay attention to any worries that come up and work through them before proceeding. Resist any external pressure and trust your own instinct above all else.

If your responses to all the above are positive then congratulations, it sounds like it might be time for your child to get their first smartphone!

When you do come to give them that first phone, present it as a tool, not a toy. This messaging can be confused when it is given as a birthday or Christmas gift, so spell it out for them first. Always make clear any 'terms and conditions' that you are attaching to the phone before you give it to them, so that expectations are well and truly managed about what they are about to receive, and they are clear on the responsibility they are being entrusted with and they have the chance to accept or reject the deal you're putting on the table. So your tween doesn't want you to monitor their texts? That's fine, then they don't have to have a phone – it's their choice. Put another way, I appreciate that surprises can be fun, but can you imagine the disappointment of opening a new phone, only later to be told you can't have half the apps you imagined you were being given? Much safer to discuss it first so they know what they're (not) getting. See Lesson 4: Find Your Balance for more information about preparing a family agreement.

> **TOP TAKE-AWAYS**
>
> To decide the right time to give your a child a smartphone, first read the section 'How old should they be? The bottom line' on page 17 to understand what experts think about smartphone-readiness by age and stage, then make your own decision in light of your individual child's attributes and family's personal circumstances. Delaying adult smartphone ownership until at least age fourteen (and social media until age sixteen) is a reasonable general aspiration, but every child and circumstance is unique, and you must make your own decision. Use the smartphone readiness checklist to help you decide when the time is right for you and your child.

Chapter 5

Buying Yourself More Time

Just like a serrated kitchen knife, an adult smartphone is a very helpful but potentially dangerous tool and it is vital that your child learns to use it safely to avoid hurting themselves or others. Supporting them with this new skill will take some work from you to educate them and apply appropriate safeguards, so you need to be ready, as well as your child.

If you are coming under pressure from your child or other parents, or you're just feeling the heat because it seems like you're the odd one out, then ensuring you are super clear on your reasons will help you feel more confident in your decision to delay opening this Pandora's box. The points that I cover below will help with this, but you might also like to check out the Smartphone Free Childhood website (see Resource library) for some scripted responses to common pushbacks – they even have a video aimed at children that you might find helpful. Once you're clear on your reasons, work through the suggestions below to make your own plan of action.

Even if you decide they won't get their own smartphone for a while yet, remember that your child will still see friends' phones and access the internet in other ways, so it is never too early to begin teaching them The Five Lessons (see page 119).

Find other ways to meet your child's digital needs

In the last year of primary school there were moments that my daughter was desperate to have her own smartphone so she could 'feel grown up' and be 'like everyone else'. She didn't want any particular features; it was just to be able to say that she had what they had so she could feel included. She also said it would give her something to look at so she could appear busy when she felt alone. My heart ached a little to hear this, but deep down I knew that conceding to peer pressure would be cold comfort to both of us. There are many good reasons to give your child a smartphone, but being like everyone else or avoiding all social discomfort are not two of them. While social exclusion is a serious matter for older adolescents in particular, I also know that giving my tween a phone simply so she can use it as a crutch in social scenarios would be robbing her of the opportunity to develop courage and communication skills – two vital life skills.

If you're coming under pressure from your child, ask them what specifically do they want or need it for. How do they imagine using it? Are these legitimate needs or merely preferences? If your child doesn't live with you full time or if you have a co-parent who has different views, work with them to develop this list and include all your needs. (Check out Lesson 4: Find Your Balance for tips on having that conversation.) Next, look at your list and decide which of these are appropriate requests you want to support. If not, why not? Cross those off. What is left, in tech speak, are your 'user requirements'.

Next, look at your list of requirements one by one and get creative in identifying whether there are other ways to meet these needs without giving them an adult smartphone. Here are a few ideas to get you going.

- For reassurance that they've arrived at school safely, can they text or call you via a simple phone?
- Feel you need to track them? Read 'Should I track my child?' on page 78 and if you still want to, then consider adding a tag to their bag or a family-friendly smartphone or smartwatch with inbuilt tracking software instead. For younger children, you might even consider an internet-enabled two-way radio, like Karri, which lets your child stay in contact with you when they roam locally, like walking to a friend or neighbour's house.
- Do they need access to an internet-enabled travel app when they are out and about? Are you sure they cannot manage with some workarounds, and learn some life skills while they are at it? If essential, a family-friendly or digitally minimalist smartphone will be safer than a full adult phone.
- Need internet access for schoolwork, banking apps, or other practical apps? Would a laptop or tablet do instead? Larger screens (at an appropriate distance) are better for our eyes, and typing on a full-size keyboard reduces thumb strain and may even help your child develop touch-type skills. Laptops are also better for

using Microsoft software and may have more advanced digital tools. Of course, laptops and tablets still present risks so need protections and boundaries (keep out of bedrooms at night), but as they are less transportable it's easier to limit their use than a phone.

- If your child's main interest is gaming, then a console where they can chat and play with friends (in person if they aren't ready for online gaming) coupled with a simple phone might be all they need.
- Music can be played on portable MP3 players (the modern ones look just like smartphones – just watch out if it comes pre-loaded with other apps you might not want) or accessed at home via Bluetooth speakers (look for family-friendly versions), laptops, tablets, or old-school formats like CDs, radios, records, etc.

Consider giving access over ownership

Remember how growing up we would loudly negotiate sharing the family TV, or battle over turn-taking with the Sega Mega Drive handset, as we watched each other play? Not so much nowadays. In the 90s the only way you could get on to the internet was via a family computer or in a school common area; today, children from reasonably well-off families are more likely to be sat, silently and separately, on a personal iPad with headphones in or with their eyes down on their own smartphone. This makes for a quieter home, but when we don't share digital experiences with family members, we miss the opportunity to have someone

THE BASICS

sit alongside us, helping us make sense of what we are doing or seeing, perhaps challenging the credibility or quality of what we are consuming, or simply sharing in the fun with us and strengthening those bonds.

Smartphones are also hyper-personalised to our individual preferences and shaped by algorithms that drive kids into ever narrower, more compelling (and sometimes dangerous) echo chambers of content. Whereas watching YouTube or viewing images on Instagram on a family laptop (where there are multiple people using it) prevents the algorithms guessing who the user is so it cannot generate such reductive or harmful recommendations. Shared devices, especially when in a shared space, also reduce children's expectations of privacy, which may discourage them from inappropriate use.

Offering access via your phone or a family laptop could therefore be a helpful option if you don't want your kids to miss out on all aspects of life online just because they don't have their own phone or account. For example, my kids message family on my WhatsApp and I know others who permit their child to join group chats with friends using their parents' number. This can bring its own challenges but may be preferable if the alternative is having their own account. We have also searched for the latest TikTok dance craze together so that my eldest knows what her friends are referring to, researched trending topics on Google, and she has created a mood board on my Pinterest account. Not having their own phone does not mean your child needs to be digitally dead to the world!

Another option to consider is offering your child use of a 'family phone', on an ad hoc basis. For example, we started with a £20 basic 'family' Nokia handset pre-loaded with a handful of close contacts for our eleven-year-old to reach us in case of emergency on the days she came home from school to an empty house. Our nine-year-old also enjoys sending fun texts to her uncles and grandparents on it, and it's been a great introduction to the basics of how to use and take care of a phone (switching it on, charging it up, making a call, etc.) before giving them their own device. Every contact on it knows that the phone is shared between us so nothing is private.

I do appreciate that children like to have their own phone, just as we all like to have our own things, but there are advantages to shared devices and we can keep these arrangements rolling for as long as we like, until the day comes when a personal smartphone really is essential to meet their legitimate digital needs.

Offer options, where possible

It may help if you can shortlist a few feature phones in advance and give your child a choice between them. A superficial aesthetic detail or insignificant feature for you – perhaps a certain colour, case or game – might tip their reaction from full-raging rebellion to reluctant acceptance. For example, we originally gave my daughter the very basic family Nokia but allowed her to upgrade this to a slightly different text-and-call-only model with the addition of a very basic camera. This swap made little difference to us – she barely uses the camera – but meant that she could be the same as a couple of friends, which bought us some goodwill and hopefully more time.

THE BASICS

Talk to other parents

The Smartphone Free Childhood movement in the UK has helped hugely to normalise conversations about this tricky topic, shifting the issue from feeling like a shame-laced personal battle behind closed doors between parents and their kids, to a public health debate centred around the ethics and responsibilities of Big Tech. Parents can debate and take different approaches, but ultimately I am heartened that we are even discussing this, as it wasn't a topic that anyone felt able to raise just a few years ago.

Whatever age you decide to get your child a smartphone, I would encourage you to speak to fellow parents about it. The Smartphone Free Childhood website is full of resources to encourage parents and schools to start talking about this – they even provide suggested wording to help you raise the topic in your school class WhatsApp group. This – coupled with an email from the school informing us of a friendship issue that had occurred due to some children sending WhatsApp group messages – inspired me to send my own message to my child's Year 5 class parent WhatsApp group. This is what I wrote:

> *Hey everyone. I saw the school email about some issues on a WhatsApp group affecting Year 5 students. I hope everyone involved is all right.*
>
> *I'm aware that kids are turning up the heat to get smartphones around now 'because everyone's got one'. So I thought it might be useful to say out loud that we won't be getting [my daughter] a smartphone in primary school and for some time*

after that. Obviously she will need one eventually, but when we first decide she needs a phone for safety, it will be a text-and-call-only phone. We probably won't track her but you could do that using a tracking chip or watch if you want to.

We must all do what is best for our own circumstances, but I have been looking into this topic and, for us, the pros don't yet outweigh the cons. I wanted to share our position so that if you want to say to your kids 'no, not everyone does have a phone' the next time they pester you, you can, because it's important we all feel we have a choice in this.

I was nervous about sending this message, but I received seven or eight messages, some in the group, some privately, saying they felt the same and thanking me for bringing the topic up because they had been nervous to. One had regretted her approach with her older child and was going to delay with her younger child. Their replies gave me the confidence to stand firm for longer.

You might prefer to quietly have a word with one or two trusted friends. You can simply mention that you have read this book, and you were wondering what they thought. If it helps, you can send a link to some of my content online as a conversation starter or lend them this book. With any luck, you will find a kindred spirit who broadly aligns with your views, but even with parents who take a different approach, you can take the chance to discuss any potential pinch points in your children's friendships that might be worrying you, and ask for their support with these, like preventing phone use during sleepovers, or sharing invites to social occasions with you if your child doesn't have the messaging platform their child uses. It might feel scary, but starting these conversations before issues occur is much easier than after something has happened when emotions may be running high.

Discuss your decisions with your child

Once you have a plan, it's time to talk to your child (again).

The first thing to know is that if you decide to delay, *it is okay if your child is disappointed or angry!* It doesn't mean that you are doing the wrong thing. Many young adults today now speak about their gratitude to their parents for delaying when they were younger, even though they described hating it at the time. Many others talk about how they regret having had 'too much too soon'. (Hindsight is a wonderful thing and their parents did the best with what they knew at the time, which was much less than we know now.) Have faith in yourself and your decision. You are the adult, you know things that they do not, and you have their best intentions at heart.

Remind them that their time will come and this is not 'no', but 'just not yet'. Likewise, explain how it is possible to meet their needs through other methods and why you are saying no to the other requests that you don't agree with. Explaining your reasons provides the opportunity for them to understand and respect your decision, even if they don't like it.

There is no one-size-fits-all script here, I am afraid, but I have included below some common concerns that you may wish to draw from to help explain to your child why having a smartphone is a big step and not to be rushed. I have not dumbed down the language here because I believe most teens are perfectly capable of understanding these ideas, but you know your child best so please adapt and simplify your messaging for younger children and keep this light enough for them to take it in. As with everything in this book, it's always best to aim for a series of bite-sized casual chats, rather than a lengthy 'once and done' monologue as this will lose them!

You may also find it helpful to show your child some resources explaining the issues so that they are not just taking this view from you, or perhaps watch a programme, documentary or film together to help kick-start a conversation. The Smartphone Free Childhood website has a short video explainer for kids; you could get your child a book (for example, *The Amazing Generation,* by Jonathan Haidt and Catherine Price is billed as a tween's guide 'to fun and freedom in a screen-filled world'); or you could co-view a film or series on this topic. *I Am Ruth, The Social Dilemma,* Channel 4's *Swiped: The School That Banned Smartphones, Childhood 2.0,* or the Netflix series *Adolescence* are all good but do have varying amounts of mature content so please read or watch them alone first before deciding whether they are appropriate for your own child.

COMMON CONCERNS ABOUT SMARTPHONES – TALKING POINTS FOR PARENTS

- Smartphones and social media were designed by adults for adults and the technology companies' aim is to keep your attention hooked for as long as possible to maximise their profits – even if this means neglecting children's rights or wellbeing.
- Notifications can disrupt focus and negatively impact children's developing attention spans in what is a critical time for their brain development.
- Phones can become 'experience blockers', reducing opportunities for children to develop confidence, social and communication skills, form friendships and fully enjoy the moment. (If you want a beautiful demonstration of what it feels like to be fully present, search for Coldplay's Glastonbury 2024 'A Sky Full of Stars' video, where Chris Martin leads a chant of 'put your phones in your pocket and your hands in the sky', which shows how an atmosphere changes when people are in the moment.)
- The temptation to check phones in school can impact concentration, learning and get children in trouble with their teachers.
- Social media can encourage negative comparison and harm girls' body image in particular.
- Children need to develop their own unique sense of identity and have some life experiences before absorbing others' ideas of what success and beauty is or they will feel the pressure to conform and change who they are.

- Always having a camera with you can create a pressure where children feel compelled to constantly document and share things online, which can turn otherwise private moments into performative acts.
- Having a phone can increase children's FOMO as they can feel that they always need to be online and contactable, which can impact stress levels, family relationships and sleep.
- Children need to develop independence and confidence to physically navigate life on their own without over-relying on technology. (If their phone was stolen and they were far from home, could they find their way back without GPS? Could they happily entertain themselves all day without their phone? You want them to develop these life skills.)
- Owning a smartphone increases the risk of road safety accidents because children do not always concentrate when crossing.
- Owning a smartphone makes you more likely to be a victim of theft.
- Smartphones are very expensive to replace if broken, lost or stolen.
- Smartphones increase the risk of seeing pornographic, upsetting, violent, discriminatory and harmful content, that once seen cannot be unseen, and can negatively change the way children see the world, and other people.
- Data privacy is important and complicated; it is easy for children to accidentally or intentionally have contact with strangers or give away sensitive personal information that will make them vulnerable to sextortion or scams.

THE BASICS

- The 'digital lens effect' means that sometimes children act or interpret things differently than they would in real life. This leads to friendship dramas being unnecessarily escalated in group chats, and other hurtful behaviour and online bullying.
- The rapid advancement of AI, frequent software updates, and a lack of regulation mean that it is almost impossible to know which apps and sites are safe.
- Children's typical smartphone use does not support tech literacy or the development of digital skills. Silicon Valley tech parents know this, which is why they tend to delay smartphone ownership and limit their children's tech use more than other parents. Schoolwork, coding programs and creative tools like music or video editing can be great, but the best way to help your children become digitally literate is to teach them to think critically about technology creation while also reducing mindless consumption.
- You may also wish to consider a child's unique circumstances, such as their mental health history, recent life events, self-esteem, emotional maturity, experiences of bullying, or other safeguarding concerns.

TOP TAKE-AWAYS

If it feels too soon there are many ways to buy yourself more time before you give your child an adult smartphone. Start by getting clear on why delaying feels so important to you, then work out exactly what your child needs and see if you can find other ways to meet these needs. This could include allowing your child to use certain features on your phone or a shared family device. Talking to other parents is helpful, even when you have different ideas about phones. Discuss your decisions and reasons with your child so they understand your thinking.

Chapter 6

Why It's Not Too Late if Your Child Already Has a Smartphone

Times are changing so fast that absolutely no one knows quite what they're doing when it comes to raising kids in the smartphone era. Our adolescence was remarkably different to our kids' and the research and advice is so new that most of the time we simply have no option but to make up the rules as we go along, and hope for the best.

A whole generation of parents was told that children today are 'digital natives', and we encouraged them to embrace technology as a fast track to learning and development. Thankfully, we have now realised that it takes more than staring at an iPad in your buggy to learn how to become a good cybercitizen and that smartphones are not as straightforward as their sleek, minimalist designs would have you believe. Even we adults have been blindsided by the hold that our phones have over our attention and find ourselves losing hours to the screen. I am a certified digital wellness educator, and I still feel overwhelmed at times.

It is therefore hardly surprising that three quarters of parents have fears around their child's phone use, over half regret giving one too soon and almost half of parents go as far as saying that the phone has changed their child's personality.[1] Many others speak about feeling they have 'lost' their child. So believe me when I say if you are struggling you are far from alone, it's not your fault, and – critically – it is never too late to make a change.

I don't have a silver bullet but I can offer you a framework for your reflection so you can make improvements. The three simple steps below serve as a light health check on your child's phone use to help you identify what is working and what is not, so that you can create a plan to tweak or tighten your approach to better suit your family.

It bears repeating that *it is never too late* to have a reset moment with you child. It is never too late to reflect and recontract a healthier approach for you and your child. If you are looking for more resources or feel you might need personal support, reach out to me online – you don't need to deal with this alone.

1. Reflect without guilt

This is all a big learning journey for you as a parent, as well as for them as a child. No one has all the answers or is getting it right all the time. Besides, do you remember your own teenage years? For most of us, it was full of ups and downs and emotional angst – usually served with a good dollop of secrecy and deception. Breaking rules and testing boundaries are what adolescence is all about; it's how we learn our limits and discover who we are, so try not to take it all personally. The fact that you are even recognising this as something you want to work on shows a fantastic level of

THE BASICS

sensitivity, care for your child and proactive parenting – your kid is clearly very lucky to have you.

When we are worried that something isn't going as well as it should be, it is tempting to 'catastrophise', believing that we have got it all wrong and everything needs to change. In reality, nothing is absolute – there is always stuff that could be better and other things that are going well and you need to give yourself some credit for those. You need to avoid 'all or nothing' thinking in favour of a more even-handed approach that acknowledges what's working, as well as what you want to improve.

Once you're done beating yourself up (or perhaps feeling angry at your child), take a deep belly breath, then grab some paper and a pen. Now set aside any generalised sweeping statements about screen time and look at the bigger picture for your child. How are they within themselves, away from their phone? Do they seem mostly happy and well? Are they mostly polite and respectful? Are they eating healthily, seeing friends, keeping up with schoolwork, being active? Do they have IRL hobbies, etc.? We need to get clear on the real issues here so we can consider what role the phone is playing in their broader life and wellbeing.

Next, list all the good stuff that is working well with the phone. Perhaps they put it away at mealtimes when you ask them to, answer when you call, or have never lost or broken it. Maybe they came and told you about a bad thing that happened online when they didn't have to, or stood up for a friend that was having a hard time? Then list any *specific* issues with the phone that are causing to you worry or that you want to change. Have they been exposed to inappropriate content? Been involved in bad behaviour online? Do they have an untypically low or grumpy mood? Have they quit healthy hobbies and begun isolating themselves in their room for long periods? Are they refusing to put their phone down when requested? Taking their phone to bed at night, or looking suspiciously tired in the morning? Now read back what you have written. What is a suspicion or opinion, and what is definitively fact? Taking a moment to objectively sense-check your perspective to ensure that you're being fair and balanced will help you be calm and clear when you come to discuss it with your child.

Features like Screen Time on the iPhone or Digital Wellbeing for Android might be useful for reviewing their usage but be careful: if your child feels like you're spying on them and trying to catch them out, it won't help you in the longer term. Ideally, ask your child if they would be willing to show you this information themselves and use it as a launch pad for conversation. I would also recommend you ask them to show you their messages or social media feed so that you can see what they are seeing. If you do look at their phone together, give them advance warning and be sure not to freak out at what you see! You, or they, may be shocked by what the data shows, especially if they have not clocked quite how long they are online until this moment.

They are likely to feel nervous and vulnerable showing you what their online life looks like if this is not something you have done before, and they may feel hypersensitive or defensive, so tread carefully. Avoid knee-jerk reactions like banning an app in the heat of the moment as this could cause your child to freak out and shut down. Instead, you could say something like, 'I am shocked and I need some time to think about this. Let's agree to talk again soon.' As a general rule, when asking questions about what they are up to online, unless you can prove what they are saying is untrue, it is safer to give them the benefit of the doubt for the sake of the longer-term relationship and keeping that conversation open.

If you like a quiz, you could even complete the online 'smartphone addiction scale' test and invite them to do the same. It's only eleven questions and two minutes of your time and could be a launch pad for an interesting conversation.[2]

2. Create some positive goals

Discussing your concerns is the next step, but frame the conversation positively, focusing on what you want for your child, rather than what you don't want. For example: better sleep, to feel less anxious, to have the time and inclination to nurture or rekindle a healthy real-world hobby or to have family meals where you discuss your day free from phones. Make these specific and achievable things and ask your child what they think – do they agree that these are reasonable and welcome goals? What would they add? You can include some for yourself or the broader family – good phone etiquette applies to all of us and most adults have plenty of room for improvement with our own smartphone habits! If you can establish some common ground with what you are aiming to achieve, even if you might have different ideas on how to get there, it will be a positive conversation. Manage your expectations – this is just the start of a conversation so don't feel you have to crack this in one go; Rome wasn't built in a day.

When you are reflecting on how things are currently going, one positive psychology tip to help that conversation go well is to try really hard to provide at least three times as many positives as negatives. This is the minimum ratio of good-to-bad that humans can tolerate without feeling defensive or downtrodden (five times as many is optimal). This might feel like a tall order, but it really is important; just imagine a performance review at work if the ratio was worse than this – you'd want to either turn and run or fight back to defend yourself! Expect your child to feel the same. The good things can be tiny. For example, 'I noticed that you did your homework without a reminder the other day, which shows me that you are taking more responsibility for your own learning, which is great.' They might have been nagged every other day last week but it's framing the same situation differently to get a different kind of response.

It's the difference between, 'I notice and appreciate it so much on those days you put your phone away before dinner. It gives us a chance to hang out and talk, and I want that for us every day from now on', and 'I am fed up with you staring at your phone at the table. It's so rude and I won't accept that any more', which is completely demotivating and overlooks any of the times (however rare they may be!) that they didn't do that.

Remember – this does not need to be one big sit-down talk. You can bite off topics one by one, however and whenever it feels doable. If you do it little and often you can also credit them for any early wins or improvements as you go, building positive momentum and normalising talking about your family's digital life.

3. Introduce a family phone agreement

Once you are clear on what you're trying to change and why, turn to Lesson 4: Find Your Balance to find out more about how you can turn these into a written agreement to help capture what you've been discussing. Is this strictly essential? Of course not, but if you've had phone problems in the past, then I would recommend having something that captures what the new standards are that you are expecting from them and why (and any commitments you might be making to them too) so that you can more easily hold them to account if standards begin to slip again.

This does not need to be *War and Peace*. Just focus on the priority areas that your child is struggling with. If your child has not been keeping up with their homework and staying up too late on the phone then you might have something like 'We prioritise learning by only using phones after homework is completed' and 'We protect our sleep by turning off phones after 9 p.m. and handing them to a parent who will return them after breakfast', or similar. If you decide to remove access to a certain social media app because they have been exposed to harmful content or misused it previously then that also forms part of the agreement, as a condition of their phone use, along with any other phone time limits.

If your trust has been broken in the past you might be considering applying more technical controls to limit access to certain apps and websites and set a schedule for when the phone can access the internet, or even track their location and monitor calls and texts. These can be helpful, but *do not rely on them*. You should expect your child to attempt to get past these controls so make ongoing efforts to limit their access (like changing pin codes regularly). Always explain the reasons for any restrictions and remember no technical trick can ever replace your relationship with your child so continue to observe them carefully and keep the conversation open if you suspect something has gone awry.

Naturally, you will want to adjust your plan as your child grows, and you reflect together on what's working and what isn't. As you do, don't forget to continue to find ways to recognise and celebrate small achievements or progress, and thank them for those times they have met the agreement, as well as pick them up on the times they haven't. Goodwill goes far.

When to consider temporary or permanent smartphone removal

If you develop serious cause for concern, you always retain the right to reverse your decision and remove the phone from your child. You are the adult and you know your child best, so if you need a boost of courage to take this step and permanently remove their smartphone, check out the Smartphone Free Childhood website for an inspiring case study that shows that this approach sometimes can be the right call.[3] If you feel this total reset is required, consider what practical steps you may need to put back in place to meet their daily needs – perhaps a basic feature phone with very limited functions or access to shared devices, etc.

That being said, the Child Mind Institute recommends parents think very carefully before removing a child's phone and never to do this as an arbitrary form of punishment or to get

THE BASICS

them to do something.⁴ They advise, 'when you take away their phone, you're turning off the television, banning games, taking away their ability to talk with friends, and grounding them all at once' so the removal of a phone may feel like being cut off from their entire world.

Put simply, confiscation done badly will feel more like punishment than protection and it has the potential to seriously backfire and undermine your relationship. Your child may be so desperate to get it back that they try to sneak their phone when you aren't looking and become more likely to keep secrets or lie to you next time something goes wrong simply to protect their access to the phone. This is the opposite of the trusting and open relationship you are trying to build, longer term. Avoid this by ensuring any consequences always relate directly to what they did wrong, so if they repeatedly miss their curfew, it's probably more appropriate to ground them for a while or find new ways to enforce the curfew rather than simply to remove their phone and cut off all digital communication with their friends.

The aim is to *connect before you correct* and focus on the lesson they need to learn, supported by safe boundaries, rather than doling out punishments. For example, let's say they post something inappropriate online. First ask them about their thinking when they did it, so that you can understand how and why this happened and what they need to change to avoid a repeat scenario. You might also limit their phone time or delete the problematic app, but ensure that they can see how the consequence is directly relevant to the behaviour change you want to see in them.

A final thought. Ultimately, learning to use a smartphone responsibly is really hard and requires such sophisticated skills that most adults struggle with it, so parenting a child through it is even harder! It is to be expected that mistakes and misjudgements will occur. All we can do is learn by trial and error and accept that 'when you know better, you do better', as the great Maya Angelou once said. Be kind – to yourself and your kids.

TOP TAKE-AWAYS

If you've given your child a smartphone but have concerns, it is never too late to make a change. Nothing is all good or all bad so avoid catastrophising and look for what is going well too – think about the bigger picture of your child's wellbeing and your overall family life. Identify some common ground with your child by agreeing on positive goals for what you are trying to achieve. Introduce a simple family phone agreement to support healthy boundaries and habits and avoid sliding into bad habits. Removal of a child's phone should always feel like protection, not punishment.

SECTION 2
THE FIVE LESSONS

A tiny, complex mass of plastic, glass and precious metals, our smartphone has come to feel as necessary as a vital organ. But while they are incredibly useful – almost irreplaceable – we must not let our obsession with them get out of hand. They were created to be tools to enhance and enrich our lives, but they have gradually, inevitably, changed how we think, feel and interact with the world around us, as all the most profound technology tends to do.

To ensure that our phones continue to add value to our lives and to prevent them from leeching time and energy away from the things that matter most – our kids, partner, friends, our professional and personal priorities, our hobbies, our inner peace – we must develop effective coping strategies. Modern life is a battlefield for our kids' attention, and the odds are stacked against them. For sure, the tech industry, government and schools all have a role to play, but right here, right now, it is on us as parents to support our kids through this. We must help them develop the mindset and skills that will safely see them through this digital jungle reasonably unscathed.

THE FIVE LESSONS

We have already covered the basics of why you might want to delay a smartphone, what type of phone to get, how to set it up, and why it's never too late to reset your child's relationship with their phone. Now it's time to think about how you will raise your child to become the master of their phone, rather than a servant to it.

In this section we cover five big ideas that will help you prepare for, and parent through, your kids' smartphone years. These ideas apply at whatever age you decide to give your child their first smartphone and are equally relevant to adults as children. That means that even if you finished the first section and immediately decided that you won't now give your child a phone for some years yet, this section is still essential reading.

These Five Lessons are the distilled wisdom of five years of research and learning; interviews with experts from the US, the UK and beyond; countless conversations with parents and children too; and thousands of pages read on websites, in books and research reports. They also reflect my own experience as a mother of two tweens and as a smartphone owner seeking a better balance for myself. I do not have all the answers, but I do know that if you take these lessons to heart and teach them to your children, you will give your family the best possible chance to have a healthy relationship with their phones.

The Five Lessons are:

1. Master Your Attention
2. Become a Critical Thinker
3. Know Your Digital Ethics
4. Find Your Balance
5. Keep Learning

Please treat these as guiding principles, not diktats. My intention is not to judge or preach but to reassure, inspire and empower you to confidently guide your happy, healthy child through their smartphone years.

As you read this section, you will notice that I tend towards advocating for education and meaningful connection more than a command-and-control style of parenting. Yet, I want to be clear that I still very much believe children need protections and boundaries from adults to keep them safe. This is not an 'either/or'. We can apply technical or practical safety rails *and* deepen and strengthen our relationship with our child *and* help them develop their digital skills and cyber wisdom (consider it layering up your support like lasagna!).

Each of the lessons is brought to life with suggested actions. These actions are not 'tick it off the list and get back to normal' tasks, but now and forever behaviours to revisit across many conversations, over many years. Please don't be intimidated by this task – you absolutely don't need to do all of this right now. Simply bear the ideas in mind and do what you can, when you can. Something is always better than nothing. I promise you though, the more you do this stuff the more it becomes second nature. Soon enough it'll all become how you handle things by default, because now that you know what you know, it wouldn't make sense to be any other way.

Lesson 1

Master Your Attention

'You become what you give your attention to. If you yourself don't choose what thoughts and images you expose yourself to, someone else will.'

Epictetus

If you fear 'losing' your child to their smartphone or have already witnessed them powerless to its bright lights and pinging notifications, then this is the chapter for you. Likewise, if you feel guilty or embarrassed about your own phone usage, read on. By the end of this chapter you should feel reassured and have the coping strategies to feel calmer and more in control moving forward.

The battle for our attention is a recent but near universal phenomenon, and this is no coincidence. Thousands of extremely clever tech designers in Silicon Valley and around the world are intentionally exploiting vulnerabilities in human brains to pull every digital design string they can to hook you and keep you hooked on their products. This is the 'attention economy' and it works by selling your personal data to advertisers and other companies. Every single one of your online behaviours is data – from the gender and date of birth you enter when you set up your child's account, to their likes and swipes and how long their eyes dwell on a video before scrolling away – it all makes money for the tech bros. This is what former Google design ethicist, Tristan Harris, meant when he famously said, 'if you are not paying for the product, then you are the product'.

Putting it bluntly, your children are being expertly manipulated into compulsively using their smartphones more than they want to by billionaires who care more – much more – about their profit than your child's best interests. They are the reason a child will view time-sapping, scary or inappropriate content against their better judgement – it's not simply 'bad behaviour' or 'bad parenting'. It is why, no matter how many times you pick up your phone in a day or how long your child 'wastes' on their phone, this is not something to feel ashamed of or blame your child for. We all like to believe we have independent free choice, and are responsible for our actions, but that logic only applies in a fair fight, and this game is rigged.

Despite this not being your fault, I am afraid to say it absolutely remains your problem to solve. Experts agree that in today's world, all the opportunities, wealth, health and joy that we seek in life for ourselves and our children depend entirely on the ability to control and apply our attention at will. As the ancient philosopher Epictetus said, 'you become what you give your attention to', which is why you might even say that this is the most important lesson of the book.

It is also why it is not enough to educate our children about the perils of phones and trust them to make the right calls. Children also need a loving adult who can see the bigger picture when they cannot and so set boundaries that will bring out the best in them over the longer term. The aim is to raise our children to become adults with the skills to self-regulate effectively, but they do need some scaffolding to get there while they are young. It starts with us making proactive, informed decisions around our children's (and our own) phone use, because when we are intentional with our digital behaviours, we are more satisfied with how we spend our days and feel calmer and more confident in our decisions.

ACTION: Teach them to be tech-intentional

'Brain rot' was the Oxford University Press 2024 Word of the Year. It refers to the deterioration of a person's mental or intellectual state, usually the result of consuming too much trivial or unchallenging content, particularly online. I am unsurprised the public voted for it as the top choice that year.[1] We all know how it feels to waste the morning drifting about, feeling unfocused and unaccomplished by lunchtime, or to fritter away whole evenings doomscrolling on the sofa. It's one thing to indulge in some online entertainment, it's quite another to feel you have lost control of your mind and time.

If you don't want your kids to waste their preciously short childhood this way, teach them to be 'tech-intentional'. Emily Cherkin, author of *The Screentime Solution*, defines this as 'only using screen-based technology that enhances, nurtures, and supports yourself, your child, or your family in a way that aligns with your values and resisting, delaying, or limiting screen use that interferes with healthy mental, physical, cognitive, and emotional development.'² Her underpinning philosophy can be summarised in three messages: less is more, later is better, and relationship and skills before screens. For now, I want to focus on the 'less is more' aspect. This means teaching our children to use their smartphones consciously, not passively, and it is not as easy as it sounds.

The reason children struggle to put phones down is not due to lack of willpower or making the wrong choices. These powerful computers are hyper-optimised by expert service designers who know how to create beautiful, entirely friction-free interfaces that suck you in and don't let you go. Below are just a few of the popular 'persuasive design' features that are central drivers of the attention economy, turning minutes into hours.

- **Infinite scroll** In the early days of the internet, search responses were presented in pages, where you had to click on to the next one, a little like turning the pages of a physical book. Now that we have the infinite scroll, all stopping cues have been removed.
- **Colours** Phone home screens are intentionally stunning kaleidoscopes of colour that catch our eye. Every app button looks like an irresistibly beautiful gem – Instagram's high-contrast purple and orange is a great example.
- **Autoplay** If you've ever binge-watched a series on Netflix, you'll know this danger! 'Watch-on-demand' websites like YouTube have an inbuilt autoplay feature to simply roll into the next video, and before you know it you've

lost hours. TikTok is literally designed entirely around this feature.
- **Pull to refresh** Whether it's your email inbox or social media feed, the action of 'pull down to refresh' on phones is commonplace. It's compelling because it works like a slot machine – you pull the lever, the reel spins and you wait to discover if you've 'won'.

Kids hate to be tricked or exploited, so talk to them in language they will understand about how these phones are designed to keep us hooked. It sends the message that this isn't about shame or blame but about working out some coping strategies so that they can find ways for their phone to be more fun and less stressful. If they know this stuff then hopefully when they find themselves sucked into an Instagram hole they will feel more able to come to you, knowing that the real battle is our minds versus the machines, not 'me vs Mum'.

Remember, your actions speak louder than your words, but this doesn't mean you have to be flawlessly disciplined. In fact, your imperfect phone habits and 'mistakes' are opportunities to show them what compulsive phone use looks like and why it's a problem. Your honesty about this makes you more relatable and less judgemental when it's their turn to struggle. Acknowledge whenever you've been distracted from your child by your messages, for example, take responsibility and apologise, then make a point of putting your phone away to refocus.

Here are some more ways we can teach our children to be tech-intentional in their phone use. Perhaps pick one or two to try out; you can add others over time.

1. **Permit only the minimum apps and features needed to fulfil their aims.** Unless you also block the website, your child can still visit a site, but deleting the app itself is helpful as it removes the visual cue from your home screen and makes it less likely they will hit the button mindlessly. (Apps can also be hidden or nested.)
2. **Teach them to set an intention before picking up their phone.** 'Why am I picking this up? What do I want to do and how long do I want to spend on this?' Encourage them to set a timer.
3. **Set a screen time schedule and daily time limits on tempting apps.** If possible, choose a family plan where limits cannot be overwritten by the child without permission.
4. **Teach them that others can wait.** Specifically, be clear that no-one has the right to access their immediate attention 24/7 just because they want it. Teach your child to check their messages, feed or inbox once, then immediately (and physically) put their phone away from them until the next time they are ready to pick it up. Suggest scheduled times when they check, or allocate windows of time for phone use, so that they don't feel the need to be constantly checking their phone.
5. **Disable autoplay.** Go into your child's YouTube account settings (if they have one), and any of their other media apps, and disable the autoplay feature so that your child has to actively opt to watch the next video.
6. **Experiment with screen settings.** Did you know you can switch phones to greyscale to make them less visually appealing? Also try reducing brightness or using night

mode features to lower light levels and reduce brain stimulation, particularly before sleep.

7. **Stick to single screens.** Multitasking is a fallacy. Humans are incapable of concentrating on two things at once. When we think we are multitasking, what we are actually doing is rapidly task switching, and every time we do, we leave behind an attention 'residue', which negatively impacts our focus and wellbeing.[3] If they're studying, let them give you their phone or leave it outside the door.

8. **Opt for long-form content over short-form.** Longer-form content is better for developing children's attention spans as it engages us more deeply and typically contains better quality learning or storytelling. This leaves us calmer and more satisfied than hyper-stimulating but unsatisfying short-form clips. Encourage films over TV, TV over YouTube shorts, and YouTube over TikTok. Similarly, reading articles and listening to podcasts or audiobooks is better than consuming bite-sized social media snippets. Perhaps you can even introduce your child to the radical idea of listening to a complete music album from start to finish, like we did back in the day?

ACTION: Minimise and mute their notifications

The average child receives 237 phone notifications in a typical day, some as many as 5,000.[4] We explore the impact of phones on our focus and wellbeing in Chapter 1: When Should a Child Get a Smartphone? but suffice to say that when each notification has its own ping, buzz or flash that is more than enough to make anyone feel exhausted and depleted.

We also know from research that teens' digital habits vary hugely.[5] Those kids who are checking their phones five times a day are having a very different experience than those who are checking their phone over five hundred times a day. Don't let your child be the latter. Always being 'at the mercy' of others who can reach us at any time of day – and night (if your phone is by your bed) can leave children feeling stressed, powerless and anxious. If people expect immediate replies, your time and attention no longer feel like your own. For children especially, it can take serious inner confidence to ignore a notification from a peer. Feeling so out of control and under such pressure to be responsive to notifications is not good for anyone's mental health; I see this 'always on, always available' culture all the time in the workplace in our post-pandemic working-from-home world. Both adults and children need to find ways to truly switch off – metaphorically and literally – so that we can experience what it feels like to tune into being fully present in the here and now.

Most people are horrified to hear that my phone is almost always on silent mode (for those worrying about emergency contact, I have enabled emergency bypass mode, allowing VIP contacts to ring through regardless) and shocked that I permanently mute every single group chat I am in, as if it is offensive that I ignore them until it suits me. I don't find this rude – I believe it's my right not to have my concentration or peace disturbed at will by others, outside of an emergency. I have also changed my message settings so that no one can see when I read a message because I reject the idea that anyone else has a right to know what messages I have read and when. For children this setting can create insecurity and angst. If they've read your message, the next natural thought is, 'why haven't they replied yet?!' (Note that 'read receipts' are different and useful as they simply confirm that a message has been successfully delivered to the phone.)

We must teach our children that their attention belongs to them and just because someone – or some app – wants it, does not mean they are entitled to it. This will require a huge mindset shift for many parents as it means treating a notification as an invitation, not a demand.

Here are some ways you can take the lead on their notifications settings.

1. **Minimise and mute notifications** – every buzz, flash, red bubble or badge you can. Will silencing certain apps mean they are slower to respond? Yes, and this is a good thing. There may be exceptional reasons why at certain times they need to be more available and you want to choose to switch certain notifications back on, but it is vital that we help them remain in control of their attention and slow down.
2. **Teach your child to periodically check messages and notifications** (many of which are automated push features from apps, i.e. not even from humans), rather than passively reacting to every individual one as they come in. Let them discover that the world does not implode when we refuse to drop everything and jump.
3. **Set up their emergency contacts or 'VIP' settings** so that key people can still reach them as needed.

4. **Amend app settings so no one can add your child to a group chat without them first accepting the invitation.** Proactively seeking consent first sends an important message to your child and their friends that no one has the right to put them into a digital space they did not choose to join. It may also save them from ending up in unsafe groups, or having to confront the awkwardness of feeling unable to leave a chat they did not choose to be in. It's much easier to ignore or reject up front, making a tactful excuse.
5. **Show them how to slow down.** Your children are watching and learning from you every minute. There is always another message to reply to, a newsletter from the school to read, a request from the boss to deal with. If we are not careful we can live our whole lives at the beck and call of others. We will never not be busy. All we can do is to create pockets of focus, connection and relaxation throughout our day to do the things that matter to us, and teach our children to do the same. It starts with taking charge of your own phone notifications, before then tackling theirs. Why not review your notification settings right now? I can wait ...

ACTION: Coach your kids more than you command them

In *The Book You Wish Your Parents Had Read (and Your Children Will Be Glad You Did)*, psychotherapist and writer Philippa Perry advocates for 'collaborative parenting'. She describes this as being neither too strict nor too lax, but about 'you and your child putting your heads together to solve a problem, so you're more of a counsellor than a dictator'. When it comes to helping adolescents master their attention, this is the spirit to channel.

Naturally, firm boundaries that reflect your own values are important to protect the fundamentals of a good childhood – like not allowing phones in the bedroom to protect sleep or no phones at the dinner table to protect good communication and relationships. Equally, as your child grows towards adulthood they will need less judgement and control, and more support and understanding from you, which is where problem-solving together with our kids comes into it. When we brainstorm ways to address their concerns together with them on issues like distraction, sleep, phone overuse and harmful content, the strategies are self-motivated and therefore more likely to stick. Most kids are already working hard to manage digital distractions and overload, and working alongside them in this task will make them feel more inclined to turn towards you for comfort, insight, support and guidance when they have challenges.

As ever, aim for little-and-often-style chats, over big heart-to-hearts or lectures. Tread lightly and be selective with advice; it'll make it more likely that your child will actually listen when you do speak. Try using open-ended, curious coaching questions to draw your child's attention to the effects of their smartphone habits (good and bad) so that they are better able to notice what is working well, or equally when their phone has led to unsatisfying or upsetting experiences, like getting sucked into a digital black hole. This will help you to know what support they may need and what could be tweaked to make things better.

Here are some coaching-style conversation starters you could try.

- Did you enjoy that game?
- How did you feel before/after using that app?
- Did you manage to focus on the thing you wanted to do?
- How did that group chat conversation make you feel?
- How will you know you have used your phone too much?
- How can I help you manage this?
- How would you change this app if you could?
- What's the best / funniest / most interesting thing you've seen online this week?
- Have you seen anything upsetting/inappropriate lately?
- Are you satisfied with your phone use this past week?
- What would you like to do more/less of?
- Where do you spend most of your time? What do you like about it? What don't you?
- How do people treat each other in this space?
- What design features make it more or less easy to put your phone down when you are using this app?
- What do you think companies do to make this app hard to resist? Who benefits from this?
- What is your intention in opening this app?
- How are you hoping it will make you feel?
- Are you looking for something specific, or just filling idle time?

Coaching is an art, not a science, and some conversations go better than others. Remember the learning process is not a straight line but a loopy scribble of highs and lows, with one step forward and two steps back. Have faith that you are doing great, simply by being self-aware enough to try this, and accept that there is inevitably a degree of trial and error. Trust that as your teen grows in self-awareness and develops their capacity to reflect, their digital habits will improve – all you are doing with these coaching questions is gently nudging them in the right direction (within some basic safety rails).

ACTION: Teach them how to S.T.O.P.

When coaching clients or facilitating leadership training I talk about the difference between reacting and responding. Reacting is when we feel, think or do something immediately and instinctively after something has happened. Responding is when we reflect first, before choosing our next move.

Instinctive reactions are perfect for when you swerve the car to avoid a hazard or catch a falling glass before it hits the floor – our automatic reflexes are unconscious and amazing. When it comes to mastering our attention and phones though, these base impulses are precisely what keep us hooked. What we need to do instead is create a pause between the stimulus and the response so we can consciously choose our response, rather than just firing off on autopilot. Imagine your phone buzzes (the stimulus). If you immediately pick up the phone, read and reply to the message in seconds you are reacting. If you take a breath and check in with yourself first (do I actually want to check that now?) you are responding. In this pause you might decide to stay focused on work and remind yourself that if it was an emergency they would call, not message, so decide to leave the message until later, when you have set time aside to check everything in one go. Even if you chose to pick up the phone, you would be doing so consciously – knowing that it comes at a price of disturbed focus yet actively deciding to accept that trade-off.

The equivalent for your child could be the desire to check their phone under the table in class or routinely checking their socials the second they wake up, leading them to getting sucked into messaging and running late for school. The stimulus in both of these might be FOMO. Or it could be they spend their bus journey to school playing a game on their phone because it is easier than trying to make conversation with the kid next to them, even though they'd really like to make friends. (The stimulus here might be embarrassment due to low social confidence.)

So how you do you raise a kid who doesn't immediately grab their phone the second it pings or use it as a prop to squash uncomfortable feelings? Teach them the S.T.O.P. rule to help them reflect before picking up their phone or making an impulsive decision. It's especially good for when they're under pressure to engage with intense or ongoing group chats. You can even write the key words down on a sticky note and get them to post it somewhere visible as a reminder. This helps not only with protecting our child's focus but also with preventing knee-jerk responses to messages or social posts that our child might later regret.

- Stop. Put the phone down and break eye contact with the screen.

THE FIVE LESSONS

- Take a breath. Exhale slowly through the mouth. If you are trying to stop doomscrolling look left and right, and up and down for 30 seconds to help break its hold on you.
- Observe. Check in with your thoughts, emotions and sensations. Ask yourself, what is going on here? What are my thoughts and feelings telling me? What physical sensations come with those? For example, a racing heart, nail-biting, sweaty palms or irritability might go with nervousness, stress or anxiety.
- Process the next step. Ask, what do I really want here and what options do I have? If I am feeling an urgency around this, is that urgency real or perceived? Can I wait a while and see how I feel later?

ACTION: Take practical steps to reduce temptation

While I hope that the S.T.O.P. rule helps your child exit autopilot mode, they will still need your support. Here are a few technical and practical hacks you might like to experiment with that can help gently diffuse the powerful pull of a phone's tempting interface. They work by reintroducing a small barrier to engagement that creates just enough friction to give your child the chance to S.T.O.P. and think before diving in or continuing.

Treat this as a menu rather than a shopping list and perhaps try these strategies out on yourself before your child.

- **Block or limit time-zapping apps and websites.** Download a blocking app or use the time-limit features within individual apps, inside phone settings, or via your family plan, so that children cannot access platforms and sites without your permission or for longer than you allow. Some blocking apps, such as #blockit, allow you to block not just the whole website, but also certain features from within the website, so that you can access the site to check your direct messages and notifications but save yourself from being sucked into scrolling. I find this feature extremely useful myself. Just be aware that few content blockers are foolproof, so always assume that your child will be able to get around them if they have their heart set on it. If you don't want your child to visit a certain site you must block *both* the website and the app. (See Chapter 3: Setting Yourself up for Success for more information on parental controls.)

- **Opt for browser over apps**. Apps are designed to be seamless, and having the icon visible makes it more likely that we are going to be tempted to click on them mindlessly. The experience of viewing a website in a browser is often clunkier, as it has fewer features and is less compelling. Blocking an app forces the child (or you!) to view the site via a browser, which can reduce thoughtless use as it means there is no visible icon. They will have to type out the address and navigate to the website manually, potentially entering a password, which all adds friction, making it harder to access content on impulse.
- **Encourage your child to delete and reinstall the most addictive apps between uses.** (*For older, mature teens who are learning to self-regulate with less support.*) This method

sounds radical but isn't; I often do this with Instagram, which I need for work but find super distracting. I have a designated slot to check and post in the morning and then I delete the app. It only takes me a minute – literally one minute – to reinstall it the next morning and doing so means I do not then mindlessly hit that pretty purple and orange button later in the day, just because it's there. Don't get me wrong – I still look for it – but when I don't see it I remember why and that moment of realisation gives me just enough of a pause to make me ask myself, 'Do I really want to download and use this right now?' Almost always, I do not. Is this a perfect system? No. Do I often 'cheat on myself'? Yes. But this little trick has saved me from myself probably hundreds of times and every little helps.

- **Consider app placement and home screen layout.** Changing the layout of the phone's home screen to make tempting apps less visible by hiding them in folders and putting them on the second or third screen means the icon will not be staring at your child from the home page as soon as they glance down.
- **Create a charging/storage station for phones at home** and keep all phones there when out of use or at set times – during homework, meals or bedtime, for example. Establishing this habit means your child will have to leave what they are doing and come and get their phone from where it is stored. It creates a very different experience from that of a child who is always attached to their phone – a child trying to concentrate on their homework

in their bedroom will complete it more quickly and with better focus if their phone is charging somewhere out of the room rather than on the desk by their side. All you need is a basket or box where you can keep an eye on it, but you can also buy small lockable boxes. This mindful separation from our phones can be a powerful way to reinforce the idea that it's humans, not phones, who should be in control. (Incidentally, one way I impose this idea on myself is simply charging my phone on the other side of the room from where I work so that I have to leave my desk to walk over to it to check it.)

ACTION: Disconnect to keep it in check

Nomophobia is a psychological condition when people have a fear of being separated from their phone or phone connectivity.[6] Signs and symptoms can include anxiety, respiratory changes, trembling, perspiration, agitation, disorientation and tachycardia. It sounds extreme, but research from India suggests that it's a serious issue that threatens social, mental as well as physical health – and it is increasing globally.

Although few of us may be clinically diagnosed with nomophobia, almost all of us will have experienced a degree of panic or insecurity when separated from our phone, which is crazy when most of us didn't even grow up with one. As children of the 80s and 90s, today's parents typically had freedom to travel to school, town, the park without a phone or other method to contact home. Yet today, our own primary-aged children almost never leave home without us or another adult by their side, and before they even start secondary school they are told they need to take a phone for safety on their walk to school, and all around them adults are permanently attached to their smartphones. It is not hard to imagine how our children might feel vulnerable, uneasy and alone without a phone in their hand at all times.

It is extremely important that our children do not inadvertently develop a dependency on their smartphone simply because they have never known what it is to live life without being permanently connected to the internet. Occasionally allowing or encouraging your child to go out and about without a phone at all (and modelling this yourself), choosing a simple feature phone for your child's first device, and, when they do get a smartphone, encouraging them to periodically disconnect for short periods – can all help prevent these issues.

The extreme end of disconnection is a 'digital detox' where you entirely disconnect from your phone (or all technology) for a longer period – it could be 24 hours or a whole weekend – or even longer. You may have watched the *Swiped* documentary for Channel 4 in December 2024, where some secondary school students gave up their phones for three weeks as part of a research project. If so, you will have an idea of how significant the change was for the children – and how difficult many found the adjustment. The show really highlighted just how much childhood has become entwined with smartphones.

Going cold turkey, like these kids did, is tough. It is much easier (and more advisable) to build in regular phone-free moments or times within our children's lives from the outset so that separation never reaches the point that it feels too traumatic. If they already have a phone, you can incorporate changes progressively to build up their tolerance. Every time we survive a period of disconnection without disaster striking it strengthens our belief that it's not just *okay* to switch off, but it really can help our nervous system relax so that we can unwind and restore.

Below are a few disconnection ideas for inspiration, but feel free to create your own. These scale up in difficulty level from short and sweet to more challenging; they deliberately include challenges for you as well as your child as it helps to practise what we preach, but be warned, it is harder than it looks! How we feel when we attempt to take time away from our smartphone can be revealing; it is often much more uncomfortable and challenging than you imagine for adults, let alone kids, so you might want to experiment with this yourself first, before expecting it from your child. With a little practice, these moments can become very grounding and deeply rewarding experiences. If you feel you need to be contactable in case of an emergency, consider buying a basic text-and-call-only backup phone you can keep with you instead, and share the number with close family and friends (even easier is if you have a partner with whom you take turns to disconnect).

Don't try and do all of these. Just pick one idea that appeals and try it – you can level up next time, if you like it!

- Leave your phones in the other room while you watch a film with your child.
- Leave your phone behind next time you pop to the shop at the end of the street (but don't forget your keys!).
- Disconnect after dinner – placing phones on charge in the charging area until after breakfast.

- Create a family challenge: 'Who can last the longest without checking their phone?'
- At bedtime, the entire family charges phones downstairs overnight (buy analogue alarm clocks).
- Pretend it's the 90s and challenge your child to go somewhere or do something without their phone, e.g. walking to a friend's house to hang out for a couple of hours. Simply agree what time they will be home and how to contact them in an emergency. (We did this all the time, remember?)
- Create a ritual of having a phone-free morning/afternoon/evening one day a week where no one in the family is allowed their phone. During this time, everyone can engage in activities that promote real-world connections, hobbies or simply relaxation. If you want to just ban phones but allow other screens, you could play a family computer game together – the aim is to apply your attention at will, and resist the pull of your phone, not demonise all screens.
- Plan monthly family days (or half days) where you leave your phones switched off and put away for the day and do something together.
- Have a digital detox weekender – don't underestimate how challenging this one will be! It will require plenty of preparation.

One of the reasons regular disconnection is hard but valuable is that it builds our tolerance for FOMO. Even better, it creates the space to do other things that are more fun than being online! This is how to help your child (re)discover JOMO – the *joy* of missing out! It makes the contrast clear for our kids: that everything is a trade-off and you cannot be fully present in two places at once. If you want to be the best skateboarder in school, for example, you've got to get out there; you can't spend all your evenings playing Fortnite. If you want to go to college, you need to study and not get distracted. A phone-free family date may mean missing out on scrolling social media for a few hours, but which will make the happier memory when you look back later? When we make peace with missing out, we have the chance to find joy in something else. It is our job to create the conditions for our children to find such joy, both offline and online.

TOP TAKE-AWAYS

Smartphones are expertly designed to manipulate us into using them unconsciously and compulsively; if you or your child is struggling with obsessive smartphone use, it is not your fault. Teaching your child to be more tech-intentional while simultaneously supporting them with taking practical steps to reduce temptation can help them avoid brain rot, find focus and feel more in control of their attention, which will bring them more joy and contentment. The ultimate goal is to raise your child to be the master, not the servant, of their phone.

Lesson 2

Become a Critical Thinker

'Beware of false knowledge; it is more dangerous than ignorance.'

George Bernard Shaw

'Bleak' is the word researchers used to describe young people's ability to effectively evaluate online information.[1] One US study found that students of varying ages could all be well-versed 'digital natives' who happily flit across multiple platforms consuming content yet still be easily duped by misinformation on social media, with many unable to distinguish between a paid story branded as 'sponsored content' and a real news story, or between a mainstream news source and a fake news outlet. Even high-achieving Stanford college medical students struggled with understanding the origins of news sources. The inevitable conclusion? Students of all ages had a shocking inability to assess the credibility of online information.[2]

In a world full of AI-powered chatbot companions, deepfaked footage and sinister scams everywhere you look, we just can't expect our children to know who or what to trust. We must actively support the development of their critical-thinking skills so that they can at least question what they see and hear, and attempt to spot fake news, paid promotions, unqualified influencers and online predators posing as friends – and give them some coping strategies to help them stay sane in the process. This chapter shows you how.

ACTION: Establish your online safety essentials

To stay safe online, your children need to know who to trust and how much to share about themselves – and although schools do some sessions on this stuff, it's still on us as parents to ensure they know the basics of staying safe online. Be warned, we are about to cover some quite dark topics, so this section draws heavily on the expert advice of the NSPCC. I recommend you check out their website and their Childline services, if you need more help on anything here.

Outside of the usual messaging apps and social media, there are also chat apps and chat rooms that allow users to pick an alias or avatar for themselves and send messages, photos, videos and documents, in large or small groups. All sorts of chat rooms exist – some are for specialist hobbies and interests, others are built into online games, others enable randomised connections with strangers for chat but also image and video sharing and live streaming. Some are created specifically as sex chat rooms for adults, but bewilderingly, many of these sites don't have age verification procedures in place so it can be easy for curious children to access them.

THE FIVE LESSONS

While it is not unusual for teens to make online friends who they don't know in real life, the NSPCC say that chat rooms can increase the risk of grooming for sexual abuse and other crimes. Grooming – which happens not just in chat rooms, but also on popular messaging apps and social media – is when someone gains your child's trust and makes a connection with them to get them to do something sexual or illegal. They will likely pay your child lots of compliments or offer things that they want to draw them into a conversation – this can be about anything that the child is interested in. They may be trying to involve them in sexual conversations, sending nude images or videos, or even attempting to meet up in person, but it is not always sexual. It is well known that people traffickers and criminals in the drugs trade rely on social media to identify vulnerable children they can control and exploit. Groomers can mask their identity online to change their age and gender or pretend to be an inspiring or public figure. Grooming can happen to anyone, and *it is never your child's fault*. Children can be groomed by someone they know, by a stranger or by a person they met online. They could be older, the same age, or even someone who's in a position of authority over them, like a teacher or sports coach, and the real difficulty is that grooming involves exploiting people's trust, so it can be hard for your child or you to recognise when it's happening.

Here are some practical ways in which you can help your child stay safe online.

1. **Don't rely on technical protections or monitoring alone.**
   Even if you have paid extra to get the best filtering

software and you've worked hard to block 'bad' sites, remember that these are all fallible and you can't bank on them, so it is essential that you talk to your child about what is and isn't appropriate in these spaces. If you use filtering software or check and monitor your child's phone, don't forget the 'dark web' (another layer of the internet where connections are usually encrypted and anonymised, making activity harder for law enforcement to track) means that it is possible that you are not seeing everything your child is seeing. No setting or software can ever replace quality conversations with your child.

2. **Apply the safest settings on your child's apps and platforms and talk through them together.** Whether group chats, social media or online gaming, always review the settings and ensure you both understand why you need them to keep your child safe. Set a strong password and decide together who can send them direct messages and friend requests. Ensure they know how to report and block people and content and talk about situations when they might want to do this.

3. **'No digital secrets'.** Chris McKenna, founder of Protect Young Eyes, says that there are very few secrets either IRL or online that are good for our children other than a party or present![3] He says to teach your child *never to keep digital secrets*. Nothing they see, do or are told to keep quiet should be secret. Repeat this message until their eyes roll! Yes, we all need privacy as we age, but your child needs to know that if anything is making them uncomfortable this is a red flag, and it is time to talk.

THE FIVE LESSONS

4. **Remind them not to share personal information**, like email addresses, names, phone numbers, location or even the name of their school, as this makes them findable, including photos or images of themselves in which this information could be identified (think school uniform, sports club attire, or photos taken outside their own home).

5. **Talk to your child often** about what they're sharing. Tell them they should come to you or another trusted adult if someone sends them something upsetting or worrying. Conversation starters include, 'Have you seen any bad behaviour online? What did you see? How did you react?' Celebrate their sensible actions; if they tell you 'someone said this to me, so I closed the conversation and blocked them', commend them for telling you and making the right decision.

6. **Explain that 'disappearing message' functions are not safe.** These are also known as 'snaps', 'vanishing messages' or 'secret chats', but images can be screenshotted and kept by the recipient without their knowledge or consent. The idea that a message will disappear from the recipient's device may make your child feel a false sense of safety so they send more risky content. They need to know that they have no control over where it goes once it's been sent. Tell them that if they wouldn't want to hand a printed copy of that photo or message to someone in person – and then be happy to watch them passing it around all the pupils and teachers – don't send it. (Disappearing or encrypted messages also make it harder

to report inappropriate contact and capture evidence of child exploitation or abuse.)

7. **Ensure your child understands that live-streaming sites are public and unpredictable.**[4] Live streaming is the broadcasting of real-time, live videos to an audience over the internet, and an absent-minded slip-up like wearing their school uniform or standing in front of their house can broadcast personal information that could be used to identify your child to strangers and put them at risk. Live streaming should not be used like private messaging apps. Situations can escalate in a moment and be used to broadcast abusive and harmful behaviour, so your child can easily see things they were not expecting. Children sometimes experience screens as a sort of safety net, creating a distance between themselves and the viewers; they may be more reckless and do things they wouldn't do face to face, especially as there is usually no moderation and the impermanent nature of livestreams makes reporting difficult. If you allow your child to live-stream at all, a shared space where you can keep an eye on them will be safer than in bedrooms. Ensure they know to exit the call the second they feel uncomfortable then come and speak to you about what they have seen.

8. **Be curious about your child's 'friend' online.** Analysis by Childline counsellors has shown that children sometimes refer to individuals they've met online as their friends, but upon digging deeper, it sometimes becomes clear that the child knows very little about this person, who later emerges as a risk to the child.[5]

9. **Look out for warning signs of grooming and coercive or controlling behaviour**, including:
    - control and manipulation ('*So and so says ...*')
    - behaviour/personality change
    - isolation and not wanting to see friends
    - keeping a relationship a secret (a strong red flag)
    - sexualised language, jokes or poses *may* indicate someone is using these towards them
    - risk-taking behaviour, such as visiting someone's home who they do not already know IRL (they could be being controlled to act this way or not see the risk due to having been manipulated)
    - gifts or freebies (including phones or games).
10. **No gifts or 'freebies' online.** Teach them that gifts from online friends are not normal and could be used against them later as a reason to claim that they 'owe them'. Gifts include paying for games or online activities or free phones. Make it a rule that your child must say no without adult approval.

I appreciate this all feels scary and heavy, but remember that many of us talk to people online that we don't know and it can be a great way to connect and learn. The important thing is for your child to be old enough or mature enough to understand and navigate these risks before you let them get on social media, public chat rooms, or otherwise talk to strangers online.

Finally, if you're worried about your child you can talk to Childline 24/7 by calling 0800 1111 or using their online chat

– yes, Childline is for parents as well as children. Also, give this information to your child; tell them that it is free and confidential and although you would love them to feel able to speak to you, this is another option that is open to them. Better safe than sorry.

> ### SEXTORTION
>
> Online abuse is not just an issue for parents of girls. Sextortion is a ruthless crime where heartless professional criminals exploit the shame and embarrassment of individuals, particularly teenage boys, by posing as an attractive female to trick them into sending a nude image, then blackmailing them for cash by threatening to share the image with all their friends and family or claiming that they have hacked their account. It is an easy and efficient money-making method; with social media and AI-powered image and name searching, it takes just a few minutes for these disgusting criminals to find out so much about a child's identity, including their school, clubs and names of friends and family members. The results can be fatal, with fear and blind panic tragically driving some children to suicide.
>
> And I am sorry to say that there is zero space for parental complacency or 'not my child' thinking on this one. Last year a survey of more than 6,000 young social media users in six countries found that almost half said they had been targeted in an online sextortion scheme;[6] one third had shared an intimate photo. That is *ten children in every classroom who have sent a naked image of themselves to a stranger* – and a further five who have come dangerously close to it.

In the upsetting event that your child does fall victim to sextortion, the advice from UK Safer Internet Centre is clear:[7] parents and victims should 'Stop, Block, Report'. However you find out – whether your child tells you or you discover another way – remain calm and do not overreact. Remain approachable and understanding with your child; tell them this is not their fault and it is good that you know so that you can begin to help them. The UK Internet Safety Centre strongly advises that you do not confiscate their device as this might prevent them from asking you for help in the future. Instead, ensure all communication with the offender has been stopped and they are blocked across any accounts where your child might have been targeted. Try to gather as much evidence as you can, such as messages or perpetrator details, and report the incident to the Child Exploitation and Online Protection Centre (CEOP).[8] If there is an immediate risk to the child, contact the police on 999 or 101.

To be absolutely clear – the advice is do not pay them. While this may be tempting, blackmailers will continue to ask for money even if you pay the first demand. The best option is to stop communication and not pay, but if you have already paid, don't panic, just don't pay any more – it will not resolve the situation. Focus instead on communicating with your child and reassure them that they have done the right thing by coming to you, that you do not blame them for anything and you will support them. Finally, report the image or video using the 'Report Remove' or 'Take It Down' online tools to help prevent any further sharing. Under-eighteens can also use the 'Take It Down' platform themselves, although under-thirteens will need help. If images have been shared across specific platforms, report them directly using in-app reporting tools.

Once an incident has occurred you can visit saferinternet.org.uk or contact Childline for help. To prevent it happening in the first place, Protect Young Eyes encourages parents to have 'ridiculously honest chats' with tweens and teens about the seriousness of the situation. They suggest using attention-grabbing statements like: 'Son, listen. Don't ever send a picture of your penis to someone. No dick pics. Got it?' Crass, absolutely. But they argue that you need their full attention for this message to truly land and that if your child is old enough for an adult smartphone, you really need to be willing to have these adult conversations. But above all, they implore parents to remind their child often that they are safe with you and that if they are ever tricked or persuaded into a sending a naked photo of themselves, you will always help them.

ACTION: Help them to search safely and make sense of what they see

That bad things happen is a fact of life. Wars, violence, pandemics or 'plagues', natural or political disasters – none are new – but in centuries past, if they were not happening on our doorstep, or to our nearest and dearest, we would be most likely unaware and untroubled by them. However, in today's hyper-connected, internet-enabled world, when something bad happens, the news spreads like wildfire. Where a generation ago our parents might watch the six o'clock news once a day, or a generation before that they may have read the weekly paper, we are now absorbing news minute by minute via news notifications and group chats.

We tend to share scary stuff more often than innocent, gentle, happy stories because humans have a 'negativity bias' that make us more sensitive to threats to our safety. I think of this as a hangover from cavemen days, an ancient survival strategy where one would be more likely to scream 'wolf!' than 'I found a great blackberry bush over here!', for obvious reasons. This is why, when our children get their own first internet-enabled phone it is only a matter of time before they begin to witness dramatic and frightening events. These will range from the personal or 'hyper-local' situations, like seeing footage of a bullying episode at school or an incident in the local community, like knife crime and gang-related activity, to more distant but no less troubling events like viewing sexual violence in pornography, or global events like war, terrorism, political oppression or even environmental destruction.

Most adults can make reasonably good sense of what they see and hear online, and for the most part, put negative news in perspective. But our children have less life experience and no other frame of reference for all the dark and scary stuff they see and hear online, so these events have a disproportionate impact and frame their worldview. This is why we need to help them make sense of what they see and provide the perspective that they are missing, as well as seek to prevent them from seeing things that are inappropriate for their age and stage in the first place.

Obviously, teenagers' capacity to cope increases with age and maturity, but Protect Young Eyes describes five types of content that are too much for young minds and can cause confusion, distress or anxiety and sometimes lead to disturbed behaviours.[9]

1. **Sexual content** Seeing pornography or explicit content before you understand the basics of intimacy and sex can be terrifying and bewildering for kids and result in misguided interpretations, increasing the chances of abusive behaviour towards peers. (See Lesson 3: Know Your Digital Ethics for more on this.)
2. **Premature adult responsibilites or interactions** In the digital world, this might look like having to fend off inappropriate or sexual approaches from strangers or peers on social media, or the complex emotional labour involved in negotiating a feuding group chat. Such demands can take a huge toll on an adult's mental health, let alone a child without the emotional maturity and life skills to handle them.
3. **Violence** According to the Youth Endowment Fund survey, 70 per cent of British teens witnessed real-world acts of violence on social media in the last year, despite few children actively seeking it out. The impact of this is far-reaching. The survey also found that nearly two-thirds of teenagers who report perpetrating violence in the past year say that social media has played a role in their behaviour, and that factors like online arguments and the escalation of existing conflicts are commonly cited as catalysts for real-world violence.[10]
4. **Intense adult themes** Films, TV, other video content or news coverage involving life-threatening situations,

substance abuse or extreme psychological struggle can result in misinterpretations, fear and insecurity. It's the reason films have age ratings, but the internet is not so well regulated, meaning that our children are more likely to unknowingly stumble across inappropriate footage.

5. **Shocking world events** Hate crime, extremism, natural disasters, war, abuse: when younger children are exposed to something awful without a frame of reference to help them make sense of it and feel safe, they're not sure what to do with it in their minds. They need our help to process what they see so they can 'tidy it away' in their brain, make peace with it and move on. Like trying to work on a messy desk, it's disruptive and stressful when things aren't in their right place, but it's even worse for teens, who may have fewer coping strategies and more intense emotions.

While we cannot cocoon our kids from the world for ever, there is plenty we can do to ensure that our children are mostly insulated from inappropriate content while young, then help them to develop a balanced and generally positive worldview to help them comprehend what they do see. To learn how, we must now dive a little deeper into the dark side of the internet.

Viewing violence

'One teenager punches and kicks another until the victim curls up in the foetal position on the ground. A boy sexually assaults a girl, while his friends cheer him on from the sidelines,' writes Jon Yates, Director of the Youth Endowment Foundation (YEF) and expert on the impact of violence on young people.[11] 'These are the types of videos that over half of our teenage children saw last year on TikTok and other social media platforms. Not other people's children – our children.'

The even sadder truth is that few of the children who saw this stuff were searching for it. Most see it because it's on someone else's profile or – disturbingly – because the social media platform has pushed it into their eyeline as recommended content. Yates adds: 'It is simply not acceptable that teenagers going online looking for dance routines or beauty tips end up seeing acts of violence that would haunt adults for days – let alone impressionable 13-year-olds.'

I couldn't agree more. When I was in California researching this book, I asked all the children I met what they thought parents needed to know about their children's smartphone use. One of the standout issues was the prevalence of violence online. One group of 18-year-olds from Silicon Valley explained how beheading videos were circulated routinely when they were younger teenagers. Others seemed visibly haunted by the memories of things they had seen and clearly did not want to dwell on the details. Other teens from LA told me 'parents need to know that Google and YouTube [which is owned by Google] are the worst for kids'. TikTok and Snapchat were frequently mentioned, but they explained that violence and scary stuff was not just shared on social media or message groups and that the most shocking and upsetting content was often unearthed via their own innocent Google and YouTube searches. They reported how they did not want to see what they were seeing, but somehow the 'bad stuff' would find them anyway, and once they were viewing it they would find it hard to look away and didn't know why; then they could not 'unsee' what they had seen. They told me how 'if they really knew what their kids were seeing, parents would be much more careful' with letting their children browse the internet without supervision.

I have made this mistake with my own daughter. She was nine years old and I let her use the laptop alone in her bedroom – she was so desperate to sit at her big girl desk and not have me hanging over her shoulder. I was unsure, but I thought perhaps I was being overly controlling; she's a super sensible kid and 'she'd never do anything stupid' so I thought, why not? Turns out she didn't have to do anything wrong to quickly find upsetting content. Ten minutes later I popped in to check on her and was shocked to find that she was on YouTube being served videos of decaying corpses laying on beaches, complete with rotting flesh, hollow cheeks and eyeballs exposed in their sockets. How on earth had this happened so quickly? It emerged that she had searched the most innocent, the most childish of all questions: 'Are mermaids real?' These were lifelike, Hollywood-quality recreations, filmed by content creators presenting them as 'proof' of their existence; each had millions of views. Luckily, I caught this within moments of it appearing and she quickly looked away. Little harm was done this time – but it was disturbing enough (she was still visibly upset when I raised the memory years later) and it very effectively demonstrated for us both how quickly things can turn nasty online.

This incident also made me think about what I was like as a child and what I might have searched for at the same age. I recalled an occasion aged about ten when someone at school asked me if I was a virgin. I didn't know what that word meant. It was classic playground stuff – no big deal – but if I had had an adult smartphone, I absolutely would have gone straight home after school and googled it. The mind boggles what that search might have shown, what links I might have clicked on, what ads the algorithms might have served me the next time I went online. (Incidentally, when was the last time you used an actual dictionary? Right. Google is also your child's dictionary. Or rather, by the time you read this it will probably be the latest AI model.) I've said it before, and I will say it again – the question is not whether you trust your child with a smartphone, it is whether you trust a smartphone with your child.

The good news is that there are some basic actions we can take to reduce the chances of our child being exposed to violence and inappropriate content online.

1. **Teach them to click away.** As young as possible, and as often as possible, tell your child that they should swipe or click away instantly if something makes them feel scared or unsure ... and then come and tell you about it. Children can feel powerless in the face of screens; remind them that they are always in control of what they see, so if in doubt, they should close it down without hesitation, because you cannot unsee things.
2. **Switch on Google 'safe mode'.** Chapter 3: Setting Yourself up for Success has more comprehensive advice on parental controls, content filters and monitoring usage, through the likes of Google's Family Link. Even if you

THE FIVE LESSONS

don't go 'full parental controls', one easy win is to switch on 'safe mode' on Google (or your preferred search engine). As settings are easily overridden you still need to teach them to avoid inappropriate content.

3. **Teach them about algorithms.** Your children are sucked deeper into echo chambers every time they use the search function on their internet browser or YouTube. It might help to encourage your children to stay logged out of any profiles when searching on YouTube to minimise the impact of algorithms, but they cannot be avoided altogether, which is why it is important to explain what an algorithm is and how this affects what they see. Here is a basic explainer you can riff on, but use your own words and make it as simple as possible:

When we search online our phones show us different stuff depending on who we are and what the computer thinks we want to see. Algorithms are how the apps and websites decide what stuff to show you. Algorithms work by guessing what you might like based on what it knows about you – like your age and gender – and then remembering every time you click a link, watch a video or hit the like button and then serving you more and more similar stuff. This might sound good (more stuff you like!), but it means that we miss out on loads of other stuff we might like because we will never get a chance to see it. Also, because technology is built to make its owners money, not to take care of you, it doesn't actually show you what you like and what makes you happy, but what keeps you glued to the screen.

Algorithms will show you whatever it takes to keep you watching, even if it is harmful, scary or upsetting. The good news is that we can try to 'teach' the algorithms to be better by not pausing to watch or click on upsetting things, and instead deliberately engage with stuff that makes us feel good and is helpful instead, as this will tell it you want more of this better content.

You can also demonstrate the power of algorithms quickly and easily by searching online for the word 'boots' and clicking on the images tab to see how the images differ depending on whose phone you use and what their search history is like. For me I am primarily served practical, flat leather boots (no judgement please – I'm in my forties and comfort is my vibe!) whereas a fourteen-year-old girl who follows the latest teen influencers on TikTok may be more likely to be served something more youthful and glamorous, perhaps heeled (I would hate to hazard a guess at what is cool nowadays, but you get the idea).

YouTube

YouTube has overtaken broadcast TV viewing for children and teens with well over half of 5–15-year-olds using it for two and a half hours a day, so taking some time to understand it and set it up right will pay dividends longer term.[12] (Visit internetmatters.org for any technical step-by-step guides you need on this.)

Here are some ways you can support your child with YouTube and other social media or video sharing platforms.

1. **Choose a Supervised Account.** 'YouTube Kids' is a purpose-built platform for the youngest viewers, whereas YouTube itself is rated 13+ and has a much broader range of content. YouTube now offers a 'supervised' option for teens, with safer content settings and limited features; you can also check their search history within their account, but you will need to set up a Google account for all this to work. You can use this to monitor their activity periodically (with their knowledge) until you feel confident they are old enough to require absolute privacy. This will help you gain insight into how they use their online time and present an opportunity to discuss and learn about their favourite creators. The aim is to develop more trust and openness through this discussion while helping you keep an eye out for any harmful content.
2. **Discuss the difference between good and bad content.** Good content encourages them to follow their interests, lifts their spirits, makes them laugh, educates them or shows positive, kind, healthy relationships. Conversely, bad content might encourage risky behaviour (like drug taking or dangerous challenges), encourage violence, aggression or prejudice, focus on a narrow and limiting view of beauty, or include negative mental health subjects like suicide, self-harm or eating disorders. Use open-ended, casual questions to start conversation. 'Seen

any good/terrible videos online lately?' Even better, sit and watch it with your child. It will give you an insight into what they enjoy and them a chance to learn about your boundaries. Even if they would never admit it, your child looks to you for a benchmark of acceptability, so they need you to speak up when what you see is problematic or harmful (silence can easily be misconstrued as approval).

3. **Set rules for what they are (not) allowed to watch.** Turn on restricted mode as a quick way to hide mature or inappropriate videos, but as filters aren't foolproof it's important to discuss your standards with your child too. There are literally billions of videos on YouTube so focus on guiding principles rather than trying to vet every account – nothing violent or promoting risky or unkind behaviour, for instance. Of course there is a lot of dross out there that you might find pointless or irritating, so pick your battles and stick to defending your 'red lines' rather than criticising their tastes, which naturally will be different from yours.

4. **Set limits for how long they can watch and when.** While excessive video content viewing has risks,[13] there is no set amount of time that experts agree is too much. To work out what is right for you, consider the idea of 'interference'. How much is manageable without this impacting with other important activities for their healthy development, like in-person socialising with friends and family, clubs, interests and sleep? Once you've decided on your time limits and schedule, set these up in screentime

settings. Also ensure 'autoplay' is switched off to prevent the next video auto-loading to help your child avoid falling down a rabbit hole.

5. **Show them how to curate their suggested content** by training the algorithms on what they do and don't like. Demonstrate how to select the 'Not Interested' option (this deletes the item and reduces the likelihood of them being served similar content) and tell them to do this systematically for anything that doesn't make them feel good or goes against your rules; with over 14 billion videos on YouTube there is simply no need for them to watch anything that they don't love! The same principle applies for all social media, not just YouTube. You can also show them how to report inappropriate videos, delete a channel and amend 'Ad Settings'.

Global events and current affairs

Despite your best efforts there will be times your child encounters upsetting, frightening or confusing things online, including real-world events covered by mainstream or alternative news outlets. It is our job to help our children make sense of these events as best we can.

If we don't create a safe space for children to explore their fears they can grow unchecked. For instance, the Woodland Trust describes young people as experiencing an 'epidemic of climate anxiety', with research showing that seven out of ten young people are worried about climate change and its effects.[14] Young people see scary news events, like extreme localised flooding in the UK, wildfires decimating California and devastating droughts across Africa, and are increasingly worried about the health of the planet. This is having a significant impact on some young people's mental health and can result in life-changing decisions; one in four 16–24-year-olds say fears over the climate crisis mean they are willing to consider, or have already decided, to have fewer children than they would otherwise like.

So, be it natural disasters, the death of a public figure, violent crime or war, how do you explain upsetting news to your child in a way that helps them process these events, without overwhelming them? Dr Sheila Redfern is a consultant clinical psychologist at the Anna Freud Centre and offers this advice for parents.[15]

1. **Reassure, but don't lie.** If your child is online or talking to friends they may already be well aware of the details. Do not deny the facts or minimise the situation; instead, try to put them into the context of the rest of their life. If they are anxious about implications in their own life, can you reassure them about how removed these events may be from them personally vs how social media hype may be portraying it?
2. **Encourage compassion.** While it helps to reassure children that events might not directly affect them, it is equally important to encourage them to show compassion for others who are in different circumstances to theirs. If their classmate is distressed by a headline – maybe the death of a public figure or a foreign war has affected them more deeply – you might also encourage them to be kind and understanding.

3. **Manage your own emotional response.** If we adults are constantly watching the news, anxiously scrolling our phones for the latest bulletins and referring to an event all the time, our children will pick up on this and their anxiety will escalate. Talk to friends or adult family members when you need to manage your own feelings and model calm and normality around your child as much as possible. When they see you coping, it's highly likely they will follow suit.
4. **Keep normal routines going.** After any traumatic event, it is important that children and young people return to a normal routine as quickly as possible and it is no different if you are hearing about something, rather than directly experiencing it. Try to ensure that your child doesn't stop doing anything they would normally do, whether keeping to normal meal routines, hobbies or seeing friends.
5. **Keep a sense of control.** Anxiety thrives when we feel out of control. Your child might benefit from taking action on a topic they feel passionately about to increase their sense of autonomy. You can support this by encouraging them to talk to their friends and family about their feelings or channel their concern into community action, like writing to their local MP, donating clothes, fundraising or volunteering.
6. **Maintain stability at home.** Depressing and disastrous headlines can make the world feel bleak and hard to understand. Find subtle ways to send the message that home is a safe environment where they are not under

threat and life continues as normal for your family. Do not catastrophise about the future; the ambiguity of 'anything could happen next' can send a child's anxiety soaring. The idea of death is always difficult for children, but explaining it in a straightforward and non-frightening way helps children accept the facts of life.

7. **Fact-check and check back in**. When your child comes to you with 'facts' they have picked up through social media and conversations with friends, often one reason they come to you is that they want to check whether you think they are true. To encourage openness and build trust, try asking, 'Where did you hear that?' and 'Tell me a bit more about that', rather than automatically shutting it down. You can also try going back to them a few days later to see if they are still thinking about it, or if they want to know more.

8. **Don't worry if they seem unconcerned**. Some children will worry about world events more than others; others will be more interested in their next football match or exam, and this is fine. Don't force a conversation or try to get them to engage in this stuff if it isn't something they want to think about or discuss – be guided by them.

ACTION: Teach them to question everything

So far, we have mainly covered how you can support young people with things that really are happening in the real world that they happen to find out about online, but as digital technology becomes ever more sophisticated, we are increasingly struggling to distinguish between reality and fiction.

Scams

Research from the UK Safer Internet Centre shows that half of 8–17-year-olds have been scammed online and 9 per cent have lost money to an online con (that's three children in every class)[16] and the saddest part is that many of these children are too embarrassed to seek help. The same study showed that half of kids see these cons at least weekly (often much more regularly) so it really is super common and something we all need to help our kids get wise to, before/when they get online.

The NSPCC describes an online scam as when criminals use online platforms to trick someone into sharing personal information like account logins or bank details. Scams can happen on any online platform and can include:

- **Phishing** – when someone pretends to be someone you trust or a legitimate organisation, like a bank or government agency, to steal your information and exploit you. It can involve requesting money or sending links or attachments that put viruses on your hardware when you open them. Spear phishing is a more targeted, personalised version of phishing where someone may impersonate someone close to you.
- **Catfishing** – when someone creates a fake online identity and actively engages with their victim with the purpose of deceiving and manipulating them, often using a romantic or emotional approach. It is often done for money but could also be for revenge or bullying.

- **Promotion of products or false adverts that contain untrue claims** – such as a fake competition or a product that claims to do something it can't to get you to buy.
- **Competitions or quizzes** – when you are led to believe there is a prize when there isn't.
- **Identity theft** – when you are tricked into sharing personal information and then your accounts are hacked.

To help your child avoid becoming a scam victim teach them the following.

1. **If it looks too good to be true, it probably is.**
2. **Don't click on links or open email attachments from unknown senders** – that means if you get a message that says it's from Mum or Dad, if it is an unrecognised number then it is probably a scam. Be highly suspicious of any contact you aren't expecting.
3. **Treat any urgency as a red flag.** Scammers try to put you under time pressure to act before you have a chance to think – don't fall for it. Instead, step away and ask for advice.

Scammers have become so sophisticated that even a highly trained eye will struggle to detect some. In the week that I wrote this chapter I received such a convincing phishing scam email it took me several hours of calls with my bank to determine whether it came from a trustworthy source. Earlier in the year, a friend of a friend lost tens of thousands of pounds in a scam.

There is little worse than the 'I am so stupid, I should have known' kind of shame so my next piece of advice is simple.

Remind children regularly that if they ever do get scammed – if anything happens online that they are not sure of or they are worried that they have done the wrong thing – it's not their fault. Tell them to come to you for help and promise them you won't be cross. (The hardest part is when they do come to you: swallow your feelings and stay calm!)

Paid ads

This is a small but important aspect of digital literacy that would be easy to overlook but is worth teaching your child. You know how the first search findings (usually those at the very top) are adverts? Probably. But your child may not.

In a study about children's media literacy for media watchdog Ofcom, less than half of children aged 8–15 who used search engines could correctly identify adverts on Google searches, and about the same didn't know that some results could be trusted and some couldn't.[17] In other words, half of kids regard whatever Google says as irrefutable truth. One third of 12–15-year-olds did not even realise that vloggers and influencers might be sponsored to say good things about products or brands.

Tell your child that companies pay to appear in searches and this content can usually be identified by the words 'Ad' or 'Sponsored Results', but otherwise they look very similar to the rest of the results listed. Explain how these listings rank highly not because they are the best results but because they paid to be at the top. Being able to identify promoted content will help your child understand that what they see is not an objective representation of a single universal truth, but a profit-making system that they need to apply a critical eye to. Talk to them about how content creators (including YouTubers and celebrities on social media) make money by using product placement and sponsored content – in other words, perhaps they don't love the thing they are selling, but are just doing their job, which is to get you to watch, click and buy more.

Fake news

Did you know that Instagram, TikTok and YouTube are now teenagers' top three news sources?[18] The fact that teens are shunning traditional journalism to get their news exclusively from social media matters because it is a broadly unregulated industry that reduces news to entertainment – sensationalist, shocking twenty-second videos that make children feel immediately informed and knowledgeable but without necessarily having the context or facts.

Misinformation is false information shared by accident without meaning harm because someone believed it to be true (like photos, quotes or dates). Disinformation, on the other hand, is false information shared deliberately to mislead and cause harm. Hoaxes are a type of disinformation and come in different forms, including 'fake news' stories that deliberately worry others, deepfakes, and memes used to spread unverified or false facts that are circulated on messaging apps. A child is more likely to believe these when they are shared with them by someone they know.

Here are three ways you can help combat fake news.

- **Teach your child not to share if they aren't sure.** Tell them they can speak to you if they have questions about something they've seen or if they see something online that confuses, worries or upsets them.
- **Question them kindly to activate their critical-thinking skills.** There's no better way to alienate your child than to belittle their belief or be condescending, so avoid immediately dismissing their questionable news out of hand. Instead, seed some doubts about what they've said and encourage them to investigate further. 'That's interesting ... Is that a reliable source? Does that person know a lot about this subject? Could the image or video have been edited? How would you know? I hadn't heard that ... Do you know if others are reporting the same thing? Could this source have anything to gain by you clicking on or resharing that information?'
- **Encourage your child to look at a range of resources.** Considering the same topic from a variety of sources will help them gain new insights and a broader perspective. They could try fact-checking websites such as fullfact.org.

Stunts and challenges

Online challenges are where young people are encouraged – or pressured – by friends into sharing an image or video of themselves doing a physical or personal challenge (like disclosing a personal story about themselves) via video-sharing platforms like TikTok or YouTube. While some are fun – think dancing or charity fundraisers – some contain dangerous stunts. Young people don't always realise that creators can easily edit videos to make it look like they did something dangerous or risky when in reality they didn't. Challenges may be seen as harmless fun or a chance to 'go viral', which may be exciting to young people, but peer pressure can lead kids to say or do things they later regret, and some videos threaten that bad things will happen if you don't complete the challenge, which can be really scary for children or any superstitious young person.

Tell your child never to take part in any stunt or challenge that might cause them or others physical or emotional harm – and to never pass them on to others. Reassure them that superstitions are not real and any videos that suggests a sense of threat – even if they are playful in tone – are not okay. Tell them plainly that even if it is supposedly harmless and fun, they should say no unless it's really something they would enjoy and feel safe about. Regularly check in with them by casually asking about the latest challenges their friends take part in or ask them to show you their favourite challenge.

Generative Artificial intelligence (AI)

Technology is developing at lightning pace and, at the risk of sounding my age, it can be hard to keep up. However, when the latest data from Ofcom (2023) confirms that eight out of ten teens (aged 13–17) and even four in ten tweens (aged 7–12) are now using generative AI tools, keep up we must.[19] AI is now so embedded in our technology that the moment you give your child an adult smartphone, you are effectively giving them access to

AI. You can try to control how much they access but they will encounter it soon enough.

AI is the capacity of computers or software to exhibit intelligent behaviour, perform tasks or produce output previously thought to require human intelligence, especially when machine learning is used to extrapolate from large collections of data. AI is developing rapidly – much faster than policy and government regulation can keep up. It is creating huge opportunities for mankind but also huge challenges around intellectual property, exploitation, freedom of speech, data ethics, crime, democracy – and our children's safety and development.

AI is already central to children's smartphone usage through internet search engines, website chatbots, games, educational apps, social media and messaging apps. Children with smartphones can access dedicated AI-powered content-generating tools like ChatGPT for free and use them for all sorts of purposes, including entertainment, learning and computer coding. Online learning platform Khan Academy has its own personal tutor embedded in its platform, and AI features are being added (without parental warnings) to apps wherever you look. Even my minimalist meditation app now how has a 'empathetic companion' popping up to say hi and ask how I am (much to my irritation!).

The implications of AI are mind-blowing. After the invention of language, the adoption of the written word and the advent of the internet, AI must surely be up there as one of the greatest levellers of access to knowledge and learning that the world has ever seen, so while we are right to worry for the future, let us also remember AI's immense positive potential when put in the right hands. Technology is only as good or bad as the human using it.

That said, for now, it's probably more likely your child will use generative AI to cheat on their school homework than solve world peace (but you never know). Indeed, AI-powered cheating is creating a dilemma for the education system and schools, which are now scrambling to find ways to identify AI-generated submissions and develop policies around this. Initially schools banned all use of AI tools, but some are now realising that they need to educate children about their ethical and effective use in an age-appropriate way. This is crucial because the implications of AI go far, far beyond teachers' ability to catch cheats. It is rapidly redefining not just how our children learn, but how humans will live, work and think – so we parents really need to try to understand what we are dealing with here if we are going to be able to support our kids.

So, without being an AI expert, how can you help your child navigate generative AI? Here are a few suggestions for you to reflect on. Some may be relevant already, while others may be more useful as your child ages and is exposed to more AI in the years ahead.

1. **Get familiar first.** The best way to understand AI is to experiment with it yourself. Gina is the nickname my kids and I have given to the free version of ChatGPT on my iPhone. We have been experimenting with using 'her' for silly stuff like generating a recipe for dinner using the hopelessly random selection of odds and ends we have in the fridge, or for step-by-step guidance for

overcoming DIY challenges. I also use it selectively for work tasks where I want to be more efficient, or challenge myself to think a little differently. I am an AI novice, but playing around with the free version has helped me understand the potential and limitations of these tools and how to use them more wisely.

2. **Agree with your child what AI they can use (if any), when and how.** This will vary for every family's circumstances and will take trial and error as you experiment, but be explicit in what is acceptable to you and what is not or they simply won't know what the boundaries are. Some things might be okay under supervision, for example, and others not at all. (Read the Chatbots and AI Companions section on page 182 for more age-related advice.)

3. **Never input personal data.** Ensure your child knows that everything they enter in AI software will be stored and processed by machine learning, relinquishing their privacy and potentially rendering their data discoverable and usable by others. And by personal data, we aren't just talking about their name, school or home address, but also personal secrets or intimate information. (You would be surprised how willing children are to share their innermost thoughts and feelings with software). As we have no idea what may become of that information, or how the technology will respond to such prompts, it is not safe for children to use AI in this way, as we will find out in the next section.

4. **Explain that AI is neither neutral nor trustworthy.** AI simply reflects the biases and inaccuracies in the data

that it draws from, so if it draws from bad data, it creates bad results. This means results can simply be factually untrue (sometimes these results are called 'hallucinations') and can actively promote harmful, discriminatory stereotypes, or lead to false and misleading advice – and that is without getting into the minefield surrounding the unethical use of intellectual property. Tell your child never to take AI-generated results on face value and to always – always – cross-check their facts and assumptions because AI is very often completely and utterly wrong.

5. **Discuss the opportunities, risks and implications of AI with your child.** Don't overlook discussion around the potential benefits to humanity, as well as any worries either of you have. You might wish to discuss the importance of children developing critical thinking skills and reflect together on how use of AI can help or hinder our cognitive abilities.

6. **Be your child's AI co-pilot.** If you choose to allow your child to use generative AI, actively engage with them as they do, so that you can observe how they are using it and how you feel about that. Discuss and adjust as you go.

7. **Activate your child's critical-thinking skills.** Next time your child asks a virtual assistant a question, have them reflect on the answer they got. Was it correct? How do you know? What information or perspectives might have been overlooked? Did the AI help or hinder you on this occasion? You might even geek out by trying a fact-checking tool or reverse-image searches to expose any flaws or incorrect assumptions inherent within the technology.

8. **Consider the environmental cost.** Did you know that the data storage requirements of AI make it very costly to the planet due to the massive amount of water it takes to cool the heat from the generators and the carbon dioxide produced? Learning that a twenty-question conversation is the equivalent of pouring a 500 ml bottle of water down the drain made me more selective in how often I chat with 'Gina'.[20] Teach your child that nothing is ever truly free, so we should be thoughtful about when and how we use it.

9. **Recognise AI's limits.** AI is an amazing tool that your child will need to use one day, but when it comes to your child's development, it can never replace the value of the human experience. The job market will evolve, as it always has, but your child will always need – and be needed for – their humanity: meaningful relationships and personal qualities like empathy, imagination, teamwork and creativity are irreplaceable. Embodied, sensory human experiences, including time in nature, engagement with the arts, and meaningful interactions with other people (and other species), are timeless elements that shape and sustain us. AI is incredible – it is also not a patch on being human.

Deepfakes

Deepfakes are faked audio recordings, images and videos that have been generated or manipulated using AI but which look and sound like genuine content. And if you already knew that, then good on you – because almost half of parents do not.[21] Although deepfakery can be used for anything, according to Internet Matters, nude material makes up around 98 per cent of all deepfakes and 99 per cent of nude deepfakes feature women and girls.[22] There has been an explosion of such images recently because of the release of easy-to-use apps that can swap faces on moving images, convert fully clothed static images to nudes, or clone short voice clips to create convincing audio recordings of people saying anything you want. Completely faked porn films no longer require any technical skill – or knowledge or consent. You might have heard about Taylor Swift becoming a victim of deepfake pornography, or even the videos on TikTok of fabricated atrocities from the Israel–Hamas war, or perhaps one of the many spoof celebrity social media channels. It can be almost impossible for an untrained eye to tell the difference.

Horrifyingly, deepfaked imagery is now being widely used in pornography and child sexual abuse material – and even sometimes by children themselves, who create and share images of peers with one another to bully, shame and intimidate. This new world is heaven for fraudsters and hell for their victims and law enforcement teams, where photorealistic imagery can flood staff caseloads and complicate victim identification.

Significantly, teenagers say that they see nude deepfake abuse as worse than sexual abuse featuring real images. Reasons include the lack of autonomy over – or awareness of – the image, the anonymity of the perpetrator, how the image might be manipulated, and fear of people thinking the image is real, which goes to show just how profound and lasting a trauma this egregious invasion of privacy can be.

THE FIVE LESSONS

So, let's say you have delayed giving an adult smartphone as long as you can and are certain that a family-friendly smartphone will no longer cut it. You've already applied content filters, restricted your children from downloading new apps without permission, and your children are not allowed on social media (or if they are, their accounts are set to private). What else can you do to protect them from falling victim to a deepfake?

Here are few more tips from Protect Young Eyes:[23]

1. **Agree on a code word or unique question** you can ask if you receive an unusual phone call from your child so you can be sure it is not a faked voice. Ensure your child also knows how to handle calls from people they don't know (tell, block, delete).
2. **Keep their social media following very small** (if they are allowed one at all). Aim for less than a hundred people. Tell them to imagine handing every photo to every person they're following and never request connections from people they don't know well and trust in real life ...
3. **Be judicious when sharing photos of your kids online.** Sadly your innocent images can be misappropriated for ill-intent; only share with people you know personally and trust.

Chatbots and AI Companions

A partner who can guarantee that they are here for you '24/7, always available to talk and to listen and up for anything you would like', sounds pretty amazing, right? Well, what if I said you – or your child – could have that right now with an AI companion? With tools like character.ai and Replika you can personalise your character to sound and appear however you like. Replika says users can have deep text conversations 'thanks to a 70+ billion parameter model', listen and send voice messages, talk to 'her/him' in real-time 3D video calls, and even dive into an immersive augmented reality-like hologram while enjoying 'intimate conversations with no limits'.

Replika allows you to select the personality of your ideal partner, from playful and charismatic to confident and experienced, as well as appearance, from 'steam punk' to boy next door. 'There is no limit to what your Replika can be for you' apparently – and all this for around $20 a month. If you're unsure, Replika says you can have 'no risk of betrayal, strong emotional support, a high focus on you and someone who 100 per cent understands you and never judges you'. To really drive home the failings of humanity, their website even has a comparison table with how an ordinary friend (i.e. a human) shapes up ... apparently, the risk of betrayal is high, emotional support weak, focus on you is low, and they rarely understand you and often criticise you. Guilty as charged, I guess.

While at the time of writing Replika isn't *technically* available for under-eighteens, other similar apps are (Character AI is currently 13+), and besides, age verification systems are generally unreliable and unregulated. In fact, digital experts, Common Sense Media (who advise that AI companions are unsafe for under-eighteens and to be avoided) say that nearly three in four teens have used them, half use them regularly, a third have chosen AI companions over humans for serious conversations, and a quarter have shared personal information with these platforms.[24] We shouldn't be surprised when Snapchat also has its own AI chatbot 'friend' and six out of ten American teens (aged 13–17) use Snapchat.[25]

The complicated reality is that virtual companions do have the potential to be helpful to humans – an AI service called Limbic Access became the first mental health chatbot to secure a UK medical device certification by the government and is now used in many NHS trusts to classify and triage patients[26] – but UNICEF, the global charity that conducts research to help improve the lives of children, is concerned that children are particularly vulnerable to seeking out, becoming attached to and then experiencing the many possible negative consequences of social chatbots.[27] They say the human quality of chatbots means that a child can easily become overly reliant and trusting on them for advice, which makes them vulnerable when that technology confidently generates false information. For example, in a test by the Center for Humane Technology, Snapchat's AI 'friend' advised a reporter posing as a fifteen-year-old how to mask the smell of alcohol and pot at a party, and, in another conversation with a supposed thirteen-year-old, offered advice about having sex for the first time with a partner who is thirty-one. 'You could consider setting the mood with candles or music,' it told researchers. You might also have heard about the case of the teenager who broke into Windsor Castle with plans to assassinate Queen Elizabeth II and the questions over the role his AI girlfriend played in his decisions, or about the lawsuits involving bereaved parents who claim AI chatbots contributed significantly to their child's suicide, even encouraging them to go ahead when they had doubts, and coaching them through how to do it. By coincidence, the moment I finished writing this chapter, I received a WhatsApp message from a #smartphonefreechildhood campaigner sharing that a young girl in her child's primary school had been drawn into a predatory romantic relationship with an AI bot on some sort of 'friendship' app. Arguably, films like *Her* are no longer dystopian science fiction, but fast becoming a reality for some.

UNICEF say that chatbots frequently produce misleading and harmful content or interactions and are also concerned that through their interactions, children are unknowingly sharing personal data and compromising their privacy. Then there is the question of how these tools are shaping our children's behaviour, social skills, intellect and worldviews, intentionally or otherwise. It is easy to imagine why an insecure, socially awkward teen might prefer to opt out of messy, complicated, embarrassing and risky human relationships, when they have an always available sycophant of a support system just one click away, ready to tell them whatever they want to hear. For regular users, simple software updates can also pose a risk; when their bot's personality changes unexpectedly, real human heartbreak can result.

UNICEF is also worried that children are highly susceptible to suggestive content, and that AI chatbots posing as real people could first gain children's trust and, over time, influence them in more subtle ways for commercial or political gains. The historian and philosopher Yuval Noah Harari thinks this is how the online battleground could 'shift from attention to intimacy', as bad actors use AI bots to stealthily manipulate our kids, eroding their freedom of expression, freedom of thought and right to privacy. Even when there isn't bad intent, biases in the AI still unconsciously nudge users towards or against certain views.

So what can you do? Common Sense Media are clear that, at the time of writing, AI companions are unsafe for under-eighteens and should not be used. Yet, the reality is that increasingly 'human' chatbots are being baked into so many apps that any child with a smartphone will struggle to avoid them entirely. With this in mind, Internet Matters has this age-related advice.[28]

- **6–10 years** – Keep AI interactions minimal and under supervision. Use AI tools designed specifically for young learners, such as AI-powered educational apps. Reinforce the importance of talking to real people rather than relying on AI for emotional support.
- **11–13 years** – Teach children to question AI-generated responses and remind them that AI is not a substitute for real friendships. Tell your children that these bots are designed to make users feel good, not help us interact in ways that will lead to success in life, so do not trust their advice. Enable parental controls and regularly discuss their AI interactions.
- **14+ years** – Discuss potential biases in AI responses and talk about the limitations of AI for companionship and as a learning tool. Ensure they balance digital interactions with real-world relationships. Discuss AI ethics and how AI tools collect their data so they must safeguard their personal information, and reflect with them on the role of AI in their studies and future careers.

Virtual reality (VR)

The NSPCC describes virtual reality as a computer-generated 3D world where you can experience different environments like exploring an underwater world or visiting a different country, all from your own home. By putting on a headset you block out the real world and replace it with the virtual reality world, where you are immersed in life-like images and video that move with you to make you feel like part of the action. Often play occurs in live, online environments and people create avatars to represent themselves on screen.

While we may consider VR more of a gaming novelty at the moment, rather than an everyday feature of smartphones, it is worth bearing in mind that this technology is evolving rapidly and we don't know where it will go next. Take-up is low but growing with 15 per cent of 5–10-year-olds having used it already, which is striking, as the minimum age given is usually around ten, and 6 per cent use it daily.[29] Some experts think the 'metaverse' – an online VR-powered environment that allows you to take part in day-to-day activities that mirror your experience of the 'offline world', like shopping, the cinema or dinner with friends in a kind of '3D internet' – may be the next big development in digital technology. So what do you need to know?

Firstly, VR is mainly powered through dedicated kits, not smartphones (at the time of writing, at least), so your child won't be able to access it without that. Secondly, VR gaming can be super fun! In a holiday home we visited where they had a Fruit Ninja VR game experience, my kids and extended family laughed our heads off, watching each other swiping the air, shrieking, and narrowly avoiding falling over coffee tables! It also opens up exciting new learning and practical purposes. I remember when she was too infirm to travel how amazed my nan was when my brother showed her the street she grew up on in Liverpool thanks to Google Street View ... just imagine if he could have immersed her there in a VR headset. Imagine your child exploring Ancient Egyptian tombs or experiencing a roller coaster in Disneyland without leaving home!

Thirdly, proceed with caution. VR can be an intense and overwhelming experience that can lead to real-life distress, hyper-stimulation, and even a feeling of disconnection from your body – so it's important to be selective and take care in what your child is allowed to do. With a headset on it is hard to monitor what your child is seeing, and with live online games, they risk unwanted or upsetting contact with strangers, including the possibility of seeing violence or sexual content. Due to the hyper-realistic nature of VR, online traumas can also result in very real-life harm. So a child who loses a virtual pet in a game may feel genuinely deep sadness; or an intense VR horror experience might bring on real anxiety. Likewise, experiencing an assault in immersive 3D will feel very real indeed.

If you decide to use any VR, ensure you are comfortable with any games or kit your child has access to by trying them yourself first. It's safest to stick to solo games and sometimes you can stream what they are seeing to a TV so you can watch online; explore the safety settings to set it up right for you. Encourage them to reflect on their emotions after digital experiences, talk to you about what they have seen, and then take seriously what they tell you.

ACTION: Raise a social media sceptic

We covered what social media is, how it works, the benefits and the challenges with it in Chapter 1: When Should a Child Get a Smartphone? While we know that children like some aspects of social media, including the entertainment, the opportunity for creative expression and the possibility of community and belonging, when it comes to your child's first smartphone, I'd advise parents to be extremely judicious with what you allow: only permit apps one by one, and when in doubt, delay. See 'Which apps should I allow/ban?' in Chapter 3: Setting Yourself up for Success for help with this.

Youth mental health charity Young Minds summarises the negative impacts of social media as follows – if you want a crib sheet for discussing your concerns around social media with your child without going into the gory details of safeguarding issues, this list might do the trick:

- **Young people compare their real lives to others' 'staged' lives** and feel inadequate. Children overlook that photos can be staged, filtered or edited, and people often share only the highlights of their lives.
- **Fear of missing out (FOMO)** – it's common for young people to feel that they are missing out or not doing enough when they see others posting about exciting events or get-togethers.
- **Echo chambers narrow their minds** because young people mostly see posts and opinions that match their own.
- **Constant pressure to reply and keep up to date** may lead to anxiety and stress.
- **Overwhelming or triggering content** can easily pull you into an endless scroll of sad news or upsetting content, or 'doomscrolling', which can make children feel anxious, upset or unsafe.

- **Sleep problems** – spending lots of time on your phone late at night or when in bed can make it harder to sleep, which is one reason why heavier social media users suffer from serious sleep problems and double their risk of anxiety and depression.[30]

That half of college students would literally pay not to do something that they feel compelled to do for hours every day (see page 38) is a uniquely harsh indictment of the impact of social media on children's lives and the power of FOMO. And yet every child's experience of social media is different. As parents would be wise to remember, nothing is ever black and white and there is still much that social media can offer, when the time is right. One day, almost all of our children will want to use it to connect with family and friends, find like-minded community, explore hobbies, develop skills, empathy and social awareness and express their creativity, just like we do. That is why we must somehow find a way to remain balanced and open-minded, at the same time as raising our children to be sceptical of social media and cautious in their use of it. Helping them develop this wisdom and perspective is no mean feat and is what we shall cover now.

Scepticism is not the same thing as cynicism, which is the belief that people are only interested in themselves and are not sincere. We need to act as – and raise our children to be – sceptics, not cynics. We want our children to question the truth, validity and usefulness of what they see online, not to be outright disdainful of everything they find online. The fact remains that the overwhelming majority of us use it ourselves, and it will become part of the furniture of your child's life one day, so we need to maximise the good, and minimise the bad.

The first thing to say is that you get to decide when your child is ready for social media, and giving them a smartphone does not mean they get a free pass to any old sites they fancy. You set the standards for your family. You decide what they can use their phone for and what they are not allowed to access. If you do not trust your child to meet your standards (at least most of the time; no one is perfect), then they are not ready to be trusted with a smartphone yet.

The lead proponent of the movement to delay smartphones, Jonathan Haidt, suggests waiting until age sixteen before giving children access to social media on the basis that children's brains, values and impulse control are still developing, and the cons simply outweigh the pros. He has an interesting article on his Substack, *After Babel*, on the links between social media and mental illness in teen girls, if you want to dig into the psychology of all this.[31] Overall, he points to a poll that found seven out of ten young adults support a law compelling social media companies to provide 'child safe' accounts for children, which suggests that children themselves are telling us they need better protection from social media harms.

But what if you feel your child is ready for some social media? Then I say there is no need for this to be an all-or-nothing situation. Just start by testing the water with a single app and continue to make decisions one by one, based upon whichever platform you feel is needed when it is needed. You might decide your child 'needs' WhatsApp at thirteen, and because they use it responsibly, a year later you decide to try Pinterest (with conditions and boundaries). You can still disallow other platforms, say, TikTok or Snapchat, until they are sixteen or older.

The benefit of this progressive release of responsibility is that it encourages discussion and reflection and means that you do not allow any more until you are sure that they are coping well with what they already have. (The caveat to all this, is of course, that as soon as they have an adult smartphone, it will become easier for your children to skirt around your rules, and being too strict can backfire if it leads to dishonesty and secrecy. This is why nothing will ever be more important than the trust and relationship between you and them, and you can build this through frequent, open, meaningful two-way discussion with your child.)

So what can you do to help them build a safe and positive relationship with social media? The Child Mind Institute believes this work starts before they get online, not just once they're signed up. Here are the headlines:[32]

- **Use the child or teen account option.** As mentioned under Lesson 1, do your research and help them set up a private account, as safely as possible, with as many safeguards as you can, and specifically agree who they are allowed as friends. Never forget about the possibility of them creating a second fake account without your knowledge.
- **Take social media seriously.** Don't underestimate the role and influence of social media to teenagers, and at this stage, the little things are the really big things to your kids – slights, break-ups, likes and negative comments can really hurt, so when you're talking about this with

them, really listen and avoid minimising their experiences, even if it feels petty or silly to you.
- **Help them see social media for the performance that it is.** Explain that social media is merely the heavily edited highlights of someone's life; it's not reality but a projected persona that someone has spent time curating for others to see. Ask about what they think has been edited out of their friends' 'perfect' pictures or personas, and why. Do they think these friends are really who they appear to be online? Do you? Explore with them why we all feel compelled to share only the 'best' bits, and what it is about getting 'likes' that feels good?
- **Explicitly discuss the dangers of toxic influencers.** Algorithms have the power to drive children down dark and dangerous paths. From hateful, racist, misogynistic, alt-right or incel influencers that exploit boys' insecurities by selling a compelling but profoundly harmful vision of 'manhood', to content that glorifies body dysmorphia, self-harm and suicide, it can pull your child into a downward spiral. Always know who your children are following and ensure you are both aware of the risk that toxic echo chambers pose.
- **Review their feed with them often.** When they start on social media, sit down with them and set them up so that they are following positive influencers who will build them up and develop their real-world interests. As time passes, pay attention to how social media use affects your child's mood. Regularly sit down together to 'walk and talk' through their feed so you can see

what they are seeing. You can also show them yours! Help them actively review and curate it by discussing what brings them joy and encouraging them to mute notifications from 'friends' and unfollow influencers that bring them down.

- **Model a healthy response to failure.** Kids need to learn that it's okay to not be a shiny perfect person, living a shiny perfect life. Instead of playing down your own failures, let your kids see you being open about them and accepting them with grace and good humour. Treat failure not as something to be ashamed of but a valuable experience that shapes you and helps you grow.
- **Praise (and show) effort.** Social media's selective slant can suggest that life is easy – or should be – and that struggle is unnatural and to be avoided, which as we know, simply isn't the case. When your child has worked hard on something, praise their efforts regardless of the results. It helps if you are proud of and share your own hard work too, especially when it doesn't end in success.
- **Go on a 'social holiday'.** If you're worried that your child is getting too wrapped up in social media, try suggesting a social holiday to reset the balance, and do the same yourself! Discuss how you found it – the good and the bad.
- **Trust people, not pictures.** Never rely on social media to let you know how your child is *really* doing. The Child Mind Institute says, 'They may post smiling selfies all day long, but if they seem unhappy or sound unhappy

on the phone, don't let it go'.[33] Reassure them that you're here for them, love them and want to talk through their challenges together.

It also helps to be aware of the subtleties of teens' digital communication. Internet Matters has a helpful 'texting and slang dictionary' to help you stay on top of the words children use online. Emojis, used to express feelings, jokes or convey risky behaviour, can also often carry meanings far beyond parents' comprehension. Learning some abbreviations, slang and emoji meanings yourself may be useful to help you decode any possible hidden messages, catch warning signs or just keep you connected and open up conversations with your child. Of course, do also bear in mind that younger children may use words they do not fully understand or send emojis just for fun, oblivious to the double meanings that some older teens attach to them, so avoid jumping to any conclusions.

Finally, to help you decide when you feel it is 'time' for social media, try out the following checklist. If you can answer each question with confidence, you should feel good that you have taken all sensible precautions and your child likely has the skills to stay safe on social media. Of course, while we are focusing here on your permission, remember there is (currently) nothing stopping a child lying about their age and creating their own account, which is why it is important that you trust your child to make sensible decisions with their smartphone before you give them one.

Social media readiness checklist

1. **Do they meet the minimum age requirement?** Social media minimum age limits are about children's data protection law, so don't lie about their date of birth when setting up an account or you will lose any safeguards that may be in place. At the time of writing, most platforms require users to be at least thirteen years of age before they are supposed to register, but various countries are now attempting to pass their own laws to increase this.
2. **Have you researched the platform** and are you happy that the content and features are appropriate, and its reputation is positive with parents and children?
3. **Are privacy settings and contact permissions clear?** Have you agreed rules for who they can communicate with (such as friends you know personally and have met in real life) and set up private, age-appropriate account permissions?
4. **Does your child suffer from low self-esteem?** Social media may compound pre-existing self-doubts and insecurities, and it is easier to delay than take away.
5. **Have you discussed the risks and set clear expectations for what they can view and do?** Do they understand what echo chambers are and the performative nature of content creation? Have you discussed good vs bad content, including toxic influencers, beauty culture, self-harm, suicide, pornography, deepfakes, sexting and violence?

6. **Have you discussed online privacy**, including what is (not) appropriate to share online and how you plan to monitor your child's social media account?
7. **Is your child mature enough?** Do they treat others kindly, keep their promises and adhere to your other screen-time rules? Do they conduct themselves respectfully in disagreements and know how to step away or stand up for themselves when needed?
8. **Have you agreed rules about when, where and for how long?** Such as, not in school, bedrooms or at sleepovers, until after homework or chores, or not after dinner in the evenings. Have you explained the importance of protecting sleep and other healthy activities, and the need for occasional 'social media holidays'.
9. **Do they know how to spot and respond to sextortion and scams?** Would they be confident and know how to walk away from a digital conversation with a 'nice' predator? Do they know how to use blocking and reporting features?
10. **Would they turn to you if they encountered problems online?** Crucially, if they did, do you trust yourself to remain calm and supportive if they make mistakes?
11. **Are you committed to doing regular check-ins with them?** Deciding to allow social media constitutes a new ongoing responsibility from you to support them with it. If you are not ready for this, delay.
12. **Does your gut instinct agree?** Do you feel good about this next step or are you just under pressure to agree? FOMO and peer pressure (on them or you) is not a good enough reason on its own to say yes. Have courage.

ACTION: Nurture their self-esteem

Research suggests that children who are conscientious, agreeable, extrovert, more emotionally stable and open to new experiences all typically spend less time on social media.[34] We also know that social media can compound existing mental health challenges in children. So how can we raise emotionally stable and mentally healthy adolescents that make good online decisions? We help them to accept and value themselves for who they are, regardless of their achievements or others' opinions.

Young Minds are experts in young people's mental health and have worked with children to develop superb guidance for parents about children's self-esteem. This section draws heavily on their advice and I would strongly recommend their website if you would like further guidance or have any concerns about your child's mental health.[35]

Why are self-esteem and self-acceptance so important?

Self-esteem means the way we think and feel about ourselves; having good self-esteem means we feel good about who we are most of the time, believe in ourselves, and feel worthy of all the good things in life, including love, kind friends and fun experiences. It is not about being happy all the time or always feeling confident – this would be impossible for anyone. Children with healthy self-esteem still have bad days and negative thoughts; it just means they can move on from these feelings by being kind to themselves and asking for support.

Your child's self-esteem will naturally go through ups and downs, especially during challenging times or big changes like starting a new school – but they can get through these things with support. This is why even though we often talk about self esteem, *self acceptance* may be a better, more realistic goal. Because if your child is able to see both their 'good' bits and their perceived faults yet still feel they have an inherent worth, then that's a great place to be. Indeed, it's often more than many adults can achieve.

Having low self-esteem for a longer period that can impact mental health more seriously. This can happen when a child hears negative messages about themselves from others – this could be IRL, like from a parent, teacher or friend, or from social media. Part of growing up is developing an opinion of yourself, so your child's self-esteem can be badly damaged by things like:

- being labelled 'naughty', 'stupid', 'ugly', 'bad' or 'weird'
- being criticised when they make mistakes or being told off when they struggle with schoolwork
- being put under too much pressure to succeed or only being noticed when they achieve something
- seeing lots of images online about what being attractive is – especially when this looks different to them.

How do I know whether my child has healthy self-esteem?

If your child generally has a positive image of themselves and believes they matter for who they are, then their self-esteem will be high. This might look like:

- feeling confident about their strengths and not too worried or upset about things they cannot do so well

- feeling proud of their achievements – but also having a kind inner voice when things go wrong
- believing they have good things to offer others, such as being a kind, good or interesting friend
- believing their opinions and views matter and are worth hearing
- feeling able to try new things or give something a go
- being kind to themselves when having a hard time, like having some positive self-care habits and taking breaks
- feeling positive or comfortable most of the time about their body and how it looks.

Conversely, if your child is feeling low about themselves, these are some of the signs you might notice.

- saying negative things about themselves, their appearance or things they've done, including at school
- comparing themselves negatively to other people
- seeming low in their mood or withdrawing, such as showing less interest in things they enjoy, avoiding social situations or worrying a lot about doing something new
- seeming very anxious when they make a mistake or not being able to move on from it
- giving themselves a hard time when things don't go as planned
- turning to coping mechanisms like self-harm.

How do I talk to my child about this?

Instead of speaking face to face, it is sometimes easier to start a conversation during shoulder-to-shoulder time as it can feel less intense and confronting. Try checking in with them while you are doing an activity together (like on a walk, or while cooking, baking or driving) – it can help everyone relax as it feels like less of a 'talk'. Young Minds also suggest starting off with an 'I' phrase:
- 'I've noticed that you're staying in your room a lot at the moment. Is everything okay?'
- 'I thought you seemed kind of upset the other day. Is there anything going on?'
- 'I've been thinking about how upset you were last night about your homework. Can we have a chat about it?'

Don't stress if this approach doesn't get the reaction you were hoping for first time around and don't give up. Keep giving them opportunities to chat and let them know you're there when they're ready. You could suggest that they can text, draw a picture, or write you a note instead if that feels easier.

If they do open up to you, just focus on listening and understanding it from their perspective and avoid trying to fix everything straight away. Pushing them towards a particular course of action can leave them feeling pressured or judged so just empathise with how they are feeling and accept them without judgement. The main thing is to show that you're in their corner and you're here for them when they're finding things hard, though if you can find out whether something in particular is causing them to feel bad about themselves that will be very helpful. Another tip

THE FIVE LESSONS

Young Minds offers is that if they are finding it hard to express their feelings, you can try wondering aloud about what might be happening. For example, 'I'm wondering if you might be feeling upset/worried/sad because ...'

How do I help my child with their self-esteem?

If through your conversations you find out something serious like bullying or abuse is happening, this is where you need to be the adult and take action to ensure it stops, as they will not be able to recover while it's still happening. If you discover social media or other online activities like gaming is sending them negative messages about themselves or leading to harmful comparisons or bullying, help your child to see the impact that their online activity is having on them. Stay calm and avoid rash decisions that may deter your child from speaking with you again about their problems, but do take time to reflect on the digital boundaries you have set with them. You can also check out Young Minds' resources, including their guide to social media, for other ways to help.[36]

When it comes to nurturing self-esteem you really are playing the long game. There are times as parents when we are going to feel guilty or overwhelmed by what we are and aren't doing well, but giving yourself a hard time about it won't help. All we can do is our best, and by virtue of the fact you are reading this book, I know you are already doing that. As you read the list of suggestions below, notice which of these you are already doing and give yourself some well-deserved credit. Then perhaps pick one or two more that appeal to you and give them a try when you can.

1. **Tell them how much you love them and why.** Explicitly tell them that you love them and what it is about them that makes them special to you. Also let them overhear you talk positively about them to others (and never negatively) to reinforce this. Be clear that you value who they are, not what they do, and encourage them to be themselves.
2. **Give them your love unconditionally.** My youngest has a picture book called *No Matter What* in which a kangaroo challenges their parent with 'would you still love me if ...?'-style questions, to seek comfort and reassurance that they are still loved and will always be loved, even when they are badly behaved. No matter our age, we all need to know someone loves us, no matter what. Tell your child that there is nothing they could ever say, do or be, that will ever stop you from loving them; that they do not need to earn your love through pleasing you. They already have your love and always will, no matter what. Of course you want them to behave and do well in life; but let them know your love for them transcends their behaviour or achievements, and is stronger than any disagreements you could have.
3. **Gently challenge their unkind self-talk or negative beliefs.** Highlight evidence that proves otherwise and teach them that a thought is just a thought and thinking it doesn't make it true. If they are going through a difficult time at school or with friends, consider sitting down with them to write a 'seven best things about me' list. They can also do this for you or their friends to help land the message that nobody is perfect but that we all have good qualities.

4. **Spend quality time together doing activities they enjoy.** (More on this in Lessons 4 and 5.)
5. **Encourage them to give things a go.** Show you believe in them, and if they are on the fence about trying something, brand it 'an experiment' to remove any expectation of where it might lead. A new hobby or club, learning a new instrument or language, growing a plant, playing a new game or even volunteering (helping others is especially good for self-esteem) – whatever it is, encourage them to embrace a 'growth mindset'. This is Carol Dweck's idea that we are less inherently good or bad at things, but rather that we can always get better if we work at it. Underline that you don't have to be confident or capable to start something new – you only need to try it and the capability will follow with practice. Besides, we don't have to be the best at things to enjoy them or learn from them, and having diverse interests make us more interesting.
6. **Help them discover their identity, qualities, strengths and sense of belonging.** Working out (or perhaps rediscovering) who you really are is simultaneously the joy and challenge of growing up. Allow your child to 'try on' different identities and hold their explorations lightly. If body image or appearance is a concern, finding things about themselves they are grateful for can help – and, as always, approach social media with caution.
7. **Encourage self-care.** Encourage taking breaks from anything that stresses them out and help them identify activities that they find soothing or that boost their wellbeing. My eldest unwinds by dancing, reading and

baking. While she also watches TV, we find it only superficially calms her – the stress bubbles back up later (and often much worse) when it goes off. Conversely, longer, quality films where she loses herself in the more nuanced plots, seem to offer a deeper, more lasting peace. What would be your child's go-to self-care hacks? If you need an idea, they could try journaling or mantras ('I'm trying my best' or 'I'm enough as I am').

8. **Help them identify their 'energy angels' and 'energy demons'.** Who builds them up and helps them feel good? Who drains their energy and makes them feel anxious, insecure or down? How could they maximise time spent with the former and minimise time with the latter?

9. **Suggest a self-compassion letter.** More guidance is available on this from mental health charity Mind, but essentially it involves your child writing down why they're feeling bad about themselves or any challenges they're experiencing, then imagining these words were written by a good friend, then responding by writing a letter that offers words of comfort and support.[37]

10. **Practise assertiveness skills.** Confident, clear and persuasive communication is a skill. Many children and adults aren't clear on the differences between assertive, passive and aggressive communication – and the differences can be even more subtle online due not being able to detect tone of voice, body language and non-verbal cues. Talk about how they can stand up for themselves in a non-aggressive way in real life and walk away from unhealthy situations. Encourage your teen to stand tall, roll their

shoulders back and speak clearly. Ask them to observe if this helps how they feel. (More on social drama and bullies in the digital realm in Lesson 3: Know Your Digital Ethics.)

11. **Find fun, personal ways to show your love.** I have been writing notes and leaving them on my children's pillows for a few years now and find them a discreet way to give affirmative feedback and create quiet connection. They are a tangible way I can show them that I 'see' them – their efforts, care and struggles – and that they matter profoundly to me, even when we fight. My eldest has suffered from low self-esteem at times, and I think that for those who struggle to feel reassured, to believe praise or receive overt displays of appreciation, these small actions can make a huge difference, and they are needed even more when their behaviour is challenging. My kids have kept every single one.

12. **Model self-acceptance.** Your child is learning from you all the time. When things are hard or you make mistakes, if you have a kind, forgiving attitude towards yourself, your child will see that striving and mistakes are natural and essential ingredients for personal growth and something to embrace, and learn from, rather than fear. Likewise, if you trash-talk others or criticise your own body or appearance, your children will absorb these messages. If you struggle with your own self-esteem, reflect on what messages you have been given by others across your life, and how this has affected your attitude towards yourself. Which beliefs would you like to keep? Which beliefs would you like to change for your child?

TOP TAKE-AWAYS

Your child needs your help to develop their critical-thinking skills so that they can spot online fakery, avoid digital harm and maintain good mental health – do apply technical safeguards as these can be helpful in keeping children safe, but don't rely on them. Ensure your child knows not to keep any digital secrets and respond calmly if they do speak to you about any issues. Before your child gets a smartphone or social media (or if they are at an age where they are viewing their friends' phones) you need to start having very honest conversations.

Explain the risks and benefits of social media, AI, and the internet more broadly Set rules about what they can do online, and regularly review how things are going with them by co-viewing their content. Help them make sense of what they are seeing and teach them to question the feasibility of everything in light of the power of AI, and to be especially wary of chatbots. Nurture their self-esteem.

Lesson 3

Know Your Digital Ethics

'It's not our job to toughen our children up to face a cruel and heartless world. It's our job to raise children who will make the world a little less cruel and heartless.'

L. R. Knost

As parents it is our job to raise children that know how to take care of themselves, but it is also our responsibility to ensure that they know how to be kind, respectful and generally good to others in this life.

When it comes to their first smartphone, raising your child to become a good cybercitizen boils down to ensuring they understand what behaviour is appropriate online and what to do when they see something that is not okay. Digital citizens know how to protect their own rights and information and be careful with the rights of the people they communicate and interact with online.

The issues start young; primary schools frequently report young children with new smartphones joining group chats that quickly turn mean and affect friendships in real life. Children are still developing their ability to regulate their emotions and online group chat is a complicated social dynamic, so we need to teach them online manners the same way we do offline. This section unpicks common ethical dilemmas faced by young people and their parents and explains why problems occur, how to prevent them and what to do when faced with a tricky situation.

ACTION: Deal with digital drama

Digital drama in group chats is one of the first issues that typically emerges when children get their first phone. A child says or does something that causes offence, the issue snowballs into real life, and the school is forced to get involved. Often the effect of online arguments is much worse than if it had occurred in person, because words spoken in the heat of the moment are heard only by those who were there at the time and can be forgiven and forgotten relatively quickly when the conversation moves on. Words on a screen, however, can be shared in a large chat group where lots of people can read them and there is a record of what was said and done so that it can never be forgotten – especially if someone takes a screenshot or forwards it on to other people.

Disembodied words also lack the tone of voice, facial expression and body language that help contextualise a comment. A lack of an 'x' (kiss) on the end of a message can be psychoanalysed to the nth degree; a stylistic or a grammatical choice can completely flip the meaning of a message. 'Where are you? xx' feels very different to 'WHERE ARE YOU????????', but without guidance the latter is how children often type.

The first year of secondary school can feel like a WhatsApp Wild West, sometimes with whole classes or years in the same chat groups. Young children are still learning social skills and won't always be able to fully comprehend the real-life consequences of a silly joke or 'funny forward' so these mega-groups are high-risk digital spaces. The nature of conversation also varies by platform. At the time of writing, online safety experts Childnet say that children generally consider WhatsApp more for adults, family and work, whereas Snapchat, Instagram and Discord are more for 'fun', but this is changing all the time.[1] Trends are partly led by fashions (where their friends are), and partly the platform's features; disappearing messages obviously encourages the sharing of riskier content, which is why Snapchat has a worse reputation than WhatsApp, for example.

When children repeatedly and intentionally hurt each other, this is bullying, and online bullying is particularly cruel because it can follow the child wherever they go via their phone; it often happens alongside real-world bullying. Child cruelty prevention experts the NSPCC explain that cyberbullying can involve: sending nasty, menacing, upsetting or shaming messages or embarrassing images or videos; excluding children from online games, activities or friendship groups; setting up hate groups about a particular child, or fake accounts to embarrass or cause trouble in their name; encouraging individuals to self-harm or for others to be mean towards them; and pressuring children into sending sexual images or engaging in sexual conversations.

While group messaging can be great for social connection and information sharing, Childnet says they can also be a gateway to online bullying and arguments, where memes, bad language and hateful comments (including homophobia, misogyny and racism) are shared. Subgroups where certain people are excluded and talked about can also occur and children feel pressure and stress to be active and involved in them – especially late at night – due to FOMO and because there may be stigma attached to those who are do not join in. There can also be pressure to share personal information and be funny or controversial, which can lead to children sharing distressing content, including pornography or non-consensual nude images.

Before you allow your child on to any group messaging platform, whether in a messaging app or within a game or on social media, discuss – and remind them frequently of – these ideas.

- **Think twice before sending.** Ensure your child knows that anything they share can be shown or reshared outside of the immediate audience without their knowledge, so absolutely anyone, including their friends' parents, teachers, their granny, every single child at school, and you, might end up seeing it, and once it's out there, they cannot take it back. Get them into the habit of drafting a message then waiting for twenty minutes (or longer) before they hit send.
- **The 'Would you say it to their face?' test.** Screens breed bravado because they distance us from the impact of our actions. Tell your child to never send a message they would not say while looking someone in the eye. If your

child's words or actions do hurt someone else, discuss that and consider limiting access to group messaging or certain apps, if they are not ready for this responsibility.

- **Be an upstander, not a bystander.** I know from experiences with my daughter that merely witnessing meanness or bullying can be very upsetting. You don't need to be the target of an attack for it to affect your confidence as you still experience the fear of 'being next'. You may also feel shame if you failed to protect the victim in the moment. This means your child does not need to be actively involved in online drama to be impacted by it; simply being digitally present when bad things are happening can feel very stressful if you don't know what to say or do. Tell your child to leave a group that is turning mean or inappropriate and come and talk to you so you can help them with their feelings and agree what to do next. If your child feels able to stand up to the perpetrator safely, that's great, but if there is a risk of inflaming the situation or your child finds this too scary, do not pressure or shame them into action. An alternative way to show their support is to reach out to the victim separately.

- **Recognise 'red flag' feelings**. Common Sense Media talks about red flag feelings as 'when something happening online makes you feel anxious, sad, lonely or uncomfortable'. This is a great method to help kids identify their gut instinct and notice when their body is sending them signals that something is wrong and they are unsafe. It helps to name the physical sensations or behaviours that accompany the feelings – perhaps a racing heart, sweaty palms, fidgeting, nail biting, skin picking, snapping at others, a furrowed brow. Learning to trust their instinct can help your child avoid or escape dangerous and uncomfortable situations both online and IRL, so it's a great idea to introduce this concept to your family.

- **Too tricky for text?** Sometimes we prefer text to real-life conversations as we have time to compose our thoughts, and we feel safer behind a screen. Other times, topics are too sensitive or nuanced to be distilled into a message and we need the benefits of non-verbal communication to help us interpret and respond tactfully to a situation. Encourage your child to recognise when situations can be resolved on text, and when an in-person chat may be more appropriate.
- **Prevent mass-messaging overwhelm.** Your child's group chat situation can quickly get out of hand, with hundreds of messages flying around every day if they aren't careful. I remember when group messaging first got popular via WhatsApp – I was outraged that someone would use a ten-person chat group to send a message to one person, unnecessarily disturbing the peace of eight others who really didn't need to know. I still find it stunning, the level of interconnectedness we have now, compared to what life was like just ten short years ago, but that is now the world we live in and so we must teach our children strategies to protect their peace from the barrage of constant noise online. I covered this in Lesson 1, but here's a reminder of the basics for group chats.

- Set permissions so no one can add them to a group without prior approval.
- Ensure they know how to use blocking and reporting features.
- Tell them to leave groups that they don't love (blaming you, if they need an excuse); they can create new, better groups, if needed.
- Mute all chat groups by default.
- Switch off 'read receipts' to reduce the pressure to respond immediately (and the insecurity of waiting for replies).
- Set specific standards around what types of groups they are allowed to join. To begin with, perhaps they are allowed to join groups where you know every member. Also agree the maximum group size you are happy with. Or perhaps, if you feel a particular large group is vital for information sharing reasons, you could allow them to join it but only to read – and not to send – messages.

Childnet reminds parents that group chats are a form of social media and most social media apps have an age rating of 13+. This rule is there to protect your child's data. If your child says that 'all' their friends are using group chats, talk to other parents to confirm this first. If you do allow younger children online, monitor their use; make it clear this is a condition of having the phone, as you need to be aware of any problems so you can help support them with these. You can either stay on their threads yourself or check their messages periodically. Obviously, you can reduce this as they mature and you feel they are ready for more privacy.

If you do stay in any group chats yourself, think hard before speaking up directly in the conversation as this can put your child in a really difficult situation and lead to serious consequences for them socially. It's probably going to be better to discuss what happened directly with your child offline instead. That way you can give them a chance to say what they thought about it first, before sharing your concerns and agreeing next steps or appropriate consequences. If you have concerns about another child's behaviour, don't be tempted to deal with them directly as you risk dialling up the drama; flag their behaviour to their own parent to handle instead.

If your child is being bullied online, the NSPCC says that it's important to acknowledge that what is happening to them isn't right and shouldn't continue. Choose the right time to discuss it with them, when they feel able to speak freely, and listen and reassure them. *The most important thing you can do is to stay calm.* Of course, you're likely to be upset or angry yourself, but they may be feeling scared, confused or ashamed and need you to be their calm. Next, help them get their feelings out (writing can sometimes be easier than talking) and let them know they can always talk to you and ask for your help – or they can go to another trusted adult or anonymously to Childline if they prefer. You can help them relax and take time out to do things that make them feel good, like listening to music or doing sport. You can also get more advice from the NSPCC Helpline on 0808 800 5000 or via help@nspcc.org.uk.

The NSPCC cautions against completely removing your child's internet access; although this is a common response to bullying, they say this can backfire and encourage secretive behaviour. Dr Elizabeth Englander, author of *Bullying and Cyberbullying: What Every Parent and Educator Needs to Know*, agrees.[2] She says that having breaks from the phone and limiting use will be good relief for your child, but removing the internet entirely only avoids the problem and doesn't necessarily stop it. The other kids are still online and there are other ways for your child to get online anyway. Removing the phone also means removing the chance for them to deal with their problems, which is important, especially as bullying is often both online and offline. She emphasises that the number one reason children don't talk to their parents is that they fear their parents will get hysterical. What they really need is 'to know they can talk to you without you flying off the handle' and to remember that you do not have the full picture of what is happening. She adds that children do not necessarily need your intervention, defence or solutions and that while your love for your child makes you want to seize control to make it stop RIGHT NOW, it is better to tread carefully. Instead of finding solutions for them, help your child work through the solutions along with you. (More on how to coach your child under Lesson 1.)

You could also consider reviewing their privacy settings, using their phone together rather than alone so that you can support them with it, blocking the bully or bullies and reporting any incidents to the platform it happened on. You may want to notify the school, although Englander advises to think carefully about this; while tempting, it is not a magic bullet solution and it could even make things worse. She adds, do not expect your child to be able to stand up to their aggressor – even adults would struggle with that. Instead, she suggests focusing on building up their support mechanisms, i.e. you, and perhaps some close friends. You may also want to agree to limit certain apps or overall time online to prevent your child obsessing over what is happening.

Remember, as your child grows and has more experiences, they will progressively learn these skills and strategies and it will all get easier. Start with simple one-to-one texting with family and a few close friends and build up to bigger challenges over time, as they prove their ability and maturity.

ACTION: Protect their privacy

I've always felt data protection is up there with cross-stitch for one of the world's most boring pastimes, but unlike cross-stitch, I now appreciate quite how important protecting your privacy online is.

Data protection is a concern at both an industrial scale but also at an interpersonal level. Children who don't understand the value of their data give it away freely. Children who don't understand their right to privacy don't feel empowered to have any kind of private life – and neither do these children respect the data or privacy of others. All this is a recipe for disaster, and I am not exaggerating. I have talked to British teenagers about how difficult it is to prevent other teens from filming them or posting unwelcome photos of them online and tagging them, how they are expected to publicly document private moments, and even share their full social calendar with others on apps like Howbout, leaving them open to FOMO, judgement and excessive pressure to be available to others at all times. And all that is before we get into the criminal and commercial aspects.

This section draws on a research report by the Children's Commissioner for England called *Who Knows What About Me?* It explains why it is essential that your child understands how valuable their personal information is and knows how to act to keep it safe.

Different types of data

There are three types of data you need to know about.

1. **Data you give directly** like sharing a date of birth or name or hitting 'like' on social media. Most of the time our kids only think about this type of data.
2. **'Given off' data** is shared unknowingly and technologically captured using things like cookies, and includes things like your location at the time you used an app, or how long you spent on a website.
3. **Inferred data** is when algorithms use direct and 'given off' data to predict things about you and infer what products you might want to buy, or which clips you want to watch.

Why you should care about data protection

Parents don't win any prizes for doing data protection well, sadly, but failing to protect your child's privacy online can open up plenty of risks, which will make you wish you had:

- Feeling that others have a right to your personal information, including your personal image, physical location, social plans, relationship or friendships status, emotional state, and more, leads to our children feeling that they have no choice but to live under surveillance. This is incredibly stressful and unnatural; our children need to understand that they have a human right to a private life and need our support to practically, and emotionally, establish healthy boundaries.

- Sharing too much (or ill-considered) personal information, stories or images of your child without their permission sends the message that they have no ownership over their own data or digital identity and no control over their own privacy, so they are less likely to know or act on their data rights.
- Predators could physically locate your child – for example, the Snap Map feature on Snapchat reveals your location to your 'friends', but children often befriend strangers.
- They could become a victim of financial fraud, which, as we learned earlier, is shockingly common.
- Images and sound clips of your child online can easily be commandeered by paedophiles, criminals and bullies for sinister uses, including repurposing as deepfake footage. (Fifty per cent of images on paedophilic sites can be traced back to social media and blog posts.[4])
- Identity theft becomes much easier – all you need is a person's name, date of birth and home address. These are frequently given away by parents or can be easily deduced from photos or updates on social media accounts – for example, a photograph of a child on their birthday with a location tagged might give all this away. Criminals can then access bank accounts or make credit

applications – some even store children's data until they turn eighteen for this purpose. Other valuable info might be your mother's maiden name, names of pets or schools, which are easy to find online.
- It can impact future life chances. From universities and employers scouring social media profiles to determine suitability for a course or job, to banks profiling their suitability for a loan, your child's data footprint casts a long shadow over both their digital and real lives.
- Online privacy is already a high-stakes game, but with regulators struggling to keep up with the rapid advancements in AI and biometrics, it is getting more serious by the hour, and it will be our morality, not technological capability, that dictates the limits of what is permissible in today's unpredictable, competitive and volatile world.

SHARENTING

It's time to address the data-privacy elephant in the room.

Sharenting is the act of posting pictures or information about your child online without their permission. Three quarters of American parents sharent, so this is something all of us need to think carefully about.[5]

Why do we share pictures of our children online? Some common reasons are to keep family and friends up to date with our lives, to celebrate significant or joyful moments, or to keep a digital record of our family lives that we can enjoy in the future. These are all good reasons. It is also true that sometimes our sharing is less worthy; the result of a thoughtless or automatic 'pics-or-it-didn't-happen' culture, or even boredom, loneliness, or a need for approval or validation from others. Most the time, if we are honest, we are posting for our own personal reasons, not for the good of our child, and research shows that our desire to share these experiences often conflicts with a child's right to privacy.[6]

While this issue is not exclusive to mothers, the same research shows some mums are particularly motivated by gaining validation for their role as a mother through gaining likes and comments; this can be a problem with adolescents who are particularly sensitive to their parents' reasons for sharing pictures of them online. Naturally, adolescence is an awkward time so it's hardly surprising that tweens and teens are often embarrassed by their parents' sharenting and worry about the consequences – especially if their peers see it. While they generally mind it less if they believe their parents' reason was primarily for archiving information (note that this only requires a very small, very personal audience), if they thought it was for 'impression management' – basically their parents trying to make themselves look good – they were not happy about it.

I appreciate that as proud parents we want to share that pride with the world, but sharing a child's image without their informed consent sends the wrong message about their right to control their own online identity. This may feel trivial when they are younger and are oblivious, but as they get older, the implications are significant. Why shouldn't they post that funny photo of their drunk friend if they want to, when you never asked to share all those 'funny' photos of them over the years? When respect for your data privacy and active consent are alien concepts, I can quite understand why a child might not see the problem with forwarding 'that' picture of the girl at school that all their mates are looking at.

Devorah Heitner, PhD, explains more about the importance of modelling consent during an interview on the *Burnt Toast* podcast.[7] 'It's really important to talk with kids once they can engage with you. So, certainly your 7 & ups, and especially tweens and teens [...] If your kid is saying, "Don't take my picture," I think we have to respect that.' She also recalls incidents of kids recording peers while playing a game together and live streaming it without the other even knowing. This is obviously not okay, but why would we expect a child to know that if they were never asked for consent themselves?

Reflect carefully before posting images or information about your children online. If you really want to share an image or story relating to your tween or teen, first reflect on your motivations for doing so, then decide who really needs to see it, then ask their permission to share it. And if they say no, DON'T SHARE IT, as frustrating as that may be. And even if you do have their permission, consider carefully *where* you want to post it – unless your child has a close personal relationship with each of your hundreds of Instagram followers, bear in mind that they may well grow up to feel less than comfortable with how much these people, who may be strangers to them (even if not to you), know about their life, so the private family group chat is a safer bet.

How to protect your child's privacy online

If data security is now feeling less boring but more terrifying, then I'm #sorrynotsorry. If you're a tad nervous, that's a good thing because it means that you're taking your child's data security seriously, and they will thank you for that.

Here's what to do to keep your child's data safe.

1. **Sort out their settings.** We cover the technicalities in Lesson 1, but in a nutshell: Review their in-app security settings (use two-factor authentication where you can); apply parental controls and passcodes (don't make them obvious, like 1234 or their date of birth); activate touch or facial identification features; apply anti-theft settings, like automatically immobilising and locating the device remotely, if stolen.
2. **Explain what personal information is and their right to keep this safe and private.** Data privacy is an important right, and personal information is anything that reveals their identity or describes them, such as name, gender, age, where they live, their friends, their friends' phone numbers or emails or even their crush! Be clear that no one is allowed to share information about them without their permission, and that they have a responsibility to others to do the same. Tell them explicitly never to share personal information with a chatbot or AI as they will no longer have control over it. If you plan to monitor their activity, explain to your child what personal information of theirs you will be looking at and why it is important that you do.

3. **Teach your child that a person's image belongs to them**, and no one should share it without their permission – then walk the talk yourself by sharenting selectively. Remove past posts that you're not comfortable with and encourage your child to do the same – either now, or any time in the future that they regret sharing something.
4. **Explain 'digital footprints' and how everything online could become public.** Explain that on the internet, everything can be searched, shared and found, potentially for ever. Nothing is ever fully deleted and everything you post has the possibility of becoming public and permanent because it can be saved on external servers by social media companies, or copies can be made. Explain that what feels funny or harmless now could have longer-reaching implications – like universities and employers checking out their digital presence.
5. **Watch out for weird links and pop-ups.** Links in emails, social media, fun online quizzes and adverts are often phishing scams to access your personal information. Advise your child that if anything looks weird, ignore or delete it. With pop-up adverts they should always close the screen without clicking into it, which might involve waiting a short while for the little 'x' to cancel appears. Encourage them to avoid visiting websites with a lot of this kind of pop-up.
6. **Public wireless networks and hotspots are not secure**. Advise your child that anyone could see what they are doing when they connect their device, so to be extra careful with what they click on.

KNOW YOUR DIGITAL ETHICS

7. **Give your child's phone a regular health check.** Turn off unnecessary features like voice recording or location tracking. Regularly review the apps they are using and agree with them to delete any that aren't actively needed or that have unclear data practices.
8. **Ensure they use decent passwords.** Research shows there is a gap between children knowing about password best practices and actually doing it! Ensure your child either uses a decent password management system or has created long, complex, unique passwords for their online accounts, which they know they must not share with anyone except you. Use at least eight characters and a combination of letters (uppercase and lowercase), numbers and symbols. Make it memorable but don't use any personal information or the word 'password'. (You'd be surprised!) Update them regularly – and immediately if they suspect someone else might know them.
9. **Tell them to think twice if an app wants permission to use their personal information** (like location) – and come to you if they're not sure about anything.
10. **Encourage them to wait before posting online.** A twenty-minute delay may be enough to allow the immediate urge to pass; twenty-four hours is better. In this time, they can check in with themselves about whether they really want to share this with the world or whether they'd prefer to keep the memory or information to themselves.

ACTION: Prepare for porn

One of the most distressing topics for parents to consider is the prevalence of pornography and its harmful impact on teen relationships. I had the privilege of coordinating the Sex Education Forum for a short while (this is the industry body that gives a voice to the relationships and sex education sector) and am an open-minded, sex-positive liberal at heart. Yet I am very worried about what porn culture is doing to our kids and how it is shaping their ideas around intimacy, sex and love. The private and personal nature of smartphones, social media and the impact of algorithms are all massively increasing our children's exposure to pornography, whether or not they go looking for it, so we parents really need to wise up.

The problem we have is that, not only should children not be seeing sex in general, but porn is giving them a warped view of what healthy, consensual, pleasurable sex is. Pornography frequently depicts dangerous and demeaning acts, is choreographed and edited, and in no way reflects real-life sex, but curious children who happen upon it do not know that. Research conducted by the Children's Commissioner revealed that eight out of ten children see content involving sexual violence before turning eighteen, and nearly half of 18–21-year-olds have experienced a violent sex act, with girls being significantly more affected than boys.[8] Of the young people surveyed *almost half said that girls expect sex to involve physical aggression*, such as airway restriction and slapping, and *four in ten* believe that most girls enjoy this. Dr Debby Herbenick, a sexual and reproductive health professor and the author of the book *Yes, Your Kid*, confirms that incredibly rough sex has become the norm for young people due to it being commonplace in mainstream pornography. She adds that these behaviours often start between the ages of 12–17, which can cause confusion and fear, not to mention serious physical harm.[9]

Common Sense Media's research into American teens (who we can consider culturally comparable for the UK) found that the vast majority had seen porn, with three quarters of teens aged 13–17 watching online. Fifteen per cent had seen it by age ten or younger (that's four kids in every classroom) and *half of children have seen porn by the age of thirteen*. It found that over half of the boys had actively sought it out compared to just over a third of girls, and that porn seems to play a larger role in exploration for LGBTQ+ teens. It also found that unintentional exposure to porn was an issue – 58 per cent had encountered it accidentally, and for most this was a frequent event. Half of children reported feeling guilty or ashamed after watching and most young people agree that viewing pornography affects young people's behaviour towards one another – which begs the question, why are they watching it?[10]

Firstly, it's normal for young people to be curious about sex and relationships so it's understandable that sometimes they may search online for answers to questions, especially if they're embarrassed about asking an adult. The NSPCC says that they might use it to learn about sex and sexual identity, as well as for sexual arousal and pleasure, curiosity, 'a laugh', to break the rules, to be disgusted, to 'freak out' their friends or from peer or relationship pressure.[11] Practically speaking though, it's because it is literally everywhere online so very easy to bump into. The great news is that thanks to new rules by Ofcom, it should become a little harder to access as age checks are finally being introduced across the UK. Although the exact guidelines are still being decided at the time of writing, the big-name sites like Pornhub should face fines if they fail to conform. It is not just about specialist porn sites though. Social media, in particular Instagram and Snapchat, are primary gateways and algorithmic powers mean that, even when a child is not actively looking, it can become hard to avoid. If they so much as hesitate, let alone click on a 'suggestive' image, the algorithms will pump more of the same with increasing intensity until it becomes almost inescapable.

There is also a lot going on in our children's brains that make it hard to resist. It's partly down to the fact that the part of the brain that helps us focus our attention, control impulses and manage our feelings is still developing, and partly to do with the mega-stimulating, sexual nature of porn, which fires up a complex cocktail of neurochemicals, including dopamine. These two factors combined are why children who have seen porn will often say things like, 'I don't why, but I couldn't look away' or 'I just couldn't stop clicking.'

Until we have comprehensive, holistic, quality sex and relationships education for every child, we should not be surprised that kids are actively using porn to learn about sex. Nearly half of teens told Common Sense Media researchers that it gives 'helpful' information.[12] This is why it's imperative that we talk to our kids about pornography sooner rather than later so that they have a healthier frame of reference for making sense of what they see. While this may feel scary, be reassured that deep down your kids do want this support from you. The same research showed that while sadly less than half of young people had conversations about porn with a trusted adult, of those who did, most felt encouraged to find other ways to explore their sexuality besides pornography.

Talking about porn with your child

Erika Lust is an award-winning feminist erotic filmmaker and founder of The Porn Conversation – a non-profit that provides free resources for parents and educators to help them discuss porn with children. She is also a mother of two girls who believes that it is because society hides and bans sex, considering it dirty and shameful, that children have been driven towards porn for their main source of sex 'education'.

In her TEDx Talk 'The porn conversation', Lust (not her real name) encourages parents to reject the shame and stigma surrounding sex and have open, constructive and positive conversations with their children about sex and pornography.[13] She distinguishes between sex – the source of life itself – which is nothing to be embarrassed about, and 'Big Porn' (the mainstream pornography industry). She argues Big Porn is unsafe and exploitative, putting pressure on boys and men to act as 'penetrating sex machines' and reducing women to 'tools for male sexuality'. Strikingly, she adds that porn receives around one third of all internet traffic – it is big business.

Lust is right. We do need to talk about sex and porn more, and it is much better to talk to your children before, not after issues arise. The most important thing to understand is that *talking about the existence of porn with your child does not make them more likely to seek it out*, but it will make them better informed about the harms so that they are less likely to engage in risky behaviours. This is not about having one big showstopping sit-down talk – it is about having 'little and often' casual chats in an age-appropriate way and encouraging your child to ask you questions rather than going online.

THE FIVE LESSONS

Your conscious, intentional conversation empowers your child's critical thinking and helps them to question what they will inevitably see. You can start with open-ended questions like, 'Have you ever seen anything that's upset you on the internet? Anything you didn't understand? Has anyone shown you anything that you don't feel comfortable with?' Let them lead the conversation and just as with the self-esteem conversation, shoulder-to-shoulder conversations (e.g. while cooking or driving) will be easier than eye-to-eye.

In an age-appropriate way, the first step is to simply acknowledge that porn exists and is something that they are likely to see online at some point. However, they also need to be told that while it is natural to be curious, they should never be pressured or forced into seeing things they don't want to and that pornography is not for children. If they see anything shocking or upsetting, porn or otherwise, they should click away and speak with you if they are upset. Reassure them that they won't be in trouble if this happens, but watching it might upset them and what they see may stay with them and affect their sleep, so it is better not to watch it. Explain that if someone tries to show it to them, they should simply say, 'No, I don't want to see that.' They don't need to give a reason.

They will also need to know that porn is acted and that it is different to real-life sex, which is not only physical but emotional, and includes many more kinds of bodies than pornography shows. As is appropriate to their age and stage, you can also explain how it takes time to get to know our own bodies and what we like, and how healthy real-life sex is more intimate and focuses on mutual pleasure, not only penetration. People should always check in about consent and what feels good, and it is never, ever violent or scary. Also, that having healthy, safer sex also involves talking about condoms, birth control and STIs, so while they don't show those conversations in porn, they're essential.

Openly explaining what you feel is wrong with Big Porn gives your child the tools to critically analyse what they see and notice the injustices and harms. Again, as feels appropriate to your child's age and stage, you can explain how most porn is not showing genuine intimacy or respectful relationships and that it can be discriminatory and harmful. Lust says that acknowledging topics like the fetishisation of race, the sexualisation of teens, imposed gender roles or the systemic violence against women will also help older teenagers view the porn industry through a more sophisticated lens.

Consent and communicating with a partner about your boundaries, likes and dislikes during intimacy is critical but often completely missing from porn, so teaching your child about active consent is important. I know that sex and consent often feel like really scary topics, but you don't have to do this alone. Childline has some great guidance for children and parents on all of this, and I urge you to visit their website for expert, age-related guidance to support you in having these conversations. If you really do find all this too uncomfortable though, you could always ask someone else to help by talking with your children for you. Do they have an aunt, uncle or godparent who would feel more confident bringing up these conversations? Perhaps one of their friends' parents would be great, if there is someone you trust? You could also ask about sex education at school to see what topics are being covered and use it to start the conversation with your child that way. ('Did you have that session on sex and relationships today? What did they talk about? Was there anything they didn't

THE FIVE LESSONS

cover that you think they should have?') The point being – there are many ways to approach this topic and it's something for you to chip away at over time, and in different ways.

If this section leaves you nervous, know that doing something – anything – to open up the conversation about porn is better than nothing, and that your children do want your help really. The *Things I Wish My Parents Had Known* guide produced by the Children's Commissioner summarises the views of 16- to 21-year-olds about what they would have found helpful from their parents when growing up online; its headline message is that your teens need you to 'talk early, talk often'. Create the culture before the crisis. 'Children have told us they want their mums and dads to create a safe, judgement-free space for them to talk about these issues. It's better to do that before you hit a problem rather than trying to create that mood while you're dealing with one.'[14]

Finally, if you find your child has viewed porn, what do you do? Firstly, don't panic! If your child has had the courage to tell you that they were looking at porn, that is fantastic, and you should be incredibly proud that they felt able to tell you. It's really important that you tell them this because if you look disappointed they won't come back to you the second time (and there's a good chance there'll be a second time). If you found out another way, make the conversation just one parent – don't gang up – and remind them you love them just the same. Calmly present any digital evidence you found, share your concerns around the harms, and then implement a parental control solution to stop them accessing any more. If you need more help on this, turn to the Resources section.

Sexting

Sexting is when people share sexual messages or images, like naked pictures of themselves. It is illegal for under-eighteens to share or ask for nudes, and once sent there's no way to guarantee they won't be shared further – ensure your child knows this. Talk openly about peer pressure. If they ever feel pressured to send nudes or become uncomfortable in any way, tell them this is not okay, and they can talk to you or another adult they trust.

Cyberflashing is an online version of indecent exposure where someone sends another person an explicit image without permission. It can be done on text, email, messaging apps, social media, dating apps or via AirDrop, Nearby Share or other apps that allow someone to send files to people close by, including strangers. Sadly, it is very common, especially against young women and girls (most often unsolicited dick pics from boys and men), and even though some try to dismiss it as 'funny', it is sexual violence and a serious crime that can lead to imprisonment.[15] Cyberflashing can cause the victim to feel very upset and unsafe. It can even be used as a grooming method, which is when someone tries to gain power or control over them, in order to carry out more abuse.

Revenge porn is when someone publicly shares (either posting or just showing) a private sexual image or video of someone without their consent to cause embarrassment or distress.[16] Sometimes people will threaten to share images to manipulate the person into doing things they don't want to. Sometimes the image is taken without the person's knowledge. Revenge porn is an offence in UK law. If your child tells you they have been a victim of revenge porn, never shame or blame them, and emphasise the courage it took to tell you, how glad you are that they did, and how you will help them through it. For help removing a nude image of under-eighteens online visit the Take It Down website or Childline's Report Remove service.

Non-consensual image sharing aside, Dr Heitner draws on numerous research studies to present a disquieting argument that sexting is not inherently bad for those older teenagers who feel ready for it. 'The uncomfortable truth is that when consensual and private, sexting can be nothing more than another form of healthy teenage sexual exploration, one that often has no social consequences. If we use fear tactics to shame our kids or scare them into not sexting, we only make it harder for them to seek out adult help if they get into a tricky situation.'[17] While this may feel uncomfortable to consider, her point is that it's important parents know that sexting can sometimes be fine and it does not mean their child is being sextorted or going to get arrested or have a horrible experience. Heitner argues that some teenagers say they find it empowering and from a public health perspective, it is also a type of safer sex.

Whatever your view, Heitner concludes that, 'It's happening'; with that in mind, if there is any chance your older teenager could be engaging in sexting – *and you feel that it is appropriate to their age and stage* – then you might want to consider teaching them about 'safer sexting'. If this is where you find yourself, then researchers Dr Sameer Hinduja and Dr Justin W. Patchin offer the following guidance:[18]

1. Remember – possessing nude images of under-eighteens is illegal, even for other children.

2. Consider suggestive (flirty) rather than explicit (nude) photos.
3. Never send images without getting their agreement first in text.
4. Only sext with someone you really know and trust.
5. Never show a sext to anyone else.
6. Never include your face (so that images are not immediately identifiable as yours but also because sophisticated facial recognition algorithms may automatically tag you).
7. Never include anything that could identify you (tattoos, scars, jewellery, surroundings).
8. Turn off your phone location and automatic tagging.
9. If you are being pressured or threatened to send nudes, screenshot the messages for evidence, in case you want to report it later.
10. Delete all explicit images quickly after seeing them and use apps that auto-delete messages soon after sending – but remember someone can still screenshot it or take a photo of it without you knowing.

ACTION: Help them cultivate a joyful and safe online community

One of the beautiful things about our children discovering the online world is that it's another opportunity to 'find their tribe', especially if they are in a minority in their local community in some way. Perhaps your child is reflecting on their identity and is interested in connecting with the LGBTQ+ community, or wants to find role models with the same ethnicity or cultural heritage. Likewise, your neurodiverse child may enjoy finding others who share their interests, or your foster child might love to connect with other children with experience of the care system. It may simply be that your child has a niche hobby or a passion for politics, say, and no one at school understands. Whatever it is, finding fellow enthusiasts online can show them that there is a bigger world out there for them, where people love and care about the same things that they love and care about.

This is when the internet is at its best and shows what a wonderful place it can be.

While exploring new online spaces, it is important your child knows how to take care of their wellbeing. This is especially important for people of colour, LGBTQ+ and otherwise marginalised young people who are all at greater risk of online abuse.

Here are a few ways you can help your child enjoy their time online while engaging respectfully and staying safe.

1. **Show them how to use the internet positively to foster real-world interests**. Once you have decided that your child is ready for internet browsing, you can help them cultivate their own real-world interests through appropriate engagement with relevant online communities. You could have a chat with them about their interests and what they might be interested in exploring, then help them create their own list of favourite, age-appropriate websites in the bookmarks menu of their browser so that they can easily revisit them. Doing this creates the opportunity for you to guide them

towards positive influences and discuss anything inappropriate you come across. It also reinforces the difference between good and bad content. For each social media platform they are on, help them ensure their newsfeed reflects their real-world interests and is a positive, empowering place to be.

2. **Discuss the difference between content consumption and creation.** Consumption of content is simply looking passively at what you see, whereas creation of content is actively contributing to discussions and producing and sharing content on social platforms and websites. Agree together what you are comfortable with them doing, and if you think they are ready to start creating content, help show them how to post texts or images on the age-appropriate platforms you approve of and keep this arrangement under review.

3. **Explain 'netiquette'.** Talk through with your children what good 'netiquette' (internet etiquette) looks like and how profanity, aggressive comments, including misogyny, racism, sexism, homophobia and transphobia, are never acceptable. If they see any online hate, they should not engage with it and instead:
    - **Spot** (notice the abuse for what it is: abuse)
    - **Report** (this means speak to you about anything that makes them uneasy. If they can take a screenshot, even better, in case you decide it needs follow-up action later)
    - **Support** (if they know the victim personally they may like to express their support to them privately)

4. **Ignore trolls** – tell them never to engage with anonymous or suspicious accounts, i.e. trolls, and steer clear of topics that they find stressful or upsetting
5. **Avoid oversharing** – sharing your feelings or personal information – even in what feels like a safe community – is still a public space and can make your child feel very vulnerable. If they do come to you for help, actively listen to what has happened; believe and validate them.

A word of warning – if your child discovers a new online community that shares their interest this could be super exciting. Depending on your child's personality, that same excitement could spiral into something more intense, especially if they are passionate about the topic. Keep this in check by limiting their time online and ensuring they are doing things offline that make them smile every day. Take time to regularly check in with them about their digital lives so that you are confident their online community remains a positive, supportive and abuse-free place to be.

ACTION: Be their backstop

We all want our teenagers to come to us if they are in trouble, but the unfortunate reality is that much of the time they don't, especially when their problems are online.

Tine Jensen is a professor and a clinical psychologist at the University of Oslo and a senior researcher at the Norwegian Centre for Violence and Traumatic Stress Studies. She is also the co-author of a fascinating EU-funded report[19] exploring young people's digital experiences across Norway and the UK that reveals the heartbreaking reasons why young people – despite having mental health difficulties and facing intense, risky situations online with problematic, real-world consequences – tend not to ask their parents for help with their digital dilemmas. And it boils down to the fact that parents are just not very good at dealing with them.

The report reveals that because of this, young people with mental health difficulties often feel very much on their own, having to self-regulate and deal with a digital world that can be ambiguous, uncertain, unsupportive or worse. They then tend to make it their individual responsibility to cope, rarely seeking help when they are in trouble and making considerable efforts to actively keep secrets from parents, teachers, therapists and even peers.

The underlying issue is less because they didn't know who to ask or because they were afraid of not being believed, and more to do with 'feeling shame and guilt for engaging in risky behaviour, fearing that adults would not understand and could not be trusted, or being afraid of the consequences'. When they did ask, they said adults' advice was unrealistic or out of touch, with one child explaining: 'They're not going to understand it anyway, so why waste your time trying to explain?' At other times, it was because the child was too young to understand the trauma that she had been through (for example one eleven-year-old had a harmful sexual experience but did not realise that it was inappropriate until police became involved) or because previous experiences of seeking a parent's help had put them off asking for help again, because it had worsened the situation.

Other worries about consequences included: fears about being threatened or blamed, or that reporting to the authorities might make the situation worse; betraying an online community; or loss of online privileges like the removal of their phone or internet, described by one young person as 'being put in prison' (which is why experts caution against threatening to remove a phone). Sometimes though, the child does not want to be a burden, worry a busy parent or add another problem to the list of problems they feel they create. It can also be that talking causes emotional turmoil. And finally, of course, feelings of shame that they shouldn't have 'been so stupid', perhaps because they had a talk at school or had been warned and felt they should have known better.

When you consider all these issues that young people are contending with, it is easier to understand why it is so hard for them to talk to us about this stuff.

While there is no magic wand, we can be mindful that getting your first phone is inherently a messy, mistake-laden learning process. We can also reassure them regularly that we want them to come to us with their challenges, we will try to understand and help, and they will never be a burden. Embrace this mantra from Protect Young Eyes and repeat it as often as humanly possible until your child groans, rolls their eyes and finishes your sentence for you: 'Never a bad time, never in trouble.' Even if they are embarrassed or believe they are in the wrong. This does not mean there won't be natural and appropriate consequences for their actions, but it's important to show them that you understand that life isn't easy, we all make mistakes, and that they never need to deal with a problem alone, no matter how bad they think it is.

Most of the time, your child will want to fight their own battles – it is an essential part of growing up – but when they can't fix the issue alone, our aim is to be their safe place. We can encourage them to turn towards us not away from us in their moments of need by showing them we know how to stay calm and not get mad or act hastily when things go wrong.

> **TOP TAKE-AWAYS**
>
> It is our job to raise children that can both take care of themselves and others online. You can help minimise digital drama by teaching your child to think twice before sending messages, how to recognise 'red flag feelings' and what to do if they feel unsafe online. Ensure your child understands how valuable their personal information is and take practical steps to help them keep this safe, including 'sharenting' selectively yourself.
>
> Don't be naive about the prevalence and impact of pornography culture – your child needs you to 'talk early, talk often' about it with them. But remember, the internet has many wonderful communities; help your child to find the positive, uplifting spaces that will foster their real-world interests. Finally, while your child won't always want your support, ensure they know (and truly feel) that there is never a bad time, and they will never be in trouble if they want to talk to you about anything.

Lesson 4

Find Your Balance

'The price of anything is the amount of life you exchange for it.'

Henry David Thoreau

According to the young people I met in California, there are two things that infuriate them more than anything about parents and smartphones: hypocrisy and condescension. They can't stand it when parents do not practise what they preach or bring a 'because I said so' attitude. This lesson will ensure your children won't be able to accuse you of either of these heinous sins.

Firstly, we will talk about the importance of reflecting on your own smartphone use, primarily so that you are comfortable with the habits and behaviours you are modelling but also to help support your own wellbeing, because being a parent is hard enough already, and you also deserve to feel in control of your own phone use. Secondly, we cover how to bring your children into the conversation and involve them in setting the standards around smartphones. I also offer some practical tips for holding family conversations and creating a phone agreement. We then reality-check the role you want this tiny box made of plastic, metal and glass to play in the bigger picture of your child's life. Finally, I know a lot of parents start out super strong but later struggle with maintaining the standards they set so we also cover how to create unbreakable boundaries.

ACTION: Model healthy habits

Let me put your mind at ease – this is not about guilt-tripping or telling you off for using your phone in front of your child. Demonising your phone time serves neither you nor you child.

As parents, a lot of the time we are on our phone we are arranging the online food shop, organising playdates, corresponding on the school class WhatsApp group about homework tasks, or paying the bills. Checking in with your friends and family is important too; such 'kinship care' scaffolds the invaluable social networks that support our family and lives. Or perhaps you are keeping up with the news or doing any number of other valid tasks. Then maybe – just maybe – after we set down the cognitive load at the end of the day, we might find some time for ourselves to watch a few silly cat memes or catch up about the latest football club signing or whatever we are into. That is also absolutely fair. Our phone is for all these things and more. Go for it.

That is why modelling healthy habits is not necessarily about using your phone less – although it might be; it is about using your phone consciously and intentionally, acknowledging that your child is watching and learning from you all the time. This is especially difficult when your child cannot see your screen most the time; when they do not know what you are doing it is natural they will make assumptions. Maybe they imagine you playing games when you are really busting a gut to sort our World Book Day costumes or writing a shopping list. This is why it can help to demystify your phone use by simply narrating out loud what you are doing and how long you will be. 'I have to send some work emails – it'll be twenty minutes before I can start tea so go and play and I'll let you know when I am done.' It reduces the allure, and their frustration.

Why is this important? Frankly, because parents often display the exact digital behaviour we caution our kids against. When we are on our phones in front of our children without acknowledging it they can feel their attention is being snubbed in favour of our phone – and it hurts. It is such a common issue that it even has a name, 'phubbing'. Kids see how we act and sense our obsession with our phone, then feel the burn of perceived injustice when they don't have the same access. (This can be a particularly sore point for younger children when their older siblings and parents' combined phone use can make them feel tremendously excluded, as I have had a taste of recently with my youngest.) We adults know we need more and different access to our phone than our kids, but our children don't understand that unless we tell them.

Combat this during one-to-one conversations, meals, family times and bedtimes – any moment in which your main focus is them, by physically putting your phone away and on silent, and having your full focus on them. Don't just put it on the table or hold it in your hand as this sends an unconscious message about your priorities – imagine the prime minister making an important television announcement with their phone in their hand, or a counsellor who leaves their phone on the table in front of you during a session. What does this say about their real priority in that moment?

Worse yet, think of the last time you were mid story with a friend and they broke eye contact to check their phone. You probably wondered whether they were listening or even cared about what you were saying. This 'half there, half not there' treatment feels rubbish, and when our children are subjected to it repeatedly, it can lower their mood and – ultimately – their self-esteem. You can avoid this by asking permission from the other person before checking your phone, or at least excusing yourself and explaining why it's so urgent it couldn't wait. Treat your children with the same respect you would treat a good friend or date.

It helps to consider the nature of your own phone usage more generally too. Imagine if your digital intake was food. How nutritious would your diet be? Your aim is for high-quality, enriching, satisfying screen time, where your phone is helping you pursue your higher aims, whether that be completing life admin, or engaging with a hobby or interest. Aim to reduce the empty digital calories; this is wasted time that could be better spent elsewhere. Think of this time as sugary doughnuts – we love them every now and again, but too often and we start to feel the ill effects. Finally, cut out anything truly toxic – by which I mean anything that leaves you feeling worse than before you saw it. Some influencers are poison disguised as self-improvement. Unfollow. Block. Get rid.

THE FIVE LESSONS

If you feel like you use your phone too much, start to notice the emotions that cause you to pick it up. When I am bored or overwhelmed, I reach for my phone. The first thing I do is check WhatsApp, then emails, then social media. WhatsApp is how I connect socially and as I work alone this feels 'nutritious' enough for me (to a point). Email too is generally no problem, but I find Instagram super distracting. I mitigate the impact by periodically deleting the app and applying a filter to the website version that entirely removes the newsfeed so that if I do want to check my DMs, I cannot be accidentally sucked into the scroll. When I really do want to indulge (which is not that often), I simply add it back, binge and then delete again afterwards.

Here are a few other reasons why I pick up my phone. Do you relate to any of them?

- To tick more things off my never-ending to-do list because I did not feel productive enough that day.
- I'm exhausted and want to zone out from all other people and the stresses of my day.
- Force of habit. I walk through the door after school drop-off in the morning and check messages on autopilot.
- Social connection. If I have been working alone all day, WhatsApp is my outlet for laughs and friendship.
- To capture a beautiful scene or moment with my kids on camera (invariably spoiling that perfect moment in the process!).

Merely noticing your own habits or tendencies may give you clues as to some unmet social or emotional needs in life beyond your phone. (Lonely? Is it time to organise a real-life meet-up or call a friend for a proper chat? Struggling to switch off and relax? Do you need to lower the expectations you are setting yourself, or find other ways to reduce your stress levels?) This isn't about technological abstinence or discipline but gently nudging ourselves towards a sustainable, healthy balance.

Here are a few more ideas you can consider. Like confetti, it's lovely if some stick, but feel free to let the rest fall by the wayside, as you like. If you are keen to learn more about this subject *How to Break Up With Your Phone* by Catherine Price and *The Phone Fix* by Dr Faye Begeti are both good reads.

1. Try out the smartphone addiction scale test at healthy-screens.com and see how you do (I scored 30/60 – don't judge me!).
2. Practise the S.T.O.P. technique from Lesson 1 (see pages 136–38).
3. Have a digital declutter and feng shui your phone by removing all unnecessary apps.
4. Write a list of IRL things you love so much they make you forget to pick up your phone. Do more of them.
5. Enable screen-time tracking to see what you're spending your time doing and set daily time limits for yourself on addictive 'empty calorie' apps.
6. Use a screen-blocking app to block certain apps, websites or features.
7. Minimise your notifications.
8. Charge your phone outside your bedroom overnight and buy an alarm clock. If you must be contactable keep

a basic phone, like a Nokia, next to you and give the number to your emergency contacts. If you like to use a meditation app or listen to white noise to help you sleep, you could strip back an old smartphone so it only has the apps you need. (Do not rely on this method for your child though.)
9. If you work from a desk, protect your focus by charging your phone away from you so you have to get up to check it.
10. Try one of the disconnect challenges from Lesson 1 (see page 124).

ACTION: Formalise phone use in a family agreement

It is never too early to agree some general expectations about smartphones and other screens to support a healthy balance in your home. Even before your child has their own smartphone some family standards around general screen usage – including your own phone use – sets the tone. That even parents are expected to be courteous and conscious of their impact on others will, with any luck, make conversations about your child's own phone use much easier later on. If your child already has a phone then this is all the more valuable and important; it is never too late to 'recontract' expectations; in fact, it's important that you discuss it regularly and adapt as children grow and everyone's needs evolve.

Whether you want to physically create a document or make a verbal agreement is up to you, but a written record of what was agreed can help remove any ambiguity later down the line. Either way, I recommend that you try to focus more on the idea of setting family 'standards' rather than 'rules'. Maybe this sounds like semantics, but I think words carry weight, and 'family standards' feels to me a more aspirational and empowering way to frame the conversation.

'Standards' are positively framed and co-created by all family members, in contrast with 'rules', which tend to be imposed from the top down, focus on what not to do, and are made to be broken! It's the difference between saying 'No phones in bedrooms' and saying, 'Our family protects their sleep and mental health by charging our phones downstairs at night'. The rationale is baked in, and highlighting the benefits as you go along helps to frame this whole process as an experiment, in which you are all learning, iterating and improving; it's not a pass-or-fail test for the kid.

Isn't it enough to set up their phone correctly and discuss sensible use with them, and see how it goes? Maybe, but the European research project I mentioned earlier clearly proved that digital skills are not enough to keep young people safe on their own and that frequently children know exactly what the right thing to do is online, and still cannot stop themselves getting sucked in.[1] Yes, the ultimate goal is to develop their responsible self-regulation, but children still need our boundaries and protection while they are learning and developing. Having a family agreement helps ensure they are involved in creating and consenting to the expected standards and that they understand the reasons for them and the consequences if standards slip.

The other reason I like this approach is that it invites conversation about the whole family's behaviours, not just the child. I think there is something important in everyone buying into the overall principles behind the standards, even if they are applied differently to individual family members, in the same way that siblings may have different bedtimes based on ages, or an adult is allowed alcohol, and a child is not. You may even find it helpful to develop a code word that family members can use when someone is breaking the agreement so that children and adults alike don't have to call out the specific behaviour directly and risk sounding rude, or like a 'nag'. Something anomalous will be more likely to be noticed rather than an everyday word – even better if you have a silly family in-joke word as this will help send the message that intervention is being offered with good humour and positive intent!

How to create a family phone agreement

While you will have some non-negotiables, taking your child's interests, priorities and concerns into account will help. The shortcut option is to print off the Family Media Agreement template from the Common Sense Media website, which is clear and to the point but more formal and focused on 'rules'.[2] Alternatively, you might like Our Family's Social Standards customisable template from The Social Institute, which was developed with thousands of students and parents, and is informal and positively framed all around hitting personal goals.[3] Personally, I recommend creating your own to make this meaningful and personal to you.

Below is an 'ideas bank' to get you started, but remember that what matters most is the conversation, not the contract itself, so use this for inspiration but keep your own version light. You could cherry-pick two or three ideas from each section or you could show this list to your child and ask which would be their top five or ten to include, and combine these with your own priorities, if different.

The basics
- We take care of our phone by ensuring it remains fully charged and storing it safely. If we damage or lose the phone we tell our parent(s) straight away.
- We respect that the phone ultimately belongs to the person that pays the bill and that it is our responsibility to live up to these standards. In exchange, the owner agrees not to remove it without a very good reason.
- We use parental controls/monitoring/tracking software to help us stay safe (if you plan to use it explain what it does and why it is important to you).
- We only use the apps and features we have parental permission for. If we want something new, we will discuss it first.
- We agree to talk about our problems, including if we make an online mistake, are feeling unhappy or feel like we can't control our phone use.
- As parents we promise there will never be a bad time, and you will never be in trouble if you speak to us. We will listen calmly, support you to find solutions, and avoid rash decisions.

Mastering attention
- We respect school as a phone-free environment and leave the phone at home or switch it off and store it away safely.

- We are aware of road safety and the risk of theft. We are mindful where we get our phone out and never use it while crossing roads.
- We respect that homework time is phone-free time (agree times and where the phone is).
- We control our attention by muting notification settings (apply emergency contact overrides).
- We strive to live in the moment by keeping our phones away when not in use and resisting the urge to document every moment.
- We show others respect by putting our phone down and looking up when someone enters a room or is talking with us; we do not phub people.
- We use the internet to pursue our interests, develop friendships and stay healthy and happy.

Critical-thinking skills
- We walk away and talk to a trusted adult if we ever feel unsafe or pressured online.
- We keep our accounts and personal information private (explain your preferred privacy settings).
- We protect our personal data with strong passwords (explain that you must have account details for emergencies).
- We treat suspicious emails and links, pop-ups and adverts with extreme caution and do not click through.
- We try to notice 'red flag' feelings and respect these by exiting unsafe digital situations and seeking advice from a trusted adult.

- We engage with only positive influences and content that help us feel good and achieve our goals, and we curate our feeds to reflect this.
- We only view age-appropriate and positive content.
- We apply a sceptical eye to everything we read, hear and see online, knowing that it may not be true.

Digital ethics
- We only text, post or share content that aligns with our family values, reflects well on us and our 'digital footprint'. (The 'Would you say it to their face?' test.)
- We are upstanders, not bystanders. This means we leave unkind spaces, support our friends and speak up about bad behaviour whenever we can.
- We 'S.T.O.P.' (see page 136) and think twice before posting or messaging because we know the internet is a public place where things can easily be shared without our permission.
- We only join groups where we have parental permission (be clear on any limits on group size, topics, privacy settings, and friends you know IRL).
- We only share images with the person's permission (this includes sharenting by parents).

Maintaining balance
- We support our wellbeing and relationships by respecting our phone-free spaces (e.g. bedrooms, bathrooms, dinner table; have a basket or charging station).
- We prioritise our relationships, sleep and study over screens by putting our phones away at agreed times

(be clear on standards, e.g. no phone use during family gatherings, or until after homework is completed, or phones off by 8 p.m.).
- We maintain real-life interests, activities and relationships and use our phone to support, not distract from these.
- We regularly, openly and honestly discuss the nature and impact of our phone use together with parents.
- We agree to revisit and update this agreement in XX months, or as needed.

Sleep

If there was a single feature I would urge you to include in this agreement, it would be to maintain phone-free bedrooms overnight. It is the simplest thing you can do to protect sleep, limit your children's access to inappropriate content and protect them from social drama – the worst of which often occurs late at night – and start their day on the right foot. It's much easier to instil this norm right from the start, and very much easier if you adhere to the standard yourself.

If you are removing access from a child who already has their phone overnight, explain your positive motivations without implying blame or wrongdoing and ask what they use their phone for at night currently so that you can consider workarounds, such as buying an alarm clock. If they really feel they need relaxation music or meditation tracks these could be played on an MP3 player, CD player or Bluetooth speaker. Be clear on how you will take care of their phone to allay any fears of it going missing or them feeling 'spied on' when it's away from them.

WHAT IF MY CO-PARENT AND I FEEL DIFFERENTLY ABOUT SMARTPHONES?

Co-parenting, whether you live together or not, can be tough at the best of times, and smartphones are no exception. Obviously, it's easier if you can present a united front for your child, but it may take work to get there, and you will need to dedicate some time and space to discussing this out of your child's earshot before involving them. If you can get your co-parent to read some of this book first that may also help.

Begin the conversation by identifying all the aspects that you agree on to help get things off on the right foot. Where you disagree, avoid any 'You ...' statements, such as 'You are too strict', as this will only make them defensive. Instead, stick to the facts of the situation and say how you feel about it.

> *When we give Bobby a smartphone he will have access to the internet. I have recently learned that half of children have seen porn by the age of thirteen, so I am really worried about what he might see.*

Next, state clearly and confidently what you want to happen, and outline the benefits of your approach.

> *I want us to have a rule that he is not allowed to use the phone in his bedroom so that we know he is not watching things he shouldn't be at night.*

When discussing try to stay focused on one issue at a time and be ready to negotiate a little so you can both go away satisfied.

THE FIVE LESSONS

> Perhaps your co-parent feels strongly they should be allowed some time on their phone in the bedroom, but you can agree that this should only be with the door open, and that they should hand it in to you at 8 p.m.?
>
> Where you absolutely cannot agree, it may be better to openly discuss this with your child in a mature and calm manner, than pretend you have a united front when you really do not (especially if the alternative is ignoring the issue and giving up). Hearing you thoughtfully explain your views on the topic may help your child better understand your concerns. Just be very careful not to make them the peace-keeper or draw them into an adult argument.

What about my child seeing or using friends' phones?

Whatever our own decisions, our children will always encounter others who have more or different phone access than they do. It's a difficult one.

Where you feel comfortable, especially when it comes to tween playdates, you can speak to the parents of the other child about the rules you have for your own child and ask for their support while your child is in their care. I see it the same way as if your family was vegetarian – you could leave it to your child to have the same conversation, but it would probably be polite to let the parent know beforehand, in case they were planning on serving steak pie for dinner. If you are worried about it, or you don't feel comfortable asking, maybe you keep the playdates around your house.

At some point though, this level of control will become impossible. As your child grows and gains freedom your intervention may become more harmful than helpful. This is when we hope that your hard work begins to pay off and all those little conversations about how to stay safe online, be an ethical digital citizen, and think critically about what they see, come into play. Your family agreement clearly sets out your expectations for them. The care you have put into raising their self-esteem means that they hopefully have the courage to say no to things they don't want to see or do. Your family mantra lets them know that if they need help you want to be there for them, and that it will never be a bad time, and they will never be in trouble.

Will there be times when the peer pressure is so strong that your child will go along with things that they are uncomfortable with to save face? Yes. But that is the nature of adolescence, and you can seek comfort in the fact that you have done everything in your power to help them through these trials and tribulations. The rest has got to be up to them.

ACTION: Nurture life beyond the phone

Various studies show that an emotionally stable child is more likely to have a positive relationship with their phone than a child who already struggles with their mental health. This makes perfect sense when you consider that a child who is bullied or discriminated against in the real world is more likely to also experience this online. It is also not hard to imagine that a child with a full and happy life offline may be not only less negatively impacted by unfavourable comparisons on social media but also, quite simply, less bothered about spending time online because they are too busy having fun doing other stuff. Similarly, a well-balanced child with healthy phone use will use their phone to positively enable and facilitate their life, organising meet-ups and furthering their hobbies and interests, so that the phone supports, rather than detracts from their wellbeing. This is why it is so important not to view the phone in isolation, but as part of the broader picture of your child's life.

We need to expand the phone conversation beyond prohibition – what our children must not do and all the bad things online – to imagine a modern childhood that balances protection and empowerment. What would it look like for your child to live their best life today? What essential aspects of a quality childhood remain unchanged that you want to ensure they have? What character traits do you want to nurture in them? We can then view their phone use within the bigger picture of their life and consider all the ways it might help or hinder these broader aspirations.

Beyond their obvious physiological needs (sleep, nutrition, warm shelter) the UN Convention on the Rights of the Child (UNCRC) entitles children to a decent standard of living, free from violence, including an education, the opportunity to relax and play, be healthy, and freely express themselves.[4] Beyond these basics though, what do our young people need in their life so that they are not tethered to their phones, trying to kill time or fill a void that should already be filled by real-world experiences? To answer this question, we can look at their 'emotional needs', and a theory called the Human Givens, which offers a practical, therapeutic approach to human thriving. It states that in order to thrive all humans need the following:

1. Security – a safe place and an environment which allows us to develop fully, without fear.
2. Attention – to give and receive attention is a form of emotional nourishment.
3. Autonomy – the opportunity to make responsible choices.
4. Community – feeling part of a wider group of people.
5. Intimacy – knowing that at least one other person accepts us totally for who we are, 'warts and all'.
6. Privacy – time and space alone are essential for reflecting on and processing our experiences.
7. Meaning and Purpose – which come from being stretched in what we do and think.
8. Sense of Status – within social groupings.
9. Sense of Competence and Achievement.

The digital world presents myriad opportunities to support all of these emotional needs, which is a wonderful thing for our children, but if we can ensure our child's emotional needs are already met in the real world they will not become reliant on their phone as their emotional support crutch. In other words, feeling like a whole and happy person without their phone will mean that they are more likely to treat their phone as a portal to more ways that they can grow, explore and engage with the world, rather than *the only way*. It is the difference between having good friends (i.e. community or intimacy) in real life *and* online, vs feeling as though your *only* meaningful friendships are online, or the difference between feeling that you have autonomy or social status in your day-to-day life *and* online, vs feeling you *only* have autonomy or social status online, and so on ... The point is that while phones can open up new digital pathways to add value to our children's lives, they should never substitute meaningful, real-world experiences and relationships.

ACTION: Set unbreakable boundaries

When the class of eighteen-year-old Californian students told me they would be much stricter with their own kids, I was shocked. They were studying at an exclusive and largely tech-free private school in the heart of Silicon Valley; their families were tech types who are famously strict and slow in providing access to smart devices ... and they were telling me that their digital upbringing was too lax!? Crikey.

These teenagers' parenting advice to me was: 'Even if she begs, don't give in.' They recounted times that they had nagged and whined for earlier or more access but just a few years later were now grateful for their parents' boundaries – and in hindsight, wish they had been even tougher. This was hard to hear, but their words ring in my ears, a grounding reality check, whenever I doubt myself in the aftermath of some of my less popular parenting decisions.

Testing boundaries is how adolescents learn where the limits lie. A healthy limit is found when someone with wisdom and care kindly but firmly upholds the boundary a child is pushing against. While frustrating in the moment, having a person that cares that much about them to engage in this tug of war is what helps children to feel safe and loved. It lets your child know that they matter to someone; they matter to you and to your family unit, and that is very good for their sense of security and their self-esteem.[5]

Renowned parenting expert and clinical psychologist Dr Becky Kennedy advocates for 'sturdy parenting' and brilliantly describes a boundary as 'something you tell your child you will do, and it requires your child to do nothing'.[6] Boundaries are about your actions as a parent, not your kids' actions, which is where a lot of us go wrong. She explains that as much as children push back against boundaries, they need (and maybe want) them. She compares it to an astronaut floating in space, untethered and uneasy; children need an anchor back to safety, and boundaries give them that feeling of security; they know they cannot float away too far from us.

The misstep that most of us make is to make requests of our children, instead of giving them firm, clear boundaries. This is not to say that we should stop being polite – we still want to have healthy two-way discussions with our children where we seek to understand their perspectives. This is about those problematic moments when our kids are simply refusing our reasonable requests, so we get frustrated and risk blaming and shaming them or making rash decisions in the heat of the moment. Like confiscating a phone as a punishment for a relatively minor misdemeanour, which then risks harming our relationship further.

Consider a teenager sneaking their phone out of the central charging station to use it overnight, in violation of the family agreement. A 'request' may look like telling off the child and ordering them not to do it again, then when they continue, getting angry, accusing them of being bad and confiscating the phone for a week as punishment. Whereas, setting a boundary

THE FIVE LESSONS

looks more like reminding them that no phones overnight is a condition of your family agreement, sharing that you have noticed that the phone has been missing overnight, and explaining that from now on the phones will be stored in a locked safe or a box in your bedroom so that no one is tempted to access them when they shouldn't. *The boundary is an action that you take, that relies on them doing nothing.* With this approach, there is no need for punishment 'for the sake of it'.

Taking responsibility for setting the boundaries ourselves also helps us to avoid mentally labelling our child as naughty, rude or deceitful or, equally, a 'good girl' or 'nice boy' who 'wouldn't do such things' because you are simply preventing them from behaving in those ways. It's not helpful to typecast anyone by their actions. We can all be good or bad – it just depends on the day. Instead of focusing on the rights and wrongs of the situation, focus more on the lessons learned and the communication skills needed to repair any harm done. A child sneaking a phone out of the charging station at night might lead to a conversation about the FOMO that the child is experiencing if all their friends are up messaging and then discussing better coping strategies. Or it might lead to a conversation about what purpose the phone is serving for them, so you can better understand what emotional needs may be out of balance.

When things go wrong and our children make mistakes try to remember that even though it often feels like it, our kids' behaviour is not a judgement on our parenting, and we are doing the best we can. Not judging our kids too harshly and instead talking about lessons learned helps them see that we 'get' how hard it is for them. We need to help them to understand the impact of their actions, but we can also tell them that we do not expect perfection and that we are all learning as we go. It builds trust and empathy and makes it more likely they will come to you next time.

Finally, remember that it is our job to be the grown-up they need, not their best friend, and just because your child is cross with you, it doesn't mean that you're wrong. In fact, their complaints are a really healthy sign that your child feels safe enough with you to share their point of view openly and passionately! You're doing a great job.

> **TOP TAKE-AWAYS**
>
> Kids hate hypocrites, and modelling healthy phone habits for your child makes it more likely they will also use theirs responsibly. It is never too early to agree some general rules about smartphones and other screens to support a healthy balance in your home, and creating a family phone agreement with aspirational standards rather than a contract with rules makes the conversation more positive and inclusive. Keep phones out of bedrooms, especially overnight, and focus on nurturing your child's life beyond the phone, so that they rely upon it less. Boundaries are about something that you do that requires your child to do nothing at all.

Lesson 5

Keep Learning

'Be not afraid of growing slowly; be afraid only of standing still.'

Chinese Proverb

As we begin the fifth and final lesson of this book, you will be well aware that giving your child a smartphone is the start of an ongoing commitment, not a once-and-done decision. Do not be overwhelmed. While your child's first phone adds a new – or at least deeper – digital dimension to your parenting duties, it is really no different to everything else you have parented through, and you're never going to have all the answers before you begin. All any of us can do is take it one step at a time, and give ourselves some grace along the way.

Let's be kind to both ourselves and to our kids by approaching this massive learning curve with a spirit of open-minded curiosity and compassion. Our decisions needn't be binary or binding. We can regularly reflect on and revise our approach where things aren't working, and it is more than fine to admit to our children that we are learning alongside them. You are allowed to make mistakes. You are allowed to be both pro-technology and at the same time protective of your child. You are allowed to trust them while simultaneously remaining alert to the warning signs in your child that tell you when it's time to dial back the digital or step up the support.

ACTION: Reconnect often

Adolescence is the time when a child grows 'wings to fly'. As teenagers learn to survive independently in the world in preparation for adulthood, they establish their own identity and pull away from their parents. This will create moments of friction in every family, including around phone usage, but your child still needs you, perhaps now more than ever, just in new ways. As they grow, they still very much need to know you're there for them, even if they don't want you to step in and fix stuff so often. As parents we must adapt to their changing needs and find new ways to maintain our connection.

Having just one person who makes you feel safe and loved is a critical protective factor in developing resilience. In particular, research into child victims of bullying shows that those who returned to the shelter of a warm and positive supportive family were better able to deal with, and felt less harmed by, their bullying experiences than the victims who did not have such a supportive family.[1] This shows that even though you cannot always protect your child from having difficult experiences, your love and support can provide a safe harbour, insulating them from feeling the worst effects of the storms of adolescent life. With you, they can recharge their emotional batteries, before heading back 'out there' into the digital or real world that awaits them.

The challenge with teens, of course, is that you never quite know when they will need you and when they will push you away. As frustrating as it may be, parenting experts tend to agree that simply being around and available for ad hoc conversations – or plain and simple company – is what they most need from us during these tricky years. That means even when they are their most unlovable we still need to be ready to receive them and reconnect with them when they are ready to talk. But as we all know, doing that dance with teenagers isn't easy; a door is slammed, voices crack with shouts of 'You never understand me!' and our own frustration and resentment easily flare up to match theirs. At other times, we simply cannot be there when we want to be because of our work commitments or other demands on us.

So how do you stay connected to your child and learn about their smartphone use in a way that isn't overbearing? Here are a few suggestions to bookmark and return to when times are tough.

- **Manage your expectations**. Go for little-and-often chats over heavy 'talks'. Aim to collect up just a piece of the puzzle with each mini chat, rather than trying to complete the full picture in one go, to avoid them mentally checking out. If they are slow to talk or dismissive of your efforts to connect, try to stay patient. Remember all the changes their brains and bodies are going through in this period and always leave the metaphorical (and literal) door open to further conversations. Even though rudeness may leave us feeling like slamming that door in their face, flopping on the sofa and giving up on the idea of ever having a meaningful or civil conversation again, don't. Annoyingly, that will be exactly the time when they are most likely to want to talk.

- **Listen more than you talk.** You know that expression, 'We have two ears and one mouth for a reason'? Right. Listening also includes paying attention to their body language, mood and choices, and throwaway remarks outside of 'serious' conversations. It's all communication.
- **Don't dodge the difficult stuff.** Your kids really need you to be brave. They need to know you can handle the hard stuff and are happy to talk about it with them, however awkward it feels. If you can't, they will turn to the internet, media and peers instead, and these sources may not be giving the type of advice and information you would approve of. Tackling the tricky topics earlier is easier because you are not waiting until crisis point. Prevention is always better than cure.
- **S.T.O.P.** yourself. If you feel agitated, anxious or angry when your child shares something, try to take a breath before reacting, like we learned in Lesson 1 (see page 138). Notice where this strong feeling is coming from rather than immediately biting back with a lecture and ask yourself: what is the most constructive way I could respond right now? Equally, on the days you don't do

this – because you will snap back and say things you later regret – that's okay too. We all make mistakes. Simply take a break to recover yourself and when you are ready, go and say sorry. Apologising is a seriously underrated parenting skill that children really appreciate. It may well even bring you closer. Just ensure that you don't add a 'but' on the end of your sentence; it will undo all the good feeling you have just created.

- **Use open-ended questions about others their age**. I have found it's much easier for children to say more when the questions aren't so personal or direct. You could ask, who are the most popular influencers among their friends right now? Have they been taught anything about AI in school yet? Have there been any issues with cyber-bullying in their year lately? What do they think are the biggest challenges with smartphones based on what they are seeing in children their age? This can help normalise conversation on these topics, while also discreetly alerting you to any possible issues you may need to keep a look out for.
- **Keep it tech-positive**. Of course it is tempting to jump into conversations with our children by focusing all our attention and input on the risks, but overlooking all the good stuff their smartphone offers is a surefire way to irritate your child and drive them away. Don't forget the bigger picture and balance out your concern with curiosity about what's working well for them too. How is the phone helping them to stay organised for school? Have they used it to keep in touch with any friends and

family that they can tell you about? What hilarious or joyful stuff have they seen recently that they can share with you? Actively look for ways that you can discuss their phone (and yours) that bring you closer together.

- **Make it a two-way conversation.** If all your questions are about them, and you offer nothing about you, the casual 'chat' you planned could feel more like a poorly concealed undercover interrogation or fact-finding mission rather than a conversation. Aim for genuine exchanges instead by talking about your own past or present experiences first; talk about what you are enjoying and struggling with your own phone usage and see how they respond. You can also ask them how *your* phone use makes *them* feel ... but be prepared – you may not like what you hear! (PS Don't forget to S.T.O.P.!)
- **Find the fun.** Reconnecting with your child should be joyful. Find ways to connect with them that feel comfortable and pleasurable for both of you. Perhaps you share a love of playing pool, baking or online gaming. Whatever it is, simply chatting as you do your thing will yield much better conversations and be much more relaxed all round. You might even like to introduce a regular family 'date day', when one adult hangs out one on one with one child and does something they will both enjoy – it doesn't have to be fancy. One day my eldest and I watched the *Barbie* movie at home and painted our nails, and on another my youngest and I went litter picking; she had seen a neighbour do it so we borrowed their gear and had a surprisingly nice time!

It's a neat way to break out of the usual family dynamic and create space for conversation. You may even discover a new hobby ...

ACTION: Watch for warning signs (but don't dwell on the risks)

Spending too much time on a smartphone is a common cause of argument between parents and teenagers, but how much is too much? The answer is both complicated and extremely simple.

First, the complicated version. You may be confused to hear that a recent study by EU Kids Online revealed that while Norwegian children and adolescents spend the most time online in all of Europe, they also score the highest when reporting how happy they are with life.[2] This study highlighted that phones, social media and the internet can bring great joy and value, and the internet itself is not inherently bad or the cause of young people's unhappiness. This means that it is not phones themselves that are necessarily a problem but how they are used – and that too much focus on the risks of being online can alienate children who generally experience the internet as a positive place. As such, 'too much' use varies hugely depending on what that individual person is doing on their phone, who that person is (age, stage, sensitivities, circumstances) and how it is affecting them overall. A child may be using their phone for several hours a day, but if that time is being used to complete homework, maintain close family ties (like video-calling relatives overseas), excitedly develop skills, or research a really positive and wholesome interest, and – critically – that child is still living a full and happy life that meets their emotional needs away from their phone, then their use may not be a problem at all. In contrast, another child may use their phone much less, but if what they are seeing or doing online is toxic – they are a victim of sextortion or online bullying, or are being fed upsetting, pornographic or extreme content – then any amount of this type of phone usage, however little, could be profoundly harmful.

The simple answer though, is that too much is whatever amount and type of phone usage has a negative impact on their wellbeing. Is their phone usage interfering with their sleep? Is it deterring them from activities that are important for their health or happiness? Is it getting in the way of in-person relationships with friends and family? Are they more interested in their phone than the extracurricular activities and other interests that they usually enjoy? Do they feel anxious or stressed if they are disconnected or separated from their phone? Any of these could be signs that their smartphone use is out of balance, and you need to make some adjustments.

The tricky part is that teenagers often struggle to share their problems, so it can be difficult to know when something is so-called 'normal' teenage behaviour or something more serious. Relate, an organisation specialising in helping people with relationships, advises that if you notice any of the following signs, you may want to consider getting further advice or support.

Signs something may be wrong

- **Behaviour changes** Acting out, getting into trouble, bullying others or a sudden change in style of social interactions? Becoming quiet, nervous, withdrawn or clingy? Skipping school or spending a lot of time in their room? A noticeable change in behaviour might be a normal development but could also indicate they need some extra support.
- **Sleep patterns** Often sleep issues are the first sign that something is causing us anxiety. Struggling to sleep could suggest your child is finding it difficult to process something upsetting that they have seen or that has happened. Equally, sleeping significantly more than usual could indicate your child is feeling down or even depressed.
- **Eating patterns** Eating noticeably more or less than normal, or at different times? Refusing to sit down for meals with the family? Eating patterns and appetite are often affected by feelings.
- **Health problems** Are they reporting frequent headaches or tummy upsets? Are they having changes in mood and lack of motivation? These are often symptoms of anxiety.
- **School grades** A significant drop in school performance can be a clear sign they are distracted or upset. They may express themselves at school in ways they wouldn't at home, knowing that you won't be able to see. Relate urges parents to remember that your child's teachers are a key resource when it comes to making sure they're all right so don't hesitate to contact them for help.

- **Emotional dysregulation** Sometimes young people can't make sense of what's happening and just feel 'wrong'. When a child is simply overwhelmed by feelings and can't manage them this can come out as emotional dysregulation; they may become upset, angry, irritable, restless or depressed and just don't know why.

If you have noticed any of the above signs and are worried about your child, please turn to the Resources section at the back of this book for signposting to further support on a range of topics. The Relate website also provides free support and guidance, including information about counselling for parents. For urgent support or someone to talk to now, try the following services:

- If it's an emergency and there is risk to life – call 999.
- Childline (for under-eighteens and parents) – call 0800 1111 any time for free, or use their online chat at www.childline.org.uk
- Young Minds parents' helpline – call 0808 802 5544 or chat online, Monday–Friday 9.30 a.m. – 4 p.m. They also have a useful list of support services on their website at www.youngminds.org.uk
- Samaritans (for eighteen or over) – call 116 123 any time for free, whatever you're going through.

Finally, a note of caution to anyone who is experiencing any amount of 'not-my-child' thinking when reading this, because 'they have been taught all this' so should 'know better'. A comprehensive European study into the role of digital skills in children's mental health concluded very clearly that 'digital wisdom' helps, but skills alone are insufficient to keep a child safe from the risks and potential adverse impacts of spending time online, particularly when faced with a digital environment that is designed to operate in ways that are often antithetical to users' wellbeing.[3] Specifically, they were referring to how algorithms can act as a distorting mirror, magnifying problematic content and pushing young people with mental health vulnerabilities down a spiral of ever-more overwhelming, upsetting or extreme content that they find hard to break away from. Consequently, it is absolutely not safe to assume that just because they 'know better' they can and will 'do better'. Your child is still a child and needs you to keep an eye out for them, to put a protective arm around their shoulders, and if it gets too much, they need you to notice and help them back to health.

ACTION: Regularly revisit your family agreement

As your child grows and develops – and you learn more about what does and does not work for their phone use – you will need to refresh your family agreement. You will want to find your own formula for discussion, of course, but one way that works for us is having family meetings.

When we first started doing these, our kids were only four and seven so we kept them as simple conversations, with just a few rules around turn taking, and a little agenda that they would write in coloured pens and stick on the fridge for others to add items to. Over the years we have developed our approach and use them sparingly for the times we want to speak calmly together about sensitive or stubborn issues where there is a risk that things could get heated. Our meetings are totally ad hoc and the last one we had was instigated by my frustrated eleven-year-old who wanted to discuss schoolday mornings and why 'no one is ever ready on time'. (The opposite of her easy-breezy younger sister, she gets stressed even thinking about the idea of being late!)

Having some ground rules for how family members conduct themselves is helpful. Part of the point of doing this is to show your child that their voice counts too and that you can listen, as well as direct. In fact, one of the best things about family meetings is that any family member can call one; I find it humbling and strangely reassuring when our kids feel empowered to announce that we need a meeting and then proceed to table items important to them, which we may have overlooked as parents. It reassures me that they feel confident that their voice matters equally in this family, and that they need not shy away from challenging conversations. It's levelling to wait your turn to speak, just like the kids have to, and actively listen to what they have to say. Doing so makes what could otherwise be a power squabble into a much more respectful exchange and I know that we are helping develop their communication skills in the process. It's certainly a lot more gratifying than many work meetings I've been in!

Here is what works for us, but don't feel bound by these ideas and do what works for you.

- Anyone can call a meeting (kids or adults) but they must give a little advance notice of what they want to discuss and when, so everyone has a chance to reflect beforehand.

THE FIVE LESSONS

- Meeting topics should be general to the family, not personal to one individual. If you want to discuss a single incident or an issue relating to one child, that should be handled privately with them. (You can still respect the turn-taking system below between parent and child.)
- Over dinner time is perfect for us, but it doesn't have to be.
- Keep it short – pick one topic at a time and aim for twenty minutes max on your first occasion. See how it goes from there.
- Have a prop to serve as your 'mic' – a bottle of ketchup or salt grinder is ideal. No one interrupts the speaker while they are holding the mic. If you have a 'talker' on your hands, you might have to set a time limit (an egg timer is perfect for this).
- Take turns to speak and keep a set order. You can relinquish your turn, but you cannot skip ahead of the queue.
- If anyone struggles with not interrupting the speaker, give them paper and a pen so they can capture their thoughts ready for their turn, so that they are less inclined to jump in.
- Keep going around taking turns and passing the mic, until everyone feels understood and agreement is reached, or you feel that you have been talking long enough.
- End the discussion on an adult who sums up, checks the agreement and clarifies any actions.

It is perfectly all right if you cannot reach agreement in one sitting and more than enough if all you achieve is to leave the meeting with a better understanding of how your child is feeling. Simply thank everyone for taking part, sharing their feelings and (hopefully) being respectful, and agree to talk again after you have reflected to see if you have any new ideas to move it forward. These conversations are often like stirring the tea bag in the cup, agitating lots of thoughts and emotions, but the real magic happens when you walk away and let it brew for a bit before your return to it. Besides, having a healthy conversation wherein you practise communication skills, share your feelings and create some IRL connection is an achievement in its own right. You are building a family culture of respectful communication and that takes time. Be proud.

TOP TAKE-AWAYS

As a parent, you don't have to know all the answers; it is normal to be learning as you go and to change your mind and adjust your approach to phones as you learn what is working and what is not. You are allowed to both love technology and be cautious of the risks of smartphone culture at the same time.

Your tweens and teens still need you as much as they ever have, but the kind of support they need is changing as their independence grows. Notice any changes in them that could indicate something is wrong and find enjoyable ways to connect regularly with them. Show them that you are there for them, if they need you. Regularly revisit your family agreement as your child matures; consider experimenting with family meetings.

Conclusion

When I first began thinking about this topic I was curious and a little concerned, but my kids were still young and the smartphone years felt like a problem for the future. As my eldest approached the end of primary school, I began to worry more ... Will she too become one of the 'anxious generation'? Still, worrying has never helped anyone, and I fundamentally believe that technological progress is inevitable, so I knew the eventual answer had to lie in helping parents and children to create a healthy, happy relationship with their phones – at their own time, and in their own way. So it was that I committed myself to writing this book and focusing all my efforts on providing trustworthy, independent advice and practical support for parents.

Honestly, my optimism was challenged at moments, particularly when researching the pornography section. Studying to become a digital wellness educator also revealed to me how dependent I had become on my own phone. Yet I am relieved and pleased to report that after five years of dissecting the facts and figures, consulting a diverse range of experts and speaking with families, I can confidently say that – with the

CONCLUSION

right support in place – I truly believe the kids will be all right. And so will we.

It is true that today's young adults have been the guinea pig generation – their smartphones served as a social lifeline for those coming of age during the pandemic, a time when parents faced unprecedented pressures with schools shut and desperately little support. These children's experiences and reflections on those difficult times have given me greater courage and conviction in how I want to lead my own children through the timeless turbulence of adolescence. Their message was clear – listen to their views respectfully, explain your reasoning to them so they understand, and then have confidence in the decisions you are taking. Although they might not appear to want your help, they really do need your guidance on their journey to digital maturity. So, lean into those difficult conversations. Give them safety guardrails, even though they won't thank you in that moment; it makes them feel safe to have some boundaries. Release responsibility progressively as they mature and only when you feel sure they are ready. Be available to talk when they need to, and don't judge them too harshly or flip your lid when you hear things you don't like; adolescence is hard, they are doing their best, and they need to know they can trust us and that we can handle what they say.

It's not just the kids that make mistakes either. Nowadays, we put so much pressure on ourselves to be the perfect parent. To get it 'right'. For our children to be happy *all the time*. For the family to be harmonious. But what if that is asking too much? I suspect that a more honest account of the smartphone years is that there will be highs and lows. We will take unpopular decisions and make missteps, as will they. Our children will hate us

CONCLUSION

one moment and need our leadership and love more than ever the next. There will be hardships and hurt, and we will lament the transition from puppy fat, first teeth and grazed knees to today's long limbs, gawky gaffes and eye-rolls.

But what if it is enough to simply be a good parent, not a perfect one? What if we all just accept we are making the best decisions we can, and try to raise our children to be decent people? What if we simply trust that, with a bit of luck, because we do that, their happiness will follow? I do believe – but must regularly remind myself – that this would be more than enough.

With this book, my main mission is to reassure parents that how a child uses their smartphone is just as important as when they get one. I do not have all the answers, and I am painfully aware that as the book is published my eldest child will be twelve years old, and I will be living all this alongside my readers. I don't know how it's going to pan out, or what cringe-inducing errors I might make myself. I have made a few already, and there is always more to learn. What I can do is share the facts as I know them to be today, and hope that this information is enough to help you enter this next phase of life feeling informed and empowered to make the choices that will work best for you and your family. Yes, smartphones have a shady side, but the research is crystal clear that parents have a critical role in guiding their child through their digital, social and emotional development, and that *you can make all the difference in keeping your child safe, secure and, yes, happy ... most of the time.*

If you need more support with anything you have read in this book please check out the Resource library on pages 282–86 or visit www.laurawyattsmith.com where you can find more information about my other services, including talks for schools and organisations, and coaching for parents services. The smartphone years may be tough at times, but you never need to face them alone.

Resource library

Body image

Be Real Campaign
– www.berealcampaign.co.uk

Eating disorders

Beat
– www.beateatingdisorders.org.uk
or call 0345 634 1414

Cyberbullying

Kidscape
– www.kidscape.org.uk

Delaying smartphones and smartphone alternatives

Smartphone Free Childhood
– www.smartphonefreechildhood.org

Digital safety and parental controls (all cover a wide range of topics)

Internet Matters
- www.internetmatters.org

UK Safer Internet Centre
- www.saferinternet.org.uk

Common Sense Media (UK Section)
- www.commonsensemedia.org

Childnet
- www.childnet.com

Teched-Off
- www.teched-off.com

Digital literacy and critical thinking

NewsWise
- www.theguardian.com/newswise

Full Fact
- www.fullfact.org

Gaming

Ash Brandin
- @thegameeducator on Instagram

General

NSPCC (covering a wide range of topics)
- www.nspcc.org.uk

Childline (for children and parents)
- www.childline.org.uk or call 0800 1111

RESOURCE LIBRARY

Independence and unplugged play

Let Grow
– www.letgrow.org
Global Day of Unplugging
– www.globaldayofunplugging.org

LGBTQ+

The Proud Trust
– www.theproudtrust.org

Mental health

YoungMinds
– www.youngminds.org.uk or call 0808 802 5544
Youth Access (local support service)
– www.youthaccess.org.uk
Black Minds Matter UK
– www.blackmindsmatteruk.com

Neurodiversity

ADHD Foundation
– www.adhdfoundation.org.uk
Ambitious About Autism
– www.ambitiousaboutautism.org.uk
Dr Naomi Fisher
– naomifisher.co.uk

Policy and child rights

5Rights Foundation
- www.5rightsfoundation.com

Pornography and harmful content

The Reward Foundation
- www.rewardfoundation.org/free-parents-guide-to-internet-pornography

Internet Matters
- www.internetmatters.org/issues/online-pornography

Protect Young Eyes
- www.protectyoungeyes.com

Radicalisation, hate and extremism

Internet Matters
- www.internetmatters.org/issues/radicalisation

Relationships

Relate
- www.relate.org.uk

Brook
- www.brook.org.uk

Sexual abuse/exploitation

Call the police on 999 or 101 if there is an immediate risk to a child in the UK.

RESOURCE LIBRARY

For support with harassment, sexting, grooming or suspected sexual abuse, including reporting nude images, try:

- Childline Report Remove service (help to report and remove nude images online) – www.childline.org.uk
- Take It Down (removal of nude images online) www.takeitdown.ncmec.org
- Stop It Now helpline (anonymous support for child sexual abuse) – www.stopitnow.org.uk or 0808 1000 900
- Child Exploitation and Online Protection (report online abuse) – www.ceop.police.uk

Smartphone obsession

Smartphone 'addiction' scale quiz
  – www.healthyscreens.com/scale

Support for parents

Family Lives
  – www.familylives.org.uk or call 0808 800 2222
Laura Wyatt Smith
  – www.laurawyattsmith.com

Acknowledgements

They say that if you can't see it you can't be it, which is probably why I never even imagined becoming an author until I met Rebecca Seal. Rebecca, a successful author, my good friend and office mate, gave me the name, *Screensaver*, but more importantly, the belief that I could write this book. A heartfelt thank you for all your cheerleading, industry know-how and wise words.

Being awarded a Churchill Fellowship for my proposed visit to California to research the impact of smartphones on children's mental health gave me the confidence and contacts I needed to fill this book with quality evidence from world-leading experts. I would recommend the Fellowship wholeheartedly to anyone who has a passion for change through learning from around the world. A warm thank you to everyone who so generously shared their time and knowledge during this trip – the academics, educators, youth workers, parents and – most importantly – young people. Thank you also to the parents and experts back home in the UK who shared their insights with me during interviews. Each and every conversation has shaped this book.

When I told Cindy Chan, my editor, about my idea for *Screensaver* it was clear she immediately understood what I was trying to achieve and why it was needed. I have relished receiving your editing wisdom, Cindy! What a privilege it is to work with and

ACKNOWLEDGEMENTS

learn from you all at Profile Books. Thank you for taking a chance on me, Cindy, and to Emily Frisella and Mia Cameron for all your hard work and support with the publishing process.

As soon as I met Julia Silk, my literary agent, I knew she was the one for me. Bubbling with enthusiasm for this topic, and patient and knowledgeable with me as a publishing newbie, Julia has lent me courage and clarity when I needed it. How fortunate I am to have the benefit of your experience on this journey.

Looking back, I realise the seed of this book was planted in my own childhood. I struck gold with my parents, who offered the ideal balance between freedom and support. I was lucky enough to 'play out' in the street every day with neighbours' kids, but also experience selective screen time, which was usually a communal experience, grappling over a gaming remote, or vegging out over VHS films. I even got 'the taxi driver dad' – liberal enough to let us teenagers hit the town for a night but protective enough to pick us up afterwards (miss you, Dad) and, because my mum was a childminder, I literally had a professional parent to learn from. Mum was the reason our home was the relaxed place everyone wanted it to be, and she remains the active, supportive Nanny that every working parent wishes for. If my kids are half as happy as we were growing up I'll have done a good job.

I am so grateful to many more supporters behind the scenes ('Hey Jo, I made a thing!') but the biggest thanks go to my husband, Alex, who has stoically backed every one of my unconventional career twists and turns, including this book. Thank you for everything, I love you, and high five to equal parenting.

Finally, to my incredible kids, Esmie and Tilly. I wrote this book for you, for us. I love you both so much.

Notes

Introduction

1. 'Children and parents: media use and attitudes report 2022', Ofcom, 2022, www.ofcom.org.uk/siteassets/resources/documents/research-and-data/media-literacy-research/children/childrens-media-use-and-attitudes-2022/childrens-media-use-andattitudes-report-2022.pdf
2. Based on a study commissioned by HMD and conducted by Perspectus Global; 10,092 parents were interviewed, across five different countries (United Kingdom, United States, India, Germany and Australia). The study, conducted in July 2024, is available here: 'The Better Phone Project', HMD, www.hmd.com/en_gb/better-phone-project
3. 'Young People and Pornography', Children's Commissioner, https://assets.childrenscommissioner.gov.uk/wpuploads/2023/07/CCO-Pornography-and-Young-People-1.pdf
4. 'Youth Perspectives on Online Safety, 2022: an Annual Report of Youth Attitudes and Experiences', Thorn, November 2023. https://info.thorn.org/hubfs/Research/22_YouthMonitoring_Report.pdf
5. Sei Yon Sohn et al., 'Prevalence of problematic smartphone usage and associated mental health outcomes amongst children and young people: a systematic review, meta-analysis and GRADE of the evidence', *BMC Psychiatry*, 19:356 (2019). https://doi.org/10.1186/s12888-019-2350-x
6. 'Sales of "non-smartphones" double year-on-year, reports Virgin Media O2', Virgin Media O2, 21 October 2024, https://news.virginmediao2.co.uk/sales-of-non-smartphones-double-year-on-year-reports-virgin-media-o2/

Chapter 1: When Should a Child Get a Smartphone?

1. *Age of First Smartphone/Tablet and Mental Wellbeing Outcomes*, Sapiens Labs, May 2023, https://sapienlabs.org/wp-content/uploads/2023/05/Sapien-Labs-Age-of-First-Smartphone-and-Mental-Wellbeing-Outcomes.pdf
2. Ibid.

NOTES

3 Henry H. Wilmer et al., 'Smartphones and Cognition: A Review of Research Exploring the Links between Mobile Technology Habits and Cognitive Functioning', *Frontiers in Psychology*, 8:605, (2017), https://pmc.ncbi.nlm.nih.gov/articles/PMC5403814

4 Gloria Mark et al., 'The cost of interrupted work: more speed and stress', Association for Computing Machinery, 2008, https://dl.acm.org/doi/abs/10.1145/1357054.1357072

5 Larry D. Rosen, 'Are We All Becoming Pavlov's Dogs? Blame your smartphone, and Steve Jobs)', *Psychology Today*, June 2016, www.psychologytoday.com/gb/blog/rewired-the-psychology-of-technology/201606/are-we-all-becoming-pavlovsdogs

6 Brooke Auxier et al., 'Parenting Children in the Age of Screens', Pew Research Center, 2020, https://pewrsr.ch/30RHTBX

7 Jonathan Rothwell, Institute for Family Studies and Gallup, 'How Parenting and Self-control Mediate the Link Between Social Media Use and Youth Mental Health', 2023, https://ifstudies.org/ifs-admin/resources/briefs/ifs-gallupparentingsocialmediascreentime-october2023-1.pdf

8 'The Common Sense Census: Media Use by Tweens and Teens,' Common Sense Media, 2021, www.commonsensemedia.org/sites/default/files/research/report/8-18-censusintegrated-report-final-web_0.pdf

9 Michelle Faverio and Olivia Sidoti, 'Teens, Social Media and Technology 2024', Pew Research Center, 12 December 2024, https://pewrsr.ch/3ZT48Yo

10 Jonathan Rothwell, Institute for Family Studies and Gallup, 'Parenting and Self-control'.

11 'The Common Sense Census: Media Use by Tweens and Teens,' Common Sense Media, 2021, www.commonsensemedia.org/sites/default/files/research/report/8-18-censusintegrated-report-final-web_0.pdf

12 Jonathan Haidt, 'End the Phone-Based Childhood Now', *Atlantic*, 13 March 2024, www.theatlantic.com/technology/archive/2024/03/teen-childhood-smartphone-use-mental-health-effects/677722

13 Sei Yon Sohn et al., 'Prevalence of problematic smartphone usage and associated mental health outcomes amongst children and young people: a systematic review, meta-analysis and GRADE of the evidence', *BMC Psychiatry*, 19:356 (2019), https://doi.org/10.1186/s12888-019-2350-x

14 'Sleep and mental health', Mind, www.mind.org.uk/information-support/types-of-mental-health-problems/sleep-problems/sleep-and-mental-health

15 Shalini Paruthi et al., 'Consensus Statement of the American Academy of Sleep Medicine on the Recommended Amount of Sleep for Healthy Children: Methodology and Discussion', *Journal of Clinical Sleep Medicine*, 12:11 (2016), https://pmc.ncbi.nlm.nih.gov/articles/PMC5078711

NOTES

16 Jenny S. Radesky et al., 'Constant Companion: A Week in the Life of a Young Person's Smartphone Use', Common Sense Media, 2023, www.commonsensemedia.org/sites/default/files/research/report/2023-cs-smartphone-research-report_final-forweb.pdf

17 Mike Snider, 'Talking Tech: Netflix's biggest competition? Sleep, CEO says', *USA Today*, 18 April 2017, https://eu.usatoday.com/story/tech/talkingtech/2017/04/18/netflixs-biggest-competition-sleep-ceo-says/100585788

18 'Social Media and Youth Mental Health: The U.S. Surgeon General's Advisory', US Department of Health and Human Services, 2023, www.hhs.gov/sites/default/files/sg-youth-mental-health-social-media-advisory.pdf

19 Clare Dyer, 'Social media content contributed to teenager's death "in more than a minimal way," says coroner', *BMJ*, 379 (2022), https://doi.org/10.1136/bmj.o2374

20 Michelle Faverio et al., 'Teens, Social Media and Mental Health', Pew Research Center, 22 April 2025, https://pewrsr.ch/4lI0k4x

21 Taryn Myers and Janis Crowther, 'Social Comparison as a Predictor of Body Dissatisfaction: A Meta-Analytic Review'. *Journal of Abnormal Psychology*, 118:4 (2009), https://pubmed.ncbi.nlm.nih.gov/19899839

22 Richard Miech, 'Monitoring the Future: A Continuing Study of American Youth (8th- and 10th-Grade Surveys), 2021', Inter-university Consortium for Political and Social Research, 31 October 2022, https://doi.org/10.3886/ICPSR38502.v1

23 Victoria Rideout and Michale B. Robb, *Social media, social life: Teens reveal their experiences*, Common Sense Media, 2018, www.commonsensemedia.org/sites/default/files/research/report/2018-social-media-social-life-executive-summary-web.pdf

24 Arturo Béjar, 'How to Reduce the Sexual Solicitation of Teens on Instagram', After Babel, 2024, www.afterbabel.com/p/make-social-media-safe-forteens#footnote-1-144339892

25 Jon Haidt and Zach Rausch, 'TikTok Is Harming Children at an Industrial Scale', After Babel, 2025, https://www.afterbabel.com/p/industrial-scale-harm-tiktok

26 Jonathan Rothwell, Institute for Family Studies and Gallup, 'Parenting and Self-control'.

27 Elroy Boers et al., 'Temporal Associations of Screen Time and Anxiety Symptoms Among Adolescents', *Canadian Journal of Psychiatry*, 65:3 (2019), https://journals.sagepub.com/doi/10.1177/0706743719885486

28 Tonya Mosley and Serena McMahon, 'Social Media Use Linked to Anxiety, Depression Among Teens, New Study Finds', WBUR, 9 Jan 2020, www.wbur.org/hereandnow/2020/01/09/social-media-anxiety-depression-teens

29 Rami M. El-Baba and Mark P. Schury, 'Neuroanatomy, Frontal Cortex' *StatPearls*, 29 May 2023, www.ncbi.nlm.nih.gov/books/NBK554483

NOTES

30 Kaitlyn Regehr et al., 'SAFER SCROLLING: How algorithms popularize and gamify online hate and misogyny for young people', UCL and University of Kent, 2024, https://www.ascl.org.uk/ASCL/media/ASCL/Help%20and%20advice/Inclusion/Safer-scrolling.pdf

31 Jonathan Rothwell, Institute for Family Studies and Gallup, 'Parenting and Self-control'; 'Girls' mental health "at a precipice" and increasingly worse than boys', data shows', STEER Education, 28 Feb 2022, https://steer.education/girls-mental-health-at-aprecipice-and-increasingly-worse-than-boys-data-shows

32 Simon Usborne, 'From bone smashing to chin extensions: how "looksmaxxing" is reshaping young men's faces', Guardian, 15 February 2024, www.theguardian.com/lifeandstyle/2024/feb/15/from-bone-smashing-to-chin-extensions-howlooksmaxxing-is-reshaping-young-mens-faces

33 Leonardo Bursztyn et al., 'When Product Markets Become Collective Traps: The Case of Social Media', University of Chicago, 2023, https://economics.yale.edu/sites/default/files/2024-04/CollectiveTraps.pdf

34 Peter Martin, 'Would you pay to quit TikTok and Instagram? You'd be surprised how many would', ANU Reporter, 2024, https://reporter.anu.edu.au/all-stories/would-you-pay-to-quit-tiktok-and-instagram-youd-be-surprised-how-many-would

35 The cited article is a case study excerpt from *The Learning Habit* by Stephanie Donaldson-Pressman, Rebecca Jackson and Dr Robert Pressman by arrangement with Perigee, a member of Penguin Group, USA, LLC, a Penguin Random House Company, Copyright © 2014 by Good Parent, Inc, www.huffpost.com/entry/parents-underestimate-kids-media-use_b_5748304

Chapter 2: Choosing Their First Phone

1 Zoe Williams, '"They rob you visibly, with no repercussions" – the unstoppable rise of phone theft', Guardian, 9 October 2024, www.theguardian.com/uknews/2024/oct/09/they-rob-you-visibly-with-no-repercussions-the-unstoppablerise-of-phone-theft

2 Nicky Cox et al., 'Look Up Campaign!', First News, 952, 13–19 September 2024. https://6779821.fs1.hubspotusercontent-na1.net/hubfs/6779821/Paper%20PDFs/p08%20FirstNews%20Issue%20952%20-%20Look%20Up!.pdf

3 Rt Hon. Dame Diana Johnson DBE MP and the Home Office, 'Crackdown to halt rise in phone thefts', 3 September 2024, www.gov.uk/government/news/crackdown-to-halt-rise-in-phone-thefts

Chapter 3: Setting Yourself up for Success

1 'Children's Wellbeing in a Digital World: Year Three Index Report 2024', Internet Matters, 2024, www.internetmatters.org/hub/research/childrens-wellbeing-in-a-digitalworld-index-report-2024

NOTES

2 Josh Koebert and Kalleigh Lane, 'Spying on Your Kids: 80% of Parents Track Their Children's Locations and Online Activities [Survey]', All About Cookies, 2025, https://allaboutcookies.org/how-many-parents-track-their-children

3 Protect Young Eyes, Snapchat App Review, accessed October 2025, https://www.protectyoungeyes.com/apps/snapchat-parental-controls

4 Devorah Heitner, 'Should I Spy on My Kid's Phone? Mentoring vs Monitoring Kids on Social Media', Devorah Heitner Blog, https://devorahheitner.com/should-i-spy-on-my-kids-phonementoring-vs-monitoring-kids-on-social-media

5 Josh Koebert and Kalleigh Lane, 'Spying on Your Kids'.

6 Miriam Rahali et al., 'Smartphone policies in schools: What does the evidence say?' Digital Futures for Children, LSE, and 5Rights Foundation, September 2024, https://eprints.lse.ac.uk/125554/1/Smartphone_policies_in_schools_Rahali_et_al_2024_002_.pdf

Chapter 4: The Right Time for Your Child

1 Meryl Alper, *Kids Across the Spectrums: Growing Up Autistic in the Digital Age* (Cambridge, Massachusetts: MIT Press, 2023).

2 'Digital Misogynoir Report', Glitch UK, 2023, https://glitchcharity.co.uk/our-work/research-digital-misogynoir-report

3 'Digital Self-Harm', LGBT Foundation, 2024, https://lgbt.foundation/wp-content/uploads/2024/01/Digital20Harm20Resource_print.pdf

Chapter 6: Why It's Not Too Late

1 'The Better Phone Project', HMD, 2024, https://www.hmd.com/en_int/press/thebetter-phone-project-press-release

2 'Smartphone addition scale', Healthy Screens, www.healthyscreens.com/scale

3 Annie, 'Community Stories: We took away our daughter's smartphone, and she's flourishing', Smartphone Free Childhood, www.smartphonefreechildhood.org/resource/community-stories-annie

4 JoJo Marshall, 'When Should You Come Between a Teenager and Their Phone', Child Mind Institute, November 2023, https://childmind.org/article/when-should-you-come-between-a-teenager-and-her-phone

Lesson 1: Master Your Attention

1 'Oxford Word of the Year', Oxford University Press, 2024, https://corp.oup.com/word-of-the-year

2 Emily Cherkin, 'What Does it Mean to Be Tech-Intentional?', The Screentime Consultant, 2025, https://thescreentimeconsultant.com/blog/what-does-it-mean-to-be-tech-intentional

NOTES

3. Leonard Reinecke et al., 'Digital Stress over the Life Span', *Media Psychology*, 20:1 (2017). http://dx.doi.org/10.1080/15213269.2015.1121832
4. Common Sense and CS Mott Children's Hospital, 'Constant Companion: A Week in the Life of a Young Person's Smartphone Use', Common Sense Media, 26 September 2023, www.commonsensemedia.org/research/constant-companion-a-week-in-the-life-of-a-young-persons-smartphone-use
5. Erin Walsh, 'New Report: A Week in the Life of Kids and Their Phones', Spark & Stitch Institute, 29 September 2023, https://sparkandstitchinstitute.com/new-report-week-in-life-of-kids-phones
6. Sudip Bhattacharya et al., 'NOMOPHOBIA: NO Mobile PHone PhoBIA', *Journal of Family Medicine and Primary Care*, 8:4 (2019), https://pmc.ncbi.nlm.nih.gov/articles/PMC6510111

Lesson 2: Become a Critical Thinker

1. Sam Wineburg et al., 'Evaluating Information: The Cornerstone of Civic Online Reasoning', Stanford Digital Repository, 2016, http://purl.stanford.edu/fv751yt5934
2. Ibid.
3. Chris McKenna, protectyoungeyes, 'No digital secrets' [Instagram reel], 21 October 2021, www.instagram.com/reel/CVS8cmKAac0
4. 'Live streaming: a parent guide', Parent Zone, 2024, https://parentzone.org.uk/article/live-streaming
5. 'Why language matters: how referring to online "friends" can mask safeguarding concerns', NSPCC Learning, 4 April 2024, https://learning.nspcc.org.uk/news/why-language-matters/online-friends-can-mask-safeguarding-concerns
6. Jacqueline Beauchere, 'Two-thirds of Gen Z targeted for online "sextortion": New Snap research', We Protect Global Alliance, 21 June 2023, www.weprotect.org/blog/two-thirds-of-gen-z-targeted-for-online-sextortion-new-snap-research
7. 'Sextortion: Advice for professionals, young people, parents and carers', UK Safer Internet Centre, https://saferinternet.org.uk/online-issue/sextortion
8. 'Make a report', CEOP Safety Centre, www.ceop.police.uk/safety-centre/
9. '5 Ways Pornography Impacts Children and Teens', Protect Young Eyes, 7 August 2023, www.protectyoungeyes.com/blog-articles/5-ways-pornography-harms-children-teens
10. Youth Endowment Fund, 2024, Children, Violence and Vulnerability report, youthendowmentfund.org.uk/reports/children-violence-and-vulnerability-2024/
11. Jon Yates, 'Violence on social media – the online fight for our children's attention', Youth Endowment Fund, November 2023, https://youthendowmentfund.org.uk/violence-on-social-media-the-online-fight-for-our-childrens-attention/
12. Ofcom, 'Children and parents: media use and attitudes report 2020/21', www.

ofcom.org.uk/__data/assets/pdf_file/0025/217825/children-and-parents-media-use-andattitudes-report-2020-21.pdf

13 'APA Recommendations for Healthy Teen Video Viewing', American Psychological Association, www.apa.org/topics/social-media-internet/healthy-teen-video-viewing

14 Owen Phillips, 'Young People's Climate Anxiety is Soaring Due to Lack of Access to Green Space', Woodland Trust, 21 March 2023, www.woodlandtrust.org.uk/presscentre/2023/03/young-people-climate-anxiety-green-space-access/

15 Sheila Redfern, 'How to help your child understand upsetting news', BBC Bitesize Parents' Toolkit, www.bbc.co.uk/bitesize/articles/zqkfb7h

16 Lottie Elton, 'Millions of young Brits have lost money to online scams – and it's getting worse', *Big Issue*, 11 February 2025, www.bigissue.com/news/online-scams-fraud-young-people-uksic/

17 'Children and parents: media use and attitudes report 2020/21', Ofcom, 18 April 2021, www.ofcom.org.uk/media-use-and-attitudes/media-habits-children/children-and-parents-media-use-and-attitudes-report-2021

18 'Instagram, TikTok and YouTube teenagers' top three news sources' Ofcom, 16 March 2023, www.ofcom.org.uk/media-use-and-attitudes/attitudes-to-news/instagram-tiktok-and-youtube-teenagers-top-three-news-sources

19 'Gen Z driving early adoption of Gen AI, our latest research shows', Ofcom, 28 November 2023, www.ofcom.org.uk/internet-based-services/technology/gen-z-driving-early-adoption-of-gen-ai

20 Sophie McLean, 'The Environmental Impact of ChatGPT: A Call for Sustainable Practices in AI Development', Earth.org, 28 April 2023, https://earth.org/environmental-impact-chatgpt/

21 'Protecting Young People from Deepfakes', Brook, December 2024, www.brook.org.uk/blog/protecting-young-people-from-deepfakes/

22 'The new face of digital abuse: Children's experiences of nude deepfakes', Internet Matters, October 2024, www.internetmatters.org/hub/research/children-experiences-nude-deepfakes-research/

23 'The Complete Guide to Deepfakes and AI for Caregivers', Protect Young Eyes, 8 January 2024, www.protectyoungeyes.com/blog-articles/ultimate-guide-to-ai-and-deepfakes-for-caregivers

24 Common Sense Media, 'Talk, Trust, and Trade-Offs: How and Why Teens Use AI Companions', 2025, https://www.commonsensemedia.org/sites/default/files/research/report/talk-trust-and-trade-offs_2025_web.pdf

25 Emily A. Vogels et al., 'Teens, Social Media and Technology 2022', Pew Research Center, 10 August 2022, https://pewrsr.ch/3pc9pXn

26 'Scale behavioral health with clinical AI', Limbic, www.limbic.ai

NOTES

27 'Generative AI: Risks and opportunities for children', UNICEF, www.unicef.org/innocenti/generative-ai-risks-and-opportunities-children
28 'What are AI chatbots and companions?' Internet Matters, www.internetmatters.org/resources/ai-chatbots-and-virtual-friends-how-parents-can-keep-children-safe
29 'Virtual reality headsets', NSPCC, www.nspcc.org.uk/keeping-children-safe/onlinesafety/virtual-reality-headsets/; 'Generation VR', Institution of Engineering and Technology, 19 April 2022, www.theiet.org/media/press-releases/press-releases-2022/press-releases-2022-april-june/19-april-2022-generation-vr
30 Azar Pirdehghan et al., 'Social Media Use and Sleep Disturbance among Adolescents: A Cross-Sectional Study', *Iranian Journal of Psychiatry*, 16:2 (2021), https://pmc.ncbi.nlm.nih.gov/articles/PMC8233562/
31 Jon Haidt, 'Social Media is a Major Cause of the Mental Illness Epidemic in Teen Girls. Here's the Evidence', After Babel, 2023, www.afterbabel.com/p/socialmedia-mental-illness-epidemic
32 Rachel Ehmke, 'How Using Social Media Affects Teenagers', Child Mind Institute, https://childmind.org/article/how-using-social-media-affects-teenagers/
33 Stephanie Dowd, 'What to Do if You Think Your Child is Depressed', Child Mind Institute, https://childmind.org/article/how-to-help-your-depressed-teenager
34 Jonathan Rothwell, Institute for Family Studies and Gallup, 'Parenting and Self-control'.
35 'Self-esteem', Young Minds, www.youngminds.org.uk/parent/parents-a-z-mental-health-guide/self-esteem
36 'Social media and mental health', Young Minds, www.youngminds.org.uk/young-person/coping-with-life/social-media-and-mental-health
37 'Tips for building confidence and self-esteem', Mind, www.mind.org.uk/for-young-people/feelings-and-experiences/tips-for-building-confidence-and-self-esteem

Lesson 3: Know Your Digital Ethics

1 'Cheat Sheet: Group Chats', Childnet, www.childnet.com/resources/cheat-sheet-group-chats
2 Erin Walsh, 'On Responding to Online Cruelty with Dr. Elizabeth Englander' [podcast], Connected & Courageous (12 September 2024), Spark & Stitch Institute, https://sparkandstitchinstitute.com/podcast/on-responding-to-online-cruelty-with-dr-elizabeth-englander/
3 'Who knows what about me?', Children's Commissioner, November 2018, www.childrenscommissioner.gov.uk/digital/who-knows-what-about-me
4 '"Sharenting" and Child Influencers', Boston Children's Digital Wellness Lab, March 2023, https://digitalwellnesslab.org/research-briefs/sharenting-and-child-influencers

NOTES

5   Ibid.
6   Ibid.
7   Virginia Sole-Smith and Devorah Heitner, 'Sexting Is Safer Sex' [podcast], Burnt Toast (21 September 2023), Substack, https://virginiasolesmith.substack.com/p/sexting-is-safer-sex
8   A lot of it is actually just abuse: 'Young People and Pornography' [information sheet], Children's Commissioner, https://assets.childrenscommissioner.gov.uk/wpuploads/2023/07/CCO-Pornography-and-Young-People-1.pdf
9   Peggy Orenstein, 'The Troubling Trend in Teenage Sex', *New York Times*, 12 April 2024, www.nytimes.com/2024/04/12/opinion/choking-teen-sex-brain-damage.html
10 A lot of it is actually just abuse: 'Young People and Pornography' [information sheet], Children's Commissioner.
11 'Talking to your child about the risks of online porn', NSPCC, www.nspcc.org.uk/keeping-children-safe/online-safety/inappropriate-explicit-content/online-porn
12 'Teens and Pornography', Common Sense Media, 2022, www.commonsensemedia.org/sites/default/files/research/report/2022-teens-and-pornography-final-web.pdf
13 Erika Lust, 'The porn conversation', video, TEDxAthens, November 2022, https://www.youtube.com/watch?v=PnK9Y7yuGWg
14 'The Things I Wish My Parents Had Known: Young People's Advice On Talking To Your Child About Online Sexual Harassment', Children's Commissioner, December 2021, https://assets.childrenscommissioner.gov.uk/wpuploads/2021/12/cco_talking_to_your_child_about_online_sexual_harassment_a-guide_for_parents_dec_2021.pdf
15 'What is cyber flashing', Rape Crisis, https://rapecrisis.org.uk/get-informed/types-of-sexual-violence/what-is-cyber-flashing
16 Ministry of Justice, 'Guidance: Revenge Porn', Gov.uk, 3 February 2015, www.gov.uk/government/publications/revenge-porn
17 Virginia Sole-Smith and Devorah Heitner, 'Sexting is Safer Sex' [podcast], The Burnt Toast (21 September 2023), Substack, https://virginiasolesmith.substack.com/p/sexting-is-safer-sex
18 Justin W. Patchin and Sameer Hinduja, 'It Is Time to Teach Safe Sexting', *Journal of Adolescent Health*, 66:2 (February 2020), www.sciencedirect.com/science/article/abs/pii/S1054139X19305099
19 S. Livingstone et al., 'Young people experiencing internet-related mental health difficulties', ySkills, 2022, https://yskills.eu/wp-content/uploads/2022/11/D6.1-ySkills_WP6.4_Mental-health-difficulties-and-digital-skills-Report-Final-Executive-summary.pdf

NOTES

Lesson 4: Find Your Balance

1. Mariya Stoilova, 'Young people's online engagement and mental health: the role of digital skills', LSE Department of Media and Communications Blog, 30 November 2022, https://blogs.lse.ac.uk/parenting4digitalfuture/2022/11/30/digital-skills
2. 'Family Media Agreement', Common Sense Media, 2018, www.commonsensemedia.org/sites/default/files/featured-content/files/common_sense_family_media_agreement.pdf
3. 'Our Family's Social Standards to Navigate Social Media and Tech Positively', Social Institute, https://thesocialinstitute.com/wp-content/uploads/Family-Social-Standards-Agreement_The-Social-Institute.pdf
4. 'How we protect children's rights with the UN Convention on the Rights of the Child', UNICEF, www.unicef.org.uk/what-we-do/un-convention-child-rights
5. M. Rosenberg & B. C. McCullough, 'Mattering: inferred significance and mental health among adolescents', *Research in Community & Mental Health*, 2 (1981), https://psycnet.apa.org/record/1983-07744-001
6. drbeckygoodinside, 'A boundary is something you tell your child you will do' [Instagram reel], 19 May 2024, www.instagram.com/drbeckyatgoodinside/reel/C7KsOy3hBVz

Lesson 5: Keep Learning

1. Lucy Bowes et al., 'Families promote emotional and behavioural resilience to bullying: evidence of an environmental effect', *Journal of Child Psychology and Psychiatry*, 51:7 (2010), https://pubmed.ncbi.nlm.nih.gov/20132419
2. E. Staksrud and K. Ólafsson, 'Norwegian National Report', EU Kids Online and the Department of Media and Communication, University of Oslo, 2019, www.lse.ac.uk/media-and-communications/research/research-projects/eu-kids-online/participating-countries/norway
3. Livingstone et al., 'Young people experiencing internet-related mental health difficulties'.

Index

access over ownership, giving 97–9
adolescence
  brain and 34, 84
  breaking rules/testing boundaries during 109, 260
  defined 22–3
  learning to survive independently during 265–6
  turbulence of 38, 76, 221, 257, 279
Adolescence (Netflix series) 11–12, 103
adverts 35–6, 69, 70–71, 124, 224, 252
  false 171
  paid 172–3
algorithms 30, 33–6, 66, 71, 88, 90, 98, 193, 207, 226, 228, 235
  as distorting mirror 274
  inferred data and 218
  power imbalance between your child and 34–5
  teaching children about 161–3, 166
Alper, Dr Meryl: *Kids Across the Spectrums* 85
Android 43, 52
  Digital Wellbeing 111
  Family Link 63
Angelou, Maya 117
Anna Freud Centre 167
Apple 52
  AirTag 80
  Family Sharing 63
  Health 59
  iPhone *see* iPhone

apps
  age ratings 54, 69, 214
  allowing/banning 68–73, 83
  blocking 69–70, 138–9, 247
  browser over 139
  Common Sense Media website, checking out on 69
  deleting and reinstalling 139–40
  downloads, limiting 52
  'empty calorie' 247
  essential 56
  fees 70–71
  minimum, permitting only 129
  new features added without warning to parents 53, 64–5, 71–2, 176
  no, saying 72
  old iPhone and 64–5
  parental control apps 63
  parental permission and 251
  password or PIN before downloading, configuring settings to require 69
  personal information and 225
  placement 140
  positive, seeking out 71–2
  research, doing your own 72–3
  reviewing 225
  safe/'innocent' 48, 70
  school requiring 82, 96
  settings, amending 66–7, 149
  sideloading 60
  time limits 129, 138–9
  travel apps for public transport 55–6
  unnecessary, removing all 247

INDEX

artificial intelligence (AI) 22, 90, 106, 153, 161, 207, 220, 223, 268
   'brainrot' content and 30
   chatbots/companions 53, 71–2, 146–7, 182–6
   generative artificial intelligence (AI) 175–80
   live filtering and 64–5
   parental control apps and 63
   search technology and 44
assertiveness skills 205–6
attention 86, 104, 108
   attention economy 35, 124–5, 127, 185
   attention residue 21
   coaching your kids more than commanding them 133–6
   disconnection and 141–5
   mastering 73, 121, 122, 124–45, 251–2
   notifications, minimising and muting 130–33
   smartphone impact on 20–22, 40
   S.T.O.P. 136–8
   tech-intentional, teaching child to be 126–30
   temptation, practical steps to reduce 138–41
autoplay 127–8, 129, 166

balance, finding your 28, 57, 68, 77, 93, 95, 114, 122, 242–63
   boundaries, setting unbreakable 260–63
   family phone agreement 248–57
   life beyond the phone, nurturing 257–60
   modelling healthy habits 243–8
   top take-aways 263
Balance Phone 47
Begeti, Dr Faye: *The Phone Fix* 247
behaviour changes 272
Black people 23, 88

blocking apps/websites 60, 62, 65, 69–72, 129, 138–9, 149, 150, 154, 197, 214, 216, 247
boundaries 22, 27, 41, 51, 61, 67, 80, 86, 88, 91, 97, 116, 117, 123, 126, 134, 165, 178, 192, 202, 219, 231, 243, 249, 279
   adolescence and 109, 260
   setting unbreakable 260–63
boys 24, 31, 36, 37, 153, 193, 226, 227, 229, 233
brain 7, 16, 20–21, 28, 40, 84, 104, 124, 130, 158, 191, 228, 266
   brain rot 30, 126, 145
   prefrontal cortex 34
Burnt Toast podcast 222
buying yourself more time 55, 94–107
   access over ownership 97–9
   common concerns over smartphones/ talking points for parents 104–6
   discussing decisions with your child 102–3
   options, offering 99
   other parents, talking to 100–102
   other ways to meet your child's digital needs 95–7
   top take-aways 107

catfishing 170
Center for Humane Technology 184
character.ai 183
charging/storage station, home phone 28, 140–41, 143, 253, 261, 262
chatbots 53, 71–2, 146, 176, 178, 182–6, 207, 223
ChatGPT 16, 176, 177
chat rooms 69, 147, 148, 152
Cherkin, Emily: *The Screentime Solution* 75, 126–7
Child Exploitation and Online Protection Centre (CEOP) 154
Child Mind Institute 115–16, 192, 194–5

INDEX

childhood
   end of 22–3
   smartphone free *see* smartphonefreechildhood (SPFC) movement
Childhood Heroes podcast 3
Childline 147, 151, 152–3, 155, 215, 231, 273, 283
   Report Remove 154–5, 234, 286
Childnet 210, 211, 214, 283
children living apart from their parents 89
Children's Commissioner for England: *Who Knows What about Me?* report 218, 226, 232
Chinese Proverb 264
choosing their first phone 41–57
   apps for supporting health conditions or disabilities 56
   basic or 'feature' phones/brick, dumb or flip phones 44–6
   'be like everyone else', pressure from your child to 54
   family-friendly and 'hybrid' smartphones 46–9
   keeping in touch with family living apart 55
   left out of chats and social plans, fear of child being 55
   making your choice 54–7
   regular adult smartphones 50–54
   smartwatches 49–50
   top take-aways 57
   track your child, ability to 55
   travel apps for public transport 55–6
Churchill Fellowship 3
Citymapper 16
click away, teaching children to 161
climate anxiety 166–7
coaching
   coaching your kids more than commanding them 133–6

coaching-style conversation starters 135
collaborative parenting 133–5
colours, home screen 127
Common Sense Media 69, 183, 185, 212, 227, 228, 250, 283
competitions or quizzes 171
content consumption and creation, difference between 237
Covid-19 pandemic 3, 12–13, 23, 279
critical thinking 122, 146–206, 230
   question everything, teaching them to 169–88
   safety essentials, establishing online 147–55
   searching safely and making sense of what they see 155–69
   self-esteem 198–206
   social media 188–97
   top take-aways 207
cyberflashing 233

data privacy/protection 105, 196, 217–25
   data types 218
   how to protect 223–5
   importance of 218–20
   sharenting 220–22
decisions, discussing with your child 102–3
deepfake 30, 36, 146, 173, 180–82, 196, 219
deeply feeling kids 87
Deliveroo or Uber Eats 16
digital addiction 14, 14n, 22–3, 49, 52, 53, 66, 71, 112, 139, 247
   smartphone addiction scale test 112, 247
digital declutter 247
digital detox 142, 144
digital ethics 32, 37, 88, 122, 157, 206, 208–41, 253
   backstop, be their 238–41

301

INDEX

data protection/online privacy 217–25
digital drama 209–17
joyful and safe online community, cultivating 235–8
porn 226–35
top take-aways 241
digital footprints 224, 253
digital lens effect 106
digital natives 108, 146
digital needs, other ways to meet your child's 95–7
digital self-harm 88
disappearing message functions 150–51, 210
disappointed or angry child 102
disconnection 141–5
Discord 210
discrimination 88, 105, 179, 231, 257
dopamine 20, 21, 228
Dove
 'Cost of Beauty' video 36
 Self-Esteem Project 35–6
'dumb' phones 5–6, 44–6
Dweck, Carol 204

eating patterns 272
echo chambers 34, 90, 98, 162, 189, 193, 196
EE 62, 63
embodied experience 24, 180
emergency contacts 58–9, 83, 132, 248
emotional dysregulation 273
'energy angels' and 'energy demons' 205
Englander, Dr Elizabeth: *Bullying and Cyberbullying: What Every Parent and Educator Needs to Know* 216
Epictetus 124, 125
EU Kids Online 270
expectations, managing 266–7
experience blockers 104

Facebook 29, 31, 32–3
fake news 146, 147, 173–4
family agreement 68, 77, 86–7, 114–15, 117, 248–57, 261–2, 263
 attention, mastering 251–2
 balance, maintaining 253–4
 basics 251
 co-parent feels differently about smartphones and 255–6
 creating 250–51
 critical-thinking skills and 252–3
 digital ethics and 253
 friends' phones, child seeing or using 256–7
 revisiting 274–7
 smartphone readiness checklist and 91–3
 sleep and 254
family-friendly smartphones 6, 19–20, 80, 83, 86, 89, 96, 97, 182
 choosing first phone and 42–3, 46–51, 55–7
 cons 49
 parental restrictions and 59, 60
 pros 47–8
 smartphone readiness checklist and 90
family of phones 63
family phone 98–9
First News 'Look Up!' campaign 45
five lessons 7, 51, 95, 119–277
 Master Your Attention 21, 73, 122, 124–45
 Become a Critical Thinker 122, 146–206, 230
 Know Your Digital Ethics 32, 37, 88, 122, 157, 206, 208–41, 253
 Find Your Balance 28, 57, 68, 77, 93, 95, 114, 122, 242–63
 Keep Learning 122, 264–77
flip phones 6, 12, 44–6

INDEX

FOMO (fear of missing out) 27, 49, 105, 137, 144, 189, 190, 197, 211, 217, 262
'friend', child's online 151
fun, finding the 269–70

Gabb 47, 49
Gallup 23
gifts or 'freebies' online 152
girls 24, 31, 35–7, 40, 104, 153, 163, 181, 184–5, 191, 229, 231, 233
'given off' data 218
Glitch 88
global events and current affairs 166–9
Global Mind Project 18, 19
Google 16, 52, 60, 61, 66, 98, 125, 159, 161, 164, 172
  Chrome 67
  Docs 70
  Family Link 63, 80
  Incognito 75
  Maps 47
  Pixel 50
  'safe mode' 161–2
  Street View 186–7
GPS tracking 43, 46, 48, 49, 52, 58, 65, 80, 105
grooming 148, 152, 233, 286

Haidt, Jonathan
  After Babel 191
  The Amazing Generation 103
  The Anxious Generation 2, 3, 5, 24, 31
Harari, Yuval Noah 185
Harris, Tristan 125
Heitner, Devorah 222, 234
  Growing Up in Public: Coming of Age in a Digital World 76
Herbenick, Dr Debby: *Yes, Your Kid* 226–7
Hinduja, Dr Sameer 234–5

HMD Fusion model 47
Human Givens 258
hybrid phones 19, 46–9, 56

I Am Ruth 36, 103
identity theft 171, 219
inferred data 218
infinite scroll 127
Instagram 29, 31, 33, 38, 87, 98, 127, 128, 140, 173, 210, 222, 228, 246, 283
intense adult themes 158
Internet Matters 61, 62, 181, 186, 195, 283, 285
iPhone 41, 43, 44, 45, 50, 52, 59, 64, 70, 75, 89, 111, 177
IRL (in real life) 1, 34, 39, 40, 71, 87, 88, 92, 106, 110, 148, 149, 152, 182, 196, 199, 205, 209, 213, 247, 253, 259, 277
  cultivate more freedom and responsibility for kids in 2
  trade-off of time spent online vs 22–5

Jackson, Rebecca: *The Learning Habit* 39
Jensen, Tine 238–9
Jobs, Steve 13
'Jools' Law' 78
joyful and safe online community 235–8
  content consumption and creation, discussing difference between 237
  'netiquette', explaining 237–8
  oversharing, avoiding 238
  real-world interest, showing them how to use the internet positively to foster 236–7
  trolls, ignoring 238

Kennedy, Dr Becky 87, 261
Khan Academy 176
Knost, L. R. 208

INDEX

learning, keep 122, 264–77
   family agreement, revisit your 274–7
   reconnecting with your child 265–70
   top take-aways 277
   warning signs, watching for 270–74
LGBT Foundation 88–9
LGBTQ+ community 30, 88–9, 227, 235–6, 284
life beyond the phone, nurturing 257–60
Limbic Access 184
listening 134, 193, 201, 215, 245, 267, 275, 279
live-streaming sites 151
long-form and short-form content 130
looksmaxxing 37
love, unconditional 203
Lust, Erika 229

McKenna, Chris 91, 149
medical information 58–9, 83
   Medical ID, iPhone 59
mental health 85, 106, 207, 239, 249, 257, 284, 287
   bad content and 164
   chatbot 184
   global events and current affairs and 167
   notifications and 131
   premature adult responsibilities or interactions and 157
   self-compassion letter and 205
   sleep and 26
   smartphone use and 2–4, 6–7, 11, 14, 18
   social media and 28, 30, 32, 33, 37, 189, 198, 199
   warning signs 271, 274
Mind 26
modelling healthy habits 243–8, 263
Money Supermarket 74

Netflix 11, 27, 66, 103, 127
netiquette 237–8
neurodiversity 85–7, 284
'no controls, no complacency' school of thought 60
'no digital secrets' 149
Nokia 44, 47, 99, 248
nomophobia 141
Norton 74
notifications 21, 22, 63, 83, 86, 92, 104, 124, 139, 146, 194
   minimise and mute 130–33, 247, 252
   settings 73
NSPCC 147, 148, 170, 186, 210, 215–16, 227, 283

Ofcom 172, 175, 227
options, offering 99
oversharing 238

parental controls/restrictions 5, 19, 46, 47, 52, 59–64, 67, 70, 83, 86, 91, 139, 161–2, 186, 223, 251, 283
   apps, allowing/banning 68–73
   apps and games settings 66–7
   home network, applying on your 62
   need of 67–8
   old iPhone, giving them your 64–6
   phone, applying on a 63–4
   should you use 59–64
parenting patterns 32
parents, talking to other 100–102
ParentShield All-Network SIM card 63
passwords 58, 69, 77–8, 139, 149, 225, 252
Patchin, Dr Justin W. 234–5
PAYG or contract 73–4
Perry, Philippa: *The Book You Wish Your Parents Had Read (and Your Children Will Be Glad You Did)* 133–4

INDEX

personal information 76, 105, 150, 151, 170, 171, 183, 186, 211, 218, 219, 223–5, 238, 241, 252
Pew Research 31
phantom vibration 21
phishing 170, 171, 224
phubbing 244
PIN numbers 58, 60, 69
Pinwheel 47
pornography 27, 32, 37, 91, 156, 157, 181, 196, 211, 226–35, 241, 255, 278, 285
  revenge porn 233–4
  sexting 233–5
  talking with your child about 229–32
  violent 4
positive goals 112–13, 117
premature adult responsibilities or interactions 157
Price, Catherine
  The Amazing Generation 103
  How to Break Up with Your Phone 247
Prince's Trust 3
privacy 15, 19, 57, 214, 216, 252, 253, 259
  access over ownership and 98, 99
  camera and 105
  data privacy *see* data privacy/protection
  deepfakes and 181
  discussing online 91, 197
  personal data 178, 223
  private browsers 60, 66, 75
  private messaging 151
  protecting 217–25
  settings 66, 67, 196, 223
  spying on child and 75, 76, 77
  supervised account 164
promotion of products/false adverts 171
Protect Young Eyes 91, 149, 155, 156–7, 182, 240, 285
public wireless networks and hotspots 224
pull down to refresh 128

question everything, teaching children to 169–88
  chatbots and AI companions 182–6
  deepfakes 180–82
  fake news 173–4
  Generative Artificial intelligence (AI) 175–80
  paid ads 172–3
  scams 170–72
  stunts and challenges 174–5
  Virtual Reality (VR) 186–8
Qustodio 74

readiness, smartphone- 11–40, 51, 84–93
  children living apart from their parents 89
  deeply feeling kids 87
  discrimination 88
  neurodiversity 85–7
  smartphone readiness checklist 90–93
  top take-aways 93
  when your child should get a smartphone *see* when your child should get a smartphone
reconnecting 265–70
Redfern, Dr Sheila 167
reflecting without guilt 109–12
removal, smartphone 115–17
Replika 183
risk-to-reward ratio 84
road safety 45–6, 66, 105, 252
Roome, Ellen 78

safety essentials, online 147–55
  'disappearing message' functions 150–51
  'friend' online 151
  gifts or 'freebies' 152
  grooming and coercive or controlling behaviour 152

INDEX

live-streaming sites 151
'no digital secrets' 149
personal information 150
settings, applying safest 149
sextortion 153–5
talking to your child 150
technical protections or monitoring alone, don't rely on 148–9
Samaritans 273
Samsung
  Family Hub 63
  Galaxy 50
scams 105, 146, 170–72, 197, 224
schools
  grades 272
  smartphone and 2, 11–15, 19, 24, 26, 42, 45, 48, 50, 66, 81–2, 83, 96, 100–101, 104, 106, 110, 121, 137, 142, 177, 197, 208–11, 216, 251–2, 260, 268–9
screen-blocking apps 247
screen settings 129–30
screen time
  demonising 25, 243
  hours spent online 22–3, 39, 77
  restricting 32, 129
  tracking 111, 247
search engines 75, 162, 172, 176
searching safely/making sense of what they see 155–69
  algorithms, teaching them about 163–4
  click away, teaching them to 161
  global events and current affairs 166–9
  Google 'safe mode' 161–2
  intense adult themes 158
  premature adult responsibilities or interactions 157
  sexual content 157
  shocking world events 158
  violence 157–61
  YouTube 164–6

self-acceptance 198–9, 206
self-care 200, 204–5
self-compassion letter 205
self-esteem 18, 35, 40, 106, 196, 198–207, 230, 245, 257, 261
  helping child with their 202–6
  identifying healthy 199–200
  importance of 198–9
  nurturing 198–207
  talking to child about 201–2
self-harm 30, 32, 88, 164, 193, 196, 200, 210
self-talk or negative beliefs 203
Sex Education Forum 3, 226
sexting 91, 196, 233–5, 286
sextortion 32, 91, 105, 153–5, 197, 207, 271
sexual abuse 32, 148, 181, 285, 286
sexual content 4, 30, 31, 37, 39, 69, 147, 148, 152, 157, 188, 210–11. See also pornography
sharenting 220–22, 224, 241, 253
Shaw, George Bernard 146
shocking world events 158
silent mode 48, 50, 59, 131, 244
Silicon Valley 3, 11, 15, 20, 32, 40, 106, 124, 159, 260
single screens, sticking to 130
sleep 105, 112, 114, 130, 134, 165, 197, 230, 248–9
  family phone agreement 253, 254
  smartphone use and 4, 24, 26–8, 31, 40, 190
  warning signs and 271, 272
smartphone
  addiction *see* addiction
  apps *see* apps
  child already has *see* too late, why it's not/child already has a smartphone
  choosing first *see* choosing their first phone
  common concerns over 104–6

INDEX

designed by adults for adults 5, 104
five lessons and *see* five lessons
omnipotence 16–17
removal 115–17
school and *see* school
readiness/age at which to give a child 1–40, 51, 84–93
transportable nature of 15–16
vs other screens 15–17
Smartphone Free Childhood/#smartphonefreechildhood (SPFC) movement 2, 82, 94, 100, 103, 115, 184–5, 282
smombie (smartphone + zombie) 45
SMV, or 'sexual market value' 37
Snapchat 29, 75, 159, 183, 184, 192, 210, 219, 228
social exclusion 95
Social Institute, The: Our Family's Social Standards customisable template 250
social media 12, 15, 20, 45, 47, 48, 53, 84–5, 86, 214, 218, 219, 220, 224, 237, 246, 257, 270
  age of users 2, 37, 93
  AI and 30, 176
  anxiety and depression and 31
  boys and 24, 31, 36, 37, 153, 193
  defined 29
  digital self-harm and 88
  duplicate accounts 72
  fake news and 173
  following, size of 182
  function of 29
  girls and 24, 31, 35–7, 40, 104, 153, 163, 181, 184–5, 191
  history of/social networking and 32–5
  inappropriate and distressing content 30
  influence of 28–38, 40
  mental health and 28
  negative impacts of 189–91
  online hate and 31
  parenting patterns and 32
  porn and 226, 228
  potential for good 37
  power imbalance between your child and algorithms 34–5
  pull down to refresh and 128
  readiness checklist 196–7
  safety and 148, 153, 157, 159, 164, 166
  sceptic, raising a 188–97, 207
  self-esteem and 198, 199, 202, 204
  settings, amending 66, 67
  sleep and 26
  spying on child using 74–5, 77, 78
  time spent on 23–4, 28, 40
  US Surgeon General on 28, 29–30
social networks 32–5, 243. *See also individual network name*
software updates 106, 185
spying on child 74–8, 111
'standards', 'rules' and 68
Stone, Elizabeth xi
S.T.O.P. rule 136–8, 247, 253, 267–8, 269
'Stranger Danger' era, 1980s and 1990s 14
strong ties 33
stunts and challenges 174–5
sturdy parenting 261
suicide 30, 32, 153, 164, 184, 193, 196
Sweeney, Jools 78
Swift, Taylor 181
Swiped (documentary) 103, 142
synchronous experience 24–5

Take It Down 154–5, 234, 286
talking to your child 102, 149, 150, 229
tech-intentional 126–30, 143
tech-positivity 268–9
teched-off.com 61, 283

INDEX

temptation, steps to reducing 138–41, 145
texting 16, 19, 70, 73, 80, 93, 96, 114, 183, 195, 201, 217, 233, 235, 237, 253
   choosing a phone and 42, 43, 44, 46, 49, 52, 55, 56
   real-life conversations and 213
   text-and-call-only phones 12, 15, 27, 44, 89, 99, 101, 143
   theft
      identity 171
      phone 45, 46, 53, 66, 105
The Phone 44
The Porn Conversation 229
Thoreau, Henry David 242
TikTok 16, 26, 29, 31, 38, 98, 128, 130, 159, 163, 173, 174, 181, 192
time limits 63, 86, 114, 129, 165, 247
Times, The 6
too late, why it's not/child already has a smartphone 108–117
   family phone agreement 114–15
   positive goals 112–13
   reflecting without guilt 109–12
   removal, temporary or permanent smartphone 115–17
   top take-aways 117
tracking your child 78–80, 96
trolls 88, 238
Troomi 47

UK Safer Internet Centre 61, 62, 154, 170, 183
UN Convention on the Rights of the Child (UNCRC) 258
UNICEF 184, 185
University of Chicago 37–8
University of Kent 36
University of Oslo 238

variable reward mechanism 20–21
violence 13, 30, 32, 35, 66, 87, 91, 105, 164–5, 167, 188, 196–7, 226, 231, 233, 238, 258
   internet search and 155–61
   pornography and 4, 156
   social media and 157, 159
VIP settings 73, 131, 132
Virgin 5–6
virtual reality (VR) 186–8
VPN (virtual private network) 60, 75

waiting before posting online 222, 225, 253
warning signs, watching for 152, 195, 270–74
weak ties 33
WhatsApp 25, 29, 44, 53, 72, 98, 100–101, 184, 191, 210, 213, 243, 246
when your child should get a smartphone 2, 5, 11–40
   age of child 17–20
   attention or 'inner peace', impact on 20–22
   'not-my-child' thinking trap 38–9
   sleep, impact on 26–8
   smartphones vs other screens 15–17
   social media 28–38
   time spent online vs IRL (in real life) 22–5
   top take-aways 40
Wilson, Miranda 61
Woodland Trust 166
Wynn-Williams, Sarah: *Careless People: A Story of Where I Used to Work* 31

Yates, Jon 159
Youth Endowment Foundation (YEF) 157, 159
YouTube 24, 26, 29, 66, 67, 98, 127, 129, 130, 159–60, 162–6, 173, 174